THE QUEEN OF HEARTBREAK TRAIL

The Life and Times of Harriet Smith Pullen,
Pioneering Woman

ELEANOR PHILLIPS BRACKBILL

TWODOT®

GUILFORD, CONNECTICUT
HELENA, MONTANA

A · TWODOT® · BOOK

An imprint and registered trademark of Rowman & Littlefield

Distributed by NATIONAL BOOK NETWORK

Copyright © 2016 Eleanor Phillips Brackbill
Maps by Melissa Baker © Rowman & Littlefield

British Library Cataloguing-in-Publication Information Available

Library of Congress Cataloging-in-Publication Data

Names: Brackbill, Eleanor Phillips.
Title: The Queen of Heartbreak Trail : the life and times of Harriet Smith
   Pullen, pioneering woman / Eleanor Phillips Brackbill.
Description: Guilford, Connecticut : TwoDot, 2016. | Includes bibliographical
   references and index.
Identifiers: LCCN 2015027949| ISBN 9781493019137 (hardcover : alkaline paper)
   | ISBN 9781493019144 (e-book)
Subjects: LCSH: Pullen, Harriet S. | Women pioneers—Alaska—Skagway—Biography. |
   Pioneers—Alaska—Skagway—Biography. |
   Businesswomen—Alaska—Skagway—Biography. |
   Hotelkeepers—Alaska—Skagway—Biography. | Skagway (Alaska)—Biography. |
   Frontier and pioneer life—Alaska—Skagway. | Alaska—Gold discoveries. |
   Klondike River and Valley (Yukon)—Gold discoveries.
Classification: LCC F914.S7 B73 2016 | DDC 979.8/03092—dc23 LC record available at
http://lccn.loc.gov/2015027949

∞™ The paper used in this publication meets the minimum requirements of American National Standard for Information Sciences—Permanence of Paper for Printed Library Materials, ANSI/ NISO Z39.48-1992.

In memory of Harriet Stuart Pullen Phillips

Contents

List of Illustrations

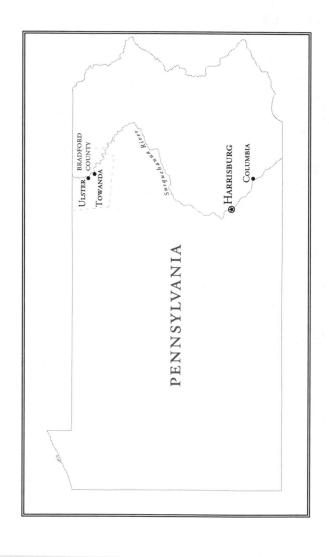

WISCONSIN

Mississippi River

GRANT
COUNTY
● Mount Hope
● Lancaster
● Platteville

⊛ MADISON

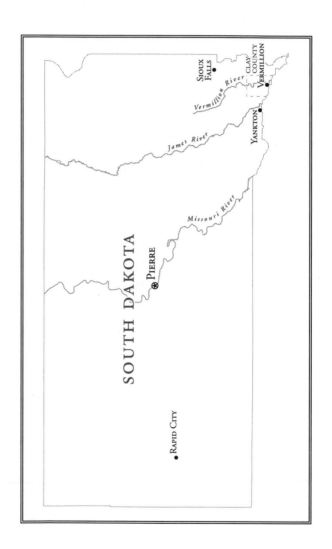

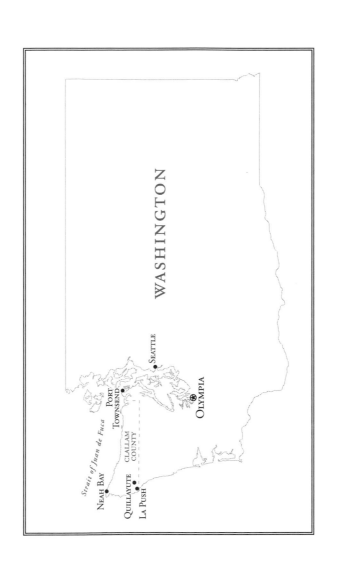

Family Tree

Smith

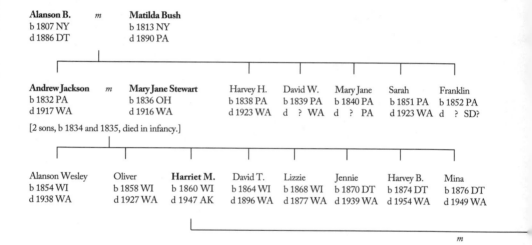

Alanson B.   *m*   **Matilda Bush**
b 1807 NY   b 1813 NY
d 1886 DT   d 1890 PA

Andrew Jackson *m*	**Mary Jane Stewart**	Harvey H.	David W.	Mary Jane	Sarah	Franklin
b 1832 PA	b 1836 OH	b 1838 PA	b 1839 PA	b 1840 PA	b 1851 PA	b 1852 PA
d 1917 WA	d 1916 WA	d 1923 WA	d ? WA	d ? PA	d 1923 WA	d ? SD?

[2 sons, b 1834 and 1835, died in infancy.]

Alanson Wesley	Oliver	**Harriet M.**	David T.	Lizzie	Jennie	Harvey B.	Mina
b 1854 WI	b 1858 WI	b 1860 WI	b 1864 WI	b 1868 WI	b 1870 DT	b 1874 DT	b 1876 DT
d 1938 WA	d 1927 WA	d 1947 AK	d 1896 WA	d 1877 WA	d 1939 WA	d 1954 WA	d 1949 WA

m

Pullen

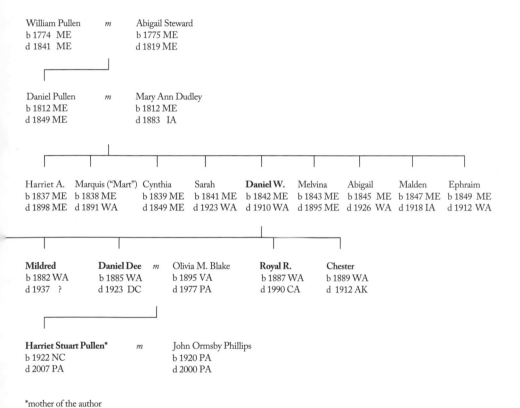

William Pullen   *m*   Abigail Steward
b 1774 ME   b 1775 ME
d 1841 ME   d 1819 ME

Daniel Pullen   *m*   Mary Ann Dudley
b 1812 ME   b 1812 ME
d 1849 ME   d 1883 IA

Harriet A.	Marquis ("Mart")	Cynthia	Sarah	**Daniel W.**	Melvina	Abigail	Malden	Ephraim
b 1837 ME	b 1838 ME	b 1839 ME	b 1841 ME	b 1842 ME	b 1843 ME	b 1845 ME	b 1847 ME	b 1849 ME
d 1898 ME	d 1891 WA	d 1849 ME	d 1923 WA	d 1910 WA	d 1895 ME	d 1926 WA	d 1918 IA	d 1912 WA

Mildred	**Daniel Dee** *m*	Olivia M. Blake	**Royal R.**	**Chester**
b 1882 WA	b 1885 WA	b 1895 VA	b 1887 WA	b 1889 WA
d 1937 ?	d 1923 DC	d 1977 PA	d 1990 CA	d 1912 AK

Harriet Stuart Pullen*   *m*   John Ormsby Phillips
b 1922 NC   b 1920 PA
d 2007 PA   d 2000 PA

*mother of the author

INTRODUCTION

In 1897, Harriet Smith Pullen left her farm on the Olympic Peninsula to seek her fortune in Skagway, Alaska, during the Klondike Gold Rush. The daughter of westwarding, homesteading pioneers who moved three times across the continent looking for land, Harriet established and managed one of Alaska's best-known hotels for fifty years, achieving near-legendary status in Alaska. But unlike the many, mostly male, stereotypical figures of the American West, she did it while building a business, homesteading and running a ranch, and raising and educating four children. A famed raconteur, she controlled her life story through numerous interviews with authors who have told pieces of her Skagway story. I wanted to find the whole story—how she got to Alaska, where she'd come from, why she stayed, and who she really was.

My initial goal in researching the life of Harriet Smith Pullen was to remove the fiction from the fact. I decided instead to keep the stories, whether apocryphal or not, and place them in a documentable historical context. Although history, on one level, is always someone's opinion, this book presents the events of Harriet Smith Pullen's life as comprehensively and accurately as possible, while accounting for her own efforts to control her storied legacy.

Note: Bracketed dates reference quoted passages from A. J. Smith's diary. I have maintained original spelling, punctuation, and grammar in all quotations throughout the book.

CHAPTER ONE

Queen of Heartbreak Trail

ONE EVENING IN 1948, HARRIET PHILLIPS, A NEWLYWED IN HER Detroit apartment, tuned in a radio play, *Queen of Heartbreak Trail*, the story of Harriet Smith Pullen. Radio dramas had been all the rage for a number of years. The war was over, Harriet Phillips's husband was safely home from army service in Europe, and she was in the last weeks of her first pregnancy. Life for them was all about the future. The *Queen of Heartbreak Trail*, on the other hand, was about the past—Harriet's past, and her family's past—for Harriet Smith Pullen was her grandmother, a pioneer in the Klondike Gold Rush of 1897. The play began:

NARRATOR: 1897, the year gold was discovered in the Klondike. It was midsummer of that year when Harriet Pullen first saw the Coast of Alaska. [*boat whistle*]

HARRIET: I took the boat up from Seattle, jam-packed with prospectors—hard, cruel men mostly, who came looking for something—gold, success, adventure. But not me. All I wanted was a job. I had to have a job, because—well, I had my reasons. Four good ones.

The steamer pulls into the harbor and Harriet maneuvers her way through a throng of men and, with no available wharf, climbs down a ladder slung over the side of the boat. A man named Mac approaches her and offers her a job, which she accepts on the spot.

MAC: Where're you gonna live? In a tent?

HARRIET: An old miner who owns a cabin on the beach is going back to the States. It has only one room, but—

MAC: Any furniture?

HARRIET: It's got a stove.

MAC: Nothing else?

HARRIET: No.

MAC: Not a bed nor a table nor a chair. You call that a home for your children?—Mrs. Pullen, I can't figure you out. You look like something out of a tea party—but you talk like Mrs. Daniel Boone!

HARRIET: Do I? Mr. Mac, all I know is, I'm going to build a new life for me and my children. . . .[1]

Queen of Heartbreak Trail, starring Irene Dunne, a much-admired singer and, at the time, a four-time Best Actress Academy Award–nominated movie star,[2] was a thirty-minute episode in the thirteenth season of NBC's *Cavalcade of America*, a weekly series dedicated to documenting dramatic moments in American history through stories of individual courage and enterprise. Actors in leading roles during the 1947–48 season alone included other red-carpet luminaries such as Lucille Ball, Lionel Barrymore, Jackie Cooper, Henry Fonda, Helen Hayes, William Powell, and Robert Taylor. The show lasted for eighteen seasons, from 1935 to 1953, followed by five years as a television program. The sponsor was the DuPont Company, the "Maker of 'Better things for better living . . . *through chemistry.*'"[3] The company's goal in sponsoring *Cavalcade* was to improve its public image through moving stories of American heroism.[4]

Just before the war, Harriet Phillips had left her North Carolina home to spend a summer waiting on tables at the Pullen House, Harriet Smith Pullen's celebrated Skagway, Alaska, hotel. Harriet Smith Pullen was widely known in Alaska, but most people in the lower forty-eight had barely heard of her. Young Harriet was, to put it mildly, stunned when she heard those words, "the story of Harriet Pullen."

After listening to the play, Harriet wrote to the National Broadcasting Company, which forwarded her letter to DuPont. A company representative responded with information about the origins of the play and a copy of its script. He also offered to send her a broadcast recording, made to order at either "78 or 33-1/3 r.p.m."[5] She chose the 78.

Today, the audio recording is readily available online at an Irene Dunne material website,[6] but during my childhood, my parents had to put that 78 on the turntable for my siblings and me to hear the play. This radio drama contained, in essence, the family lore about my great-grandmother Harriet Smith Pullen, supplemented by a few of my mother's memories. Periodically, my mother found other published accounts of Harriet's participation in Alaska's rough-and-tumble Klondike Gold Rush years. They rekindled the stories, but I had paid them little attention, mostly just glancing at the things my mother gathered and tucked away.

As a child, I thought of that 78 rpm record, the first in my mother's ever-growing collection of published stories about my great-grandmother, as a rare and old-fashioned family treasure. The play and the recording certainly gave credence to the family lore, but then, maybe the radio play *was* the family lore. The story I remember was the *Queen of Heartbreak Trail* version. There were aspects of it, however, that didn't add up. Harriet Smith Pullen didn't just land on the Skagway shore out of nowhere and start turning obstacles into opportunity. In the family version of the tale and in this radio play, it was difficult to determine how much had actually happened, and how much was invented. Being on the radio didn't make it true. How this and other stories, many of them quite romantic, might have been overstated and, more importantly, what might have been left out, I did not know. I decided to find out.

In 2004, my husband and I made plans to travel from our home in New York State to Seattle to attend a professional conference. Recalling that Harriet Smith Pullen's venture in Alaska followed an extended stay on her property in La Push, Washington, on the Olympic Peninsula, I decided we should drive there so I could see for myself where she'd lived. To prepare for the trip, I leafed through the family history files that my mother had assembled and that I had recently acquired. There I found photographs of Harriet Smith Pullen's house and property in La Push.

After arriving in Seattle, we rented a car and drove 150 miles toward La Push and the Pacific Coast. As we neared the sea, the harvested evergreen timber stands ebbed and flowed, depending on the age of the trees. In some spots where the trees were the oldest, their limbs formed a vaulted corridor that blotted out the sky. As we emerged from the dark, dripping forest of sheltering Douglas firs, red cedars, and hemlocks, scented with the woodsy aroma of decaying vegetation, we drove into the grayness of the tiny village of La Push, arranged haphazardly along a vast stretch of sky and Pacific Ocean, also gray on this overcast February day. Mist rose from the water's surface. Shag birds dove for smelt. Gulls swooped and squawked in the sky. The smell of the sea filled the soggy air. Beyond the beach we could see several small but tall, rocky, pointy islands topped with fir trees.

A marina of fishing boats filled the small harbor along one side of the main street. On the other side stood simple one-story, wooden houses painted in various neutrals and a few pastels—a drab and cheerless scene. There were broken-down cars and boats in people's yards, old tires and other debris piles, a few trailers, and a school. Devoid of trees, the village's landscape included a network of streets, rimmed at the far edges by dark pillar-straight evergreens standing like sentinels. It was not only a quiet and isolated place, but it was also empty, in the middle of a dreary and damp weekday afternoon.

I was eager to find the location—or possibly even a remnant—of my great-grandmother's house, the grand Victorian overlooking the Pacific, pictured in the old photographs. The several islands that dot the sea in one of them made me think we would be able to ascertain exactly where the house once stood. In the foreground of another photograph, a man stands with a hoe, a woman picks berries, and two children attend to a family pet. Someone had labeled the people and even the dog in the picture. The bearded man is A. J. Smith; the woman is his daughter, Harriet Smith Pullen; the children are two of Harriet's sons, Dee and Chester, with the dog, Heck. Looming in the distance is the large, imposing house, high atop a hill.

My husband and I drove up and down the streets of the tiny settlement, looking for some sign of life, finally parking and asking a man if he knew where the Pullens' house had been. He did not, but directed us to the Quileute Resort—an RV park and a row of cabins strung along the beach. Inside the resort's office, behind a glass-topped curio case, stood two women. Behind them was a display of posters and photographs. We engaged the women in conversation, asking if they knew where the Pullens' house had once stood. They did not, but the minute they heard the Pullen name, their faces lit up. I explained that my mother was a Pullen. One of them responded, "Oh, then, are you enrolled?"

Enrolled. Enrolled in what? At first, I had no idea what she meant, but I quickly realized she was asking if I was a member of their Quileute tribe. I was taken aback and mumbled, "I don't think so." No one in my genealogy-obsessed, ten-generations-on-both-sides-American, WASP family had ever breathed a word about Native American ancestry.

At that moment, into my mind's eye flashed several photographs of my great-grandmother dressed in Indian ceremonial attire. People would look at them and say, "Oh, was your great-grandmother a Native American?" I would reply, "No, she just knew some Native Americans." But the stories I heard were always cloaked in vagueness. The woman pointed to several photographs behind her and told us, "Here she is, Lillian Pullen, our tribal elder. We looked up to her. It's too bad you didn't come here sooner because she died just a few years ago." The woman offered to try to find Lillian's son, to introduce us to him and perhaps other members of the Pullen family. My husband and I needed to return to our conference, so we had to forgo any introductions. I later wrote to Lillian's son but never received a reply.

As we left the gray village with the wide-open skies and drove back into the dark, lush, and sheltered forest again, I asked myself, "How did this Quileute family on the Pacific Coast acquire the name Pullen? Was I part Native American?" I began to wonder about the radio play, and all the bits and pieces of family lore I had heard over the years. I wanted facts—not only the facts of Harriet Smith Pullen's life in Alaska and this newest mystery, but also the truth about other things I'd heard about the Pullen family.

As soon as I returned home from Seattle, I began reading through my file of family papers—reminiscences from Harriet's son, her granddaughters, and anonymous writers, as well as numerous published accounts of Harriet's Alaska story. What my early research revealed was a storyline that deviated sharply from the one I had always been told. It was time to begin some serious detective work.

In order to understand Harriet Matilda Smith Pullen's story, I thought it important to investigate her family of origin. Not one word had ever been mentioned in my family about Harriet's forebears, except the comment, "Harriet was born somewhere in the Midwest." I found in my files a one-page statement written in 1879 by Harriet's father, Andrew Jackson (A. J.) Smith, when he was forty-six. In it, A. J. outlined the basic dates and facts of his life—his birth in New York State, his marriage, the places he had lived as he migrated west, the jobs he had held, the basic facts of his Civil War military service, and his current circumstances living with his wife and seven surviving children in Washington Territory. From those bare, vital facts, I began putting together the story of Harriet's youth by researching what was going on among settlers during the mid-nineteenth-century westward expansion in America.

Four months into my research, something amazing happened. While looking through my mother's papers, I stumbled upon a letter from a cousin and learned that A. J. had kept a daily diary all of his adult life. After more research, I found the diary, actually four volumes of it, in the Washington State Library. They were just a part of a seventeen-box archive of material on the Smith family. It was, for me, a gold mine. Given that no one in my family had ever mentioned this man, the diaries and the other material introduced me to a complete stranger. They enabled me to go back in time to before Harriet's birth. The deeper I dug, the more nuanced the picture of the family of her birth became. The diaries opened a window into the life of Klondike Gold Rush pioneer, Harriet Matilda Smith Pullen. This is her story. It begins in Pennsylvania.

PENNSYLVANIA

Before daybreak on a cold November morning in 1853, A. J. Smith stepped aboard a raft tied up along his father's farm property in Ulster, Pennsylvania. He, his father Alanson, his brother Harvey, and eleven hired men cast off and floated down the Susquehanna River. Three rafts,

Mrs. Harriet Pullen
Skagway, Alaska.

1.1. A postcard of Harriet Smith Pullen wearing her Tlingit ceremonial shirt in Skagway, ca. 1920. AUTHOR'S COLLECTION

stacked high with boards, shingles, and lathe, freshly milled at Alanson's mill, held spartan accommodations for the men. Their destination was Columbia, near the Maryland border. The goal was to find customers for Alanson's annual yield of lumber.

During the twelve-day trip, A. J. wrote in his ever-present diary, "I like the manner of labor very much for there is new scenes presenting themselves ever hour." Speculating on the origins of what he termed the "sublime" geological history around him, he wrote, "There are several places . . . where towering hills of rocks stand up on eather side, and visible marks are left to show that these once streached acrost the river & that all the beautiful country above must have been lakes, hemmed in by mountains until the cattaract like proud Niagra, gave way, and by the rush of water for years threw the wall. The rocks on both sides are alike & stand with a slant as tho nature has had some great convultion. . . ." [November 23, 1853] He found the Pennsylvania State Capitol in Harrisburg impressive, noting that he had set his watch by the clock atop the building, which he had viewed through his spyglass.

He saw new sights that amazed him at every bend in the river, noting by name each eddy, spring, creek, pond, canal, aqueduct, waterfall, river junction, dam, island, bridge, tunnel, coal mine, ironworks, village, and town they passed. The river journey was like the peripatetic life that lay ahead of him—a life that A. J. would record and reflect upon in his journals for more than thirty years.

"THE REGULAR TAKING HOLD OF THE PEN"

The earliest existing volume of A. J. Smith's diary begins in 1853, the year of the raft trip. It and three other volumes span thirty years of A. J.'s life and twenty-three years of Harriet's, from 1853 to 1883.[7] Several volumes are missing, allegedly lost in a fire. My introduction to the diaries came in the form of a transcription, in the collections of several libraries,[8] made by A. J.'s granddaughter, Dorothy Vera Smith Klahn, who remembered him from her childhood. Only after finding the remaining original volumes of the diary in the Washington State Library, however, did I learn that she had done considerable editing.

1.2. Alanson B. and Matilda Bush Smith, A. J. Smith's parents, ca. 1853.

A. J. used his daily diary entries not only to hone his writing skills by "the regular taking hold of the pen," but also to track his accomplishments and highlight events. [Preface, 1853–54 diary] His elaborate and methodical coding system, challenging to decipher, includes a series of symbols that span the left edge of each page. His codes denote letters written and received, work done for pay, and milestones in his religious practice. For example, he noted having read the New Testament for the tenth time, an undertaking he completed on June 22, 1859. Always mindful of the details of his debts, A. J. utilized a double slash to indicate an exchange of currency or bartering. Two horizontal lines added later signify the completion of the transaction, the account squared. Large rectangles surround his recording of a death. An elongated cross set at an angle symbolizes an important occasion. Small diamond shapes denote the making of a map of the many places he traveled.

Reading A. J.'s diary is like traveling alongside him. Continually on the move, either on his own property or overland to places far-flung, A. J. tells his story and makes observations about his surroundings or events of national import. Sometimes in a diary entry, he lays out a situation in detail. Other times he is cryptic, and only by digging deeper is the reader able to understand what he is saying. The earliest diary reveals not only a twenty-year-old who would soon become a stereotypical westwarding, homesteading American pioneer, but also a complex man of many interests and talents.

"HOLINESS TO THE LORD"

Dominating A. J. Smith's recording of his life was his devout Christianity, reflected in the title he gave one of his diaries, "Holiness to the Lord." His parents were Methodists, but on February 11, 1848, at age sixteen, he "first set out to serve the Lord," as he put it. [February 11, 1870] Within four years, he had embraced the Brethren in Christ, an evangelical Protestant denomination founded in the late 1700s near Lancaster, Pennsylvania.

On a regular basis in his younger years, A. J. handed people scripture cards—small rectangles of stiff paper about two by three inches with short Bible passages printed in red or blue. He bought them in large quantities from his earmarked savings, "The Lord's Treasury," and carried them with him at all times. When he witnessed some-one committing a sin, he would "reprove" the guilty party, usually a man, and then hand him a scripture card. For example, he wrote, "I gave one card to a man that I heard swear. . . . It silenced him." [September 19, 1853]

The gesture did not always have the desired effect. While on a train, he heard a man swear several times. "I handed him my bible & pointed to the Commandment. He read & we had warm times, for he showed much impious resistance and it was so

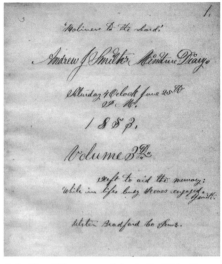

1.3. The title page of A. J. Smith's diary of 1853–1854. WASHINGTON STATE LIBRARY MANUSCRIPTS COLLECTION, A. WESLEY SMITH PAPERS, 1853–1935, M.S. 172

foolish that I should hardly think a man of sense & reason as he claimed to be would have offered them," A. J. wrote. [December 7, 1853] He encountered a similar reaction when he sharply criticized a "Materialist . . . ; his position is a very foolish one and I should think he would abandon it out of shame." [January 5, 1854]

A. J. also gave scripture cards to people who needed spiritual support or could help him spread the word of God. He regularly enclosed one in letters to his many correspondents. The thirty-five scripture cards he sent to his friend in Wisconsin, Mary Jane Stewart, were part of his effort to spread the word.

Just before the raft trip, A. J.'s father had hired a "colored man," twenty-six-year-old George W. Hill, to work on his prosperous farm.[9] A. J. reported having "a good sing" with him. [October 29, 1853] Hill became a part of the raft crew. During the trip, he and A. J. cemented their friendship. While on a layover, the two young men visited a nearby village where they bought and shared dishes of stewed oysters. Hill left

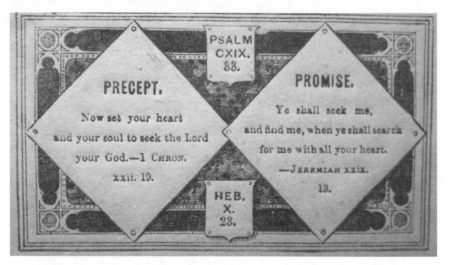

1.4. One of A. J. Smith's scripture cards from the 1850s. WASHINGTON STATE
LIBRARY MANUSCRIPTS COLLECTION, A. WESLEY SMITH PAPERS, 1853–1935, M.S. 172

his trunk in the Smiths' cabin, visited them there on occasion, and slept
on the raft with the Smiths after the other hired men had left. After
attending church together, the two friends parted company, and Hill took
the train for home.

A. J. had grown up with the Underground Railroad as a part of his
family's life. The year of his birth, 1832, was just one year after Nat Turner
led his bloody slave rebellion in Virginia—a cataclysmic turning point
in the abolitionist movement—and one year before the founding of the
American Anti-Slavery Society. By 1837, the society had more than
one thousand affiliate organizations, including one in Bradford County,
Pennsylvania, to which Alanson probably belonged. The Underground
Railroad had become an organized movement.

In the Fugitive Slave Act of 1850, Congress mandated the return of
fugitive slaves to their owners. The penalties for noncompliance were stiff.
Although on the surface this law made Underground Railroad activity
more risky, at the same time it spurred participants into more defiant
action. The moral courage required to act as an agent or conductor in
the Underground Railroad often came from religious inspiration. As a
staunch evangelical Methodist, A. J.'s father was among the pioneers of

the Underground.[10] He opposed slavery on religious grounds; to him, all people were equal before God.

Alanson put his beliefs into action by receiving fugitive slaves from a Dr. Miles Carter, who would send them north from Towanda along the Susquehanna River to Ulster. From there Alanson took them to Elmira, New York, thirty miles farther north, where they could make their way to Canada and safety.[11] To young A. J., his father's laudable work was just business as usual. During the raft trip, A. J. noted casually in his diary, "Father, Geo[rge Hill] & I walked to ... the Railroad house," three miles from their landing spot on the river, near Middletown, Pennsylvania. [November 15, 1853] Bradford County, where the Smiths lived, Middletown, and Columbia, their destination, all had long histories of antislavery sentiment.

The visit to the Railroad house, undoubtedly a station on the Underground Railroad, was a detour from Alanson's lumber-business dealings, but, for him, an important undertaking. For A. J., though, it was a place where he "heard several profane men use the name of God in vain. I threw 2 scripture cards on the flore & left." [November 15, 1853] A. J.'s father modeled for his son activism for a moral cause, but A. J. applied it in other ways.

"MY MIND IS MADE UP & SETTLED FOR ANOTHER STATE"

A. J. turned twenty-one during his Susquehanna River voyage, a coming-of-age event for him. At the end of the trip, his father granted him twenty-five dollars, the equivalent of a month's wages, to make a solo railroad excursion to Washington, DC, with stops in New York City, Philadelphia, and Baltimore.

His time in the nation's capital included visits to the US Treasury, the Patent Office Museum, the Capitol, the Smithsonian Institution art gallery, and President Franklin Pierce's house, where he shook the president's hand. He wrote that he and the president "spoke a few words, but he was preparing his 'Message' and had not time to spend with me." [December 1, 1853] On his third day in Washington, A. J. took a steamer to Mount Vernon. After touring the house and gardens, he visited George Washington's new tomb. The old one, nearby, was in a decaying condition.

He and his fellow tourists each took some small pieces of it as mementos. A. J. would give these marble tokens to a handful of relatives and friends over the ensuing months.

A. J. capped his visit to the capital with a stop at the Washington Monument, then still under construction and only 146 feet high, about one-fourth its final height.[12] On his way home, during a brief stopover in New York City, he took a horse car to the New York Crystal Palace to see the Exhibition of the Industry of All Nations, a world's fair that ran from July 1853 to November 1854.

A. J.'s grand excursion was exciting and educational, but this young man wanted land. For that quest, he would have to embark on a much bigger journey. He briefly considered going to California in the wake of the gold rush, but changed his mind during the course of the raft trip when one of his father's associates offered him a business opportunity with the promise of "wealth in early life." His father strongly urged him to consider this offer, and promised that taking it would quickly bring him prosperity. With the strength of character and self-knowledge to recognize what was right for him, however, A. J. declined. He wrote on Thanksgiving Day, "My only reply was repeated again & again. My mind is made up & settled for another state than this." [November 26, 1853]

It is unclear exactly how A. J. had made the acquaintance of his Wisconsin friend, Mary Jane Stewart, given the one thousand miles that separated them. He did have cousins in Ohio, where Mary Jane spent her early childhood. Perhaps because of the network of Brethren—Mary Jane's family and neighbors were fellow members—in Pennsylvania, Ohio, and Wisconsin, where Mary Jane moved sometime before 1850, she had had occasion to spend time in northern Pennsylvania. In any case, she was the only correspondent to whom A. J. sent postage-paid, self-addressed envelopes. The relationship blossomed through their lively ongoing exchange of daguerreotypes and letters throughout 1853. Just after Christmas that year, A. J. announced to his parents his intention to migrate to Wisconsin to join Mary Jane, where they would marry, acquire land, and begin farming.

As he readied himself for his journey west, he traded a watch for a repeating rifle. In his trunk was also a special New Year's present he had bought for Mary Jane on his raft trip—a silver pencil with a silk cord. He packed his large chest, arranging for his parents to send it later, and left home on December 27, 1853.

After twelve days in transit, A. J. arrived in Patch Grove, Wisconsin, where Mary Jane lived with her mother, stepfather, and half-siblings in a tight-knit farming community. A. J. moved in and became part of the family immediately, joining their frequent prayer meetings and working alongside the men in the community. The romance seemed cemented within just seven days of his arrival, for he penned a poem and signed it as if it were his own (and perhaps it was):

> Ex Cupids bow has long been bent:
> Th' string's just cut, the arrow's sent:
> The mark is hit; the prize is won:
> The youth is proud: for work that's done.
> (A. J. Smith)
> [January 14, 1854]

CHAPTER TWO

Wisconsin 1854–1869

ON SUNDAY, FEBRUARY 26, 1854, A. J. AWOKE BEFORE DAWN TO AN ICY cold and silvery gray day. There was already a fire going in the stove, and the women of the family were preparing breakfast at the home of his fiancée's uncle, where A. J. and Mary Jane would make their marriage vows at 7:00 a.m. They had had only a few weeks to get to know each other after their long-distance courtship, but A. J. was supremely confident in his decision to marry his seventeen-year-old sweetheart. For him, it was time to commit to a family and a life on the land.

What is most striking about the diary once A. J. settled in Wisconsin in 1854 is how much shorter the daily accounts of his life became compared to his diary entries in Pennsylvania. Not only was he married, but he was also about to take on the responsibility for his own farm. One month after his arrival he decided to stake a claim in an area seven miles from Patch Grove that would soon become the town of Mount Hope. His future in-laws planned to relocate there as well. A. J. and Mary Jane intended to live in her parents' house temporarily while A. J. worked his own nearby land. For a young man who had always wanted to be a farmer, claiming a piece of land was an important step. He was wisely starting small and could now put to use what he had learned working on his father's Pennsylvania farm.

SQUATTER'S RIGHTS

The Preemption Act of 1841 was a federal law designed to regulate the sale of public domain lands to US citizens (and those working toward naturalization), who lived on the land for at least fourteen months or worked it consistently for five years. If an individual met these criteria, he or she (widows could make a claim) could acquire title to the land for a minimal price set by the federal government. The concept of preemption rights (akin to squatter's rights) developed as a way to prevent speculators from buying up large tracts of land and to encourage yeoman farmers to establish communities. When people met the terms of the Preemption Act, they received a patent, equivalent to a deed.

As A. J. described it, his Preemption land-claim process began with a reconnaissance trip with his father-in-law to look at eighty-acre parcels they believed were available for homesteading. They each found one. The two agreed that they would work their respective claims together and split the grain harvest equally. A. J. then visited a man who wrote up his claim for a fee of ten cents. A. J. also gave him postage money and the required two-dollar filing fee. He noted in his diary, "If any one has a claim before me the money will be refunded: if I have the first claim they will send me a certificate, and I must raise $100 to pay one year from this date." He described his claim and the occasion: "There is one good spring. [A]lso a creek crossed one corner. There are but few trees, the rest is all prairie: gradual descent to the south: It all lays to the sun. Bro[ther] W[ells] & I returned home tired." [February 6, 1854]

In Pennsylvania, where A. J. had learned the business of farming from his father, the farm was ready-made. In Wisconsin, on the other hand, he had to find it, claim it, clear it, and follow all the rules the US government had set forth in the Preemption Act.

When A. J. made his Wisconsin claim, it was still winter, too early to begin planting, so he immediately commenced improving the property by splitting rails to build fences, setting fire to the prairie grasses to prepare for planting, digging out a spring, and logging. A. J. and his work partner felled trees, drew them out of the woods, and then prepared them for transport to the mill. By the end of logging season, A. J. had seventeen of his own logs awaiting the milling process. In the evenings and during inclement weather, he made an ax handle, swifts on which Mary Jane could wind yarn, rockers for a rocking chair, and a maul fashioned from an oak knot that he had found in the woods.

As spring approached, A. J. began moving household goods to Mount Hope. By mid-March, A. J. and Mary Jane had settled in the house on his in-laws' new land. The arrival from Pennsylvania of A. J.'s chest, after nine weeks in transit, aided the domestic arrangements. In it he found what he had packed before his departure, along with some items his parents had added: "one feather tick: 1 Bible: 3 Comforters: 17 yds muslin: 1 coat: [undecipherable word]: 1 sugar bowl; full of white sugar: some dried apples: some sausage: peach stones: 1 pr pants: some books, &tc &tc." [April 14, 1854]

Trading tasks with his neighbors and the men in Mary Jane's family facilitated A. J.'s homesteading process. He borrowed oxen for certain tasks and agreed to give his father-in-law five days of work and some logs in exchange for five days' work and hauling three logs to the mill, beginning a multifaceted system of bartering that would become central to his life in the future. He faithfully recorded the details in his diary. He wrote, "I worked for Mr Parsley 2/3 day with team. Mary let them have 4 fowls, 2 guineas, bush beets. I got 34 pumpkins & 7 mellons." [September 9, 1859] His trades often included both goods and services in varying combinations. Sometimes the exchange was a triad. "I split 50 rails for uncle Goff to pay Wm Hoag for one tub," he noted. [August 27, 1859]

320 ACRES

In 1855, A. J. and Mary Jane were living on and farming a different eighty acres than the ones A. J. had claimed in 1854. Then, as his prosperity increased, an optimistic A. J. acquired more land. In May 1857, the US government granted him the patents to three parcels, a total of 320 acres.[1] A. J.'s big new farm was still in Grant County, but two miles to the north of where he had first settled. He paid cash, and even though the price of Preemption land was low, he had to borrow money to pay for it.

By the spring of 1859, A. J. was building an addition to their house to make room for the family's two sons, Alanson Wesley, known as Wesley, and Oliver William, called Olly, ages five and two. A. J. now had his own pair of oxen, which he loaned to people on occasion. He was pleased, given his many acres of prairie land, that his cattle could "get plenty of grass to eat now, wild." [May 13, 1859] His assets had increased considerably. The future looked bright for the young family.

2.1. A Wisconsin farm in May 2013, on the land that was once the Smiths' homestead. PHOTOGRAPH BY THE AUTHOR

The reproving with scripture cards had ceased by this time. Instead, A. J. became an exhorter, acquiring "a written exhorters license" on August 20, 1859, and began regularly exhorting at Sunday meetings. The role of an exhorter was somewhere between a layman and the circuit preacher. On November 28, 1859, he "exhorted on experience. Christian perfection & imperfection." The exhorter offered urgent advice or warnings, often based on a Bible passage—in A. J.'s case, equally divided between Old and New Testaments. While he practiced exhorting, A. J. also began writing in his diary what appear to be drafts of sermons. He soon moved on to embrace the sermon-delivering role of a preacher. Four years later, he passed his examination and licensing requirements to become a local preacher. Religion for A. J. had taken on a new, more official form. A. J.'s increasing responsibilities as farmer and preacher left less time for journaling. The subtitle on the title page of the diary volume

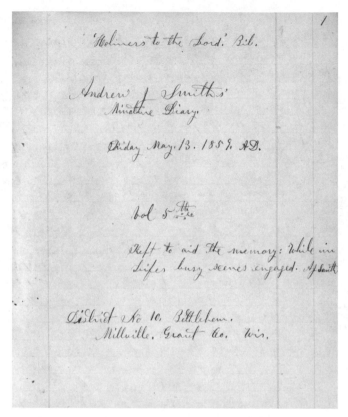

2.2. The title page of A. J. Smith's diary of 1859–1883.
WASHINGTON STATE LIBRARY MANUSCRIPTS COLLECTION, A. WESLEY
SMITH PAPERS, 1853–1935, M.S. 172

he used during this period reads, "Kept to aid the memory: While in Lifes busy scenes engaged." [1859 diary]

"FAREWELL TO MORTGAGES"
In the summer of 1859 and as the remainder of the year unfolded, A. J. noted in his diary a number of challenges that are unlike what he had reported previously. Some were minor setbacks. In June he wrote, "I planted corn all day where the gofers had pulled it out. . . . The frost of June 4th killed grass & oak leaves & sprouts 18 inches long." [June 15, 1859] He mentioned his cows, sheep, and oxen wandering off on several

occasions and the extended time it took for him to find them. He must not have had the resources to fence his new, larger property. On August 12, he had unspecified "bad luck." He noted damaging frosts that occurred in August and a killing frost in September.

By the end of the 1859 growing season, A. J.'s diary indicates that farming alone could not sustain him and his family. In November, he traded his turf-breaking plow for two sheep and a hive of bees. He may have known then that his prairie-breaking, farm-expanding days in Wisconsin were ending. In his enthusiasm for having his own land, he'd taken on more property than he could manage. With their land mortgaged to the hilt, the family was now just getting by. A. J. would have to become a wage earner. Undoubtedly, he was disappointed at his inability to live off what his own land could provide, to support his family as an independent farmer who worked only for himself.

In December 1859, A. J. began teaching school, something he had done briefly at the age of eighteen in Pennsylvania.[2] Grant County by this time had seven school districts.[3] A. J.'s new livelihood took him to teaching appointments in eight different schools over the next three years. One year his schoolhouse burned at the hands of an arsonist eighteen days into the session. He managed to find another position quickly, although the new school was farther from home (about twenty-two miles) and he could not return to his family at night. The next season he was able to find a teaching position near home. The following year, however, he was back to boarding for his teaching position. His January 3, 1862, diary entry suggests that his landlord regarded him almost as a servant. "School ect. Mr. I. L. Miles requires me to do some chores and pay One Dollar per every seven days for my board. I am at liberty to go and come at my pleasure while we mutually consent to the above." It seems the arrangement did not suit A. J., for one week later he found another place to stay and agreed to pay an additional fifty cents per week.

Mary Jane began adding to the family income by sewing for other families. A diary list of 1861 expenditures includes needles and thread, muslin and dress lining by the yard, and "2. Yds. small figured pink calico .25.," one of only a handful of times a color is mentioned anywhere in the diaries. Pink may have seemed special in that it was a color available only after the invention of aniline dyes in 1860.[4]

A. J. and Mary Jane's financial situation, on the other hand, was far from "in the pink." Unable to pay off an outstanding debt, in August A. J. renewed a mortgage to raise funds. Then, in early January 1860, the court served the Smiths with lawsuit papers, a complaint for nonpayment of a debt. In April, A. J. and Mary Jane traveled twelve miles to the sheriff's office in Lancaster, the county seat, to face the judgment. His diary entry for April 11 lays out the long-term results of his first mortgage, taken three years earlier, and conveys not only his intense frustration but also his resolve to avoid getting into debt in the future. The entry reads:

[W]ent to Lancaster. Paid D Ward   *$2.50.*
Gulop and Gleson's Judgment   *$9.46. = $11.96.*
I paid $1. to the Grant County Herald. . . .
Lancaster, Wis. Sheriff Office. Apr 11, /60 AD.
D. M. Russell versus A J Smith & Wife
    Judgment   *$72.51. cts.*
    Costs before judgment   *$32.35. cts.*
    Interest   *.75.*
    Printers fee   *3.00*
    Sheriffs fee   *6.00.*
    Clerks fee for copy & sale   *$1.95.*
    Cost to Redeem Amt.   *$116.56*
Had they proceeded to sale same $15 or $20. Must have been added to the above Amt.
S O Payne the plaintiffs Attorney let me off $5.
I then paid him $111.56 ct. He gave me a Rect in full of all demand.
    I paid J D Green for services   *.65 ct*
    J Horsefall J P,   *.50*
    B L. Loomis,   *.75.*
         Amt. $1.90

The sacrifice of my cattle   *$60.00*
4 trips to Lancaster &
2 trips to Platteville &
Six weeks time & expenses   *$25.00.*
                 Total Amt. 203.46.
    My first note, Feb. 10, 1857, $50.95 in trust at high prices has
cost me the enormous sum of $203.46.
    Farewell to Mortgages. A J Smith

The sale of the 160-acre chunk of his land was final on June 1, 1860. With the lawsuit settled and more than half of his land gone, for A. J. the following six months were challenging. He farmed the remains of his property but seemed restless and at loose ends, waiting for school to begin again in the fall. Mary Jane was pregnant. He worked occasionally for various neighbors, sold a few of his poems, worked on the road to pay taxes, and cut wood. His poem "In These Hard Times!" which he sang at the Independence Day celebration in Lancaster, tells the story of his financial situation:

HARD TIMES! Mercy on me, no mercy!
HARD TIMES! No mercy for those who are in debt.
. . . .
    My notes are due, I know that's true,
    But dollars—they are scarce and few.
. . . .
    Produce is low, you very well know,
    To settle your claims, there is no show.
Suits are commenced, our farms are fenced.
And execution must recompense—
That's how we're forced to pay.[5]
    (A. J. Smith, "In These Hard Times!")

Having sold one cow in January, A. J. had to sell another and her calf in June. In early August, he came home one day to find their cellar full of water after a heavy storm. "Lost one b[arre]l new soap, 2 bush[el] lime. Our butter & lard & Meat was flooded. S A Townsend helped me bail about 700 cubic ft. of water out of the cellar. [A] great deal of wheat is washed away & the rest is damaged very much," he wrote. [August 2, 1860]

"HARRIET MATILDA SMITH WAS BORN AT 7½ O'CLOCK PM"

It was into these deeply unsettled times that A. J. and Mary Jane's first daughter and third child was born. A. J.'s diary entry for August 12 reads, "[H]unted for the old cow—oxen & sheep. Mary is very sick—sent for Dr. Clark. [H]e was not at home. Ellery Babcock sent Daniel Garvin for Mrs Clark." The next day, he wrote:

> Mrs Clark came in the morning. Dr came about 11. o'clock. AM.
> Harriet Matilda Smith
> Was Born
> at 7½ o'clock PM. August 13th, 1860. AD.

A prayer followed:

> We thank the Lord for favors shown
> And ask thee now to bless thine own
> & May this child in early life
> Seek God and shun a world of strife

There is no indication that Harriet—known first as Matilda and later as Hattie (and sometimes Hatty)—sought God in early life, or ever, for that matter, at least not through organized religion. Nor did she shun a world of strife, for the adventurous and challenging years ahead would bring her more than her share of that.

The year 1861 found the Smiths back in Pennsylvania living with A. J.'s parents. They spent the six months of the growing season there, having rented their Wisconsin land to another farmer. During this time, A. J. learned the craft of broom making, which he would use to supplement his income from teaching. They returned to Wisconsin in the fall.

The Smiths had no horse or other mode of transportation during this time. When A. J. went to Boscobel to buy "one table $4, one bedstead

Thurs. 9. Aug. 1860. A.D.

Built 2 places to stack wheat below my house.

Fri. 10. took the top off my Barley stack, – very wet.

Sat. 11. hunted oxen most all day. fixed the Barley.

Sunday 12.

– hunted for the old cow – oxen & sheep. May is very sick – sent for Dr. Clark. he was not at home. Ellery Babcock. sent Daniel Gowen. for Mrs Clark. Geo. Cooley for Dr. Clark.

Mon. 13. Mrs Clark came in the morning. Dr came about 11. Oclock AM.

Harriet Matilda Smith
was Born.
at 7½ Oclock PM. August. 13th 1860. AD.

We thank thee Lord for favors shown
And ask thee now to bless thine own
O. May this child in early life
Seek God and shun a world of strife

My oxen & cow & one sheep came home. one did not.
(Left 7)

2.3. A. J. Smith's diary entry for August 13, 1860, the day of Harriet's birth.
WASHINGTON STATE LIBRARY MANUSCRIPTS COLLECTION, A. WESLEY SMITH PAPERS, 1853–1935, M.S. 172

$2.75, one pocket knife 25 cts, shawl 1.00, 2 butcher knives 25 cts, Powder 35 cts, cups 5, 2½ lbs shot 25 cts & a few other articles," he walked and noted that the trip home took four hours. [July 12, 1862] He also had money for necessities like new shoes for his growing children, as well as occasional luxuries, such as a two-dollar cradle rocking chair and "rattle box for Matilda [Hattie] 20 cts & 2 slates for the boys for 5 cts each," although in the latter case the presents for the children were bought with money borrowed from a neighbor. [February 7, 1861] He also bought a primary reader for Wesley, as he would do for his second son one year later, and made a little willow basket for Hattie.

A. J. was elected school clerk for a three-year term in 1862, and town clerk in 1863, offices for which he probably earned a nominal salary.[6] His duties for the latter included keeping the minutes for the town board meeting, working on maps and road books, registering voters, and issuing permits.

During the early 1860s, in addition to teaching school and serving his clerkships, A. J. also farmed on a modest scale, growing corn, wheat, hay, rye, potatoes, and broomcorn for his broom-making business.[7] He had to pay farmers with oxen to break his soil and borrow a horse to do his plowing. He also sold eggs, worked for local farmers during harvest season— grinding wheat, stacking corn, digging potatoes—and sold brooms. In the fall of 1862, he made and sold 150 brooms, using a machine to facilitate the process. In at least one instance his diary entry says "we" made brooms, which suggests Mary Jane assisted him. When the school terms began, he took his broom-making machine with him to the places where he boarded.

"WE LEFT OUR STATE, TO MEET THE FATE"

After the Smiths' return to Wisconsin from Pennsylvania, they had scaled back their farming operation and were managing to make ends meet with A. J.'s various jobs, yet difficulties would begin again for young Hattie and her family with the Civil War, which had begun in April 1861. On June 24 of that year, A. J. mentioned it for the first time when he wrote of a friend leaving for the war. In the next five months, he recorded the deaths of twelve soldiers he knew by noting the name, date, and cause of death, and surrounding each diary entry with a bold black box. More than half of the men had died of disease.

A. J. registered for the draft in June 1863 and enlisted in the Union Army's 50th Regiment Wisconsin Volunteer Infantry on March 13, 1865. Assigned to Company H, he was one of four sergeants. He spent most of his Union Army service at Fort Rice on the Missouri River, in an area that is now North Dakota. His primary assignment was to manage the fort's bakery, which produced bread for more than one thousand soldiers on a daily basis.

A. J. felt isolated in this remote place. "Comparatively we are exiled. We don't know what is going on in the world around us. We have seldom any communication from home, and as for newspaper news we get but very little, & that is so old that we are as much in the dark as ever. It is but a history of the past," he lamented soon after his arrival at the fort, in what he called his war journal. [January 1, 1866] Despite his sense of exile, there were times when A. J. seemed cognizant of and engaged in con-

temporary national issues. On February 2 he wrote, "I attended the debate last evening. Resolved that the right of suffrage should be extended to the negro. I spoke on the affirmative. The case was decided in the affirmative." Two months later Congress passed the Civil Rights Act of 1866, intended to provide full civil rights for African Americans.

A. J. made forays outside the fort to visit the Lakota people in a nearby village. He devoted five pages of his war journal to a glossary of more than one hundred English words with their Lakota-language equivalents spelled phonetically, suggesting that he had

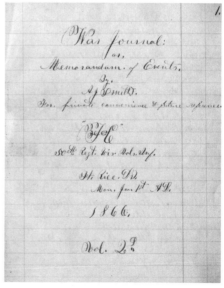

2.4. The title page of A. J. Smith's war journal of 1866. WASHINGTON STATE LIBRARY MANUSCRIPTS COLLECTION, A. WESLEY SMITH PAPERS, 1853–1935, M.S. 172

an interest in communicating with them. Among the words he listed were those for animals, people, tools, food, and common activities. A few examples as he wrote them:

"Horse"	Shun-ka-ka
"Buffalo"	Ton-tun-ka
"Rat"	E-tun-ka-tim-ka
"Soldiers"	O-ke-cha-ta
"White man"	Wa-see-che
"Arrow"	Wa-hin-ke-pe
"Salt"	Minnesque-ah
"Corn"	Wock-a-ma-zia
"To Eat"	O-tah
"Joking"	To-kin
"Buffalo robe"	She-nah

It is worth noting that "Horse" and *Shun-ka-ka* are the first words on the list, as the horse would play a significant role in the lives of the Smiths in coming years.

A. J. wrote that during one of his visits to the Lakota village he had gone into three of their tents. "The Indians seem to feel quite comfortable. I have not been in a tepee since sometime in November. I gave a Soldier cap & a piece of bread to a boy. It is lamentable to see the Image of God live in a condition that is but little above the brute creation! They are kind hearted, and if they were educated & had knowledge of God, they would be a happy people—smart & intelligent," he observed, revealing his strong evangelical bent. [January 19, 1866]

He also noted that one Indian had made a raid on other Indians nearby and "cut their teepes to pieces—killed one of their dogs & 2 of their ponies. Revenge. No one was hurt. O' that they were Christians." [January 28, 1866]

He made many observations about the daily lives of the Lakota people: "I visited Chief 'Two Bear's' tent. He has 4 wives & 7 children. 2 of his wives are at home and 2 are off hunting." [April 30, 1866]

Yesterday I saw a squaw paddle a buffalo hyde acrost the river, from E to West. 2 Indians were sitting in her boat, when she got on this side, she took her boat on her back & carried it to the tepee ½ a mile. The gentlemen Indians walked leasurely to the tepee so as to be there by the time she would have something cooked for them to eat. The women do the work & carry the burden. It is beneath the dignity of the male class to work. As soon as the female can do any thing she begins her toil, and ends it with her life. Such is man without Revelation. [May 25, 1866]

A. J. expressed empathy and concern for the well-being of his neighbors during the raw, blustery days of early spring. "The poor Indians suffer today. The Major told me that 4 died last Sunday. Many of them are in a wretched condition. Poor creatures." [April 4, 1866] His contact with Native Americans would serve him well, as he and his children would have multiple dealings with other Indian groups in the future.

HOME

The war ended in 1865, and A. J.'s impatience at being kept in the army past the armistice increased until May 17, 1866, when he noted, "I feel like a bird let out of a cage." A. J.'s regiment learned that a steamer headed for Fort Rice would soon arrive to take them home. The men were ordered to empty their straw-filled bed ticks. "We did so & now we must take the soft side of a board for our beds till we get home," he wryly commented. [May 25, 1866] Nine days after news of their impending departure, A. J. attended to some final business in the bakery. The men packed their knapsacks. After inspection, they marched to the awaiting steamer, stacked arms, loaded their gear and thirty-five cords of wood, and departed.

Arriving at St. Joseph, Missouri, the soldiers "left the boat & marched through the mud to a Depot ¼ of a mile then back to a ware house near the boat. [T]ook quarters for the night. It was very dark and we had a nasty tramp," he reported on June 11. Before boarding a train the next day, he "took a farewell drink of the muddy water of the Mo. [Missouri] River. I like it better than the well water on the shore. It is a beautiful country through which we pass. Mostly prairie. Night closes in & we are riding on a rail." [June 12, 1866] He continued describing the trip:

The corn looks well. Potatoes are in bloom. Winter wheat & Rye is headed out. Peas & red clover are in bloom. All nature is beautiful. The air is fragrant. There are a few large apple trees at Palmyra. Apples are ½ as large as hens eggs. The water is good. We came to the Miss[issippi] River about 10. AM. Crossed on a steam ferry. One of Co "D" boys was killed here a few days before, by a box falling on his head. O! how uncertain is life!!! His wife & children expect him home—that home he'll never see! How sudden & how sad, to meet such a disappointment. We left Quincy, Ill[inois] at 2. PM. I got some straw berries here. It took 2 engines to take the train up on the prairie. This is the beautifullest land I ever saw. It is under a high state of Civilization & Cultivation. We were welcomed at every station. Ladies would wave their white handkerchiefs & men would swing their hats. It makes us feel good to see Union people & know that we are welcome home. We were honored more by this people than any we have met since we have left the state of Wis[consin]. [June 13, 1866]

A. J. arrived in Chicago on June 14, 1866. He bought apples, lemons, and oranges for Mary Jane and the children. Then, with his fellow soldiers, he took the train to Madison. Still not discharged, he spent one week there and did some more shopping, haggling along the way. A. J. bought "a Straw hat .50—linen coat 2.50 & a Trunk 5.50 for $7. I bought an Album for Mary $4.50. The price was $5. Also some transparent slates for Wesley .30 Olly .25 & Hatty .25. Also some knives .35 [for Wesley] .35 [for Olly] & [brother-in-law] Olly Wells .30 & one for myself .75. Also an everlasting pencil .40 for myself. Also bought Mary Jane a Mantiller. Dress. & 2 skirts. . . . I bought my U.S. Gun $6." [June 15, 16, 1866] Two-year-old David, the Smiths' fourth child, apparently did not receive a gift. A. J. also acquired a watch and a new suit for thirty-four dollars each. He sat for his photograph, deciding to buy six prints of himself in his army uniform and eighteen in his civilian attire for six dollars. He

2.5. A. J. Smith in his Civil War uniform in June 1866, with "David Smith, A. J. Smith's brother" written on the back of a print in the Washington State Library Manuscripts Collection, whereas other prints of the photograph indicate that this is, in fact, A. J. AUTHOR'S COLLECTION spent one dollar on a copy of Lincoln's Emancipation Proclamation. He had voted for Lincoln six years earlier.

Finally, on June 20, 1866, A. J. received his discharge as a full sergeant, having served fifteen months and seven days.[8] "It has been a long year. I feel happy to be a Citizen again. To God be all the Praise," he wrote. [June 20, 1866] His discharge pay was $315.75.

After the war, A. J. lost no time in getting back to the rhythms of farming life. When he left for military duty, his children had ranged in age from one to ten years. Hattie was almost five. How the family managed throughout his time away from home is a matter of conjecture, but Wesley wrote many years later that it was during this time his mother first saw the "scar side of life, which I as a small boy shared in. We worked hard, ate hearty and slept sound when night came."[9]

Mary Jane's mother, stepfather, and siblings, who lived several miles away, undoubtedly helped them. Mary Jane did all of the chores typical of a nineteenth-century farmer's wife, including sewing most of the family's clothes. One of Hattie's sisters reported in an interview, "In the summer we wore sun bonnets. They were pretty and cute as well as useful. Mother knew how to braid hats out of oat straw, knit our stockings and spun her own yarn with a little flax wheel her own mother had given her. We had fine stockings and mittens and nice clothes. I liked those little Mother Hubbard dresses. Our stockings wore like iron."[10] According to one of her descendants, Mary Jane was also a midwife.[11]

Even though family members remembered her as being "mild and meek,"[12] Mary Jane must have been a resourceful woman of strength and forbearance, for as the family grew, A. J.'s absences continued in the years to come. If Mary Jane did not have survival skills when she married him, she surely would have developed them later. In the first twenty-nine years of their marriage, A. J. was gone for a total of nearly seven years, leaving a resilient Mary Jane, Hattie, and the other children to cope and care for the farm themselves. She surely served as a role model for young Hattie.

"I Am Going West"

After the war, there is a three-year gap in the diary. A. J. resumed writing in his war journal in May 1869 with the following three entries:

S[aturday]. 22.
I planted potatoes, finished. Sowed some Peas. Weather Pleasant.
Sun. 23.
We went to Little Green to Sunday School. . . .
M[onday]. 24.
Mary, Olly, Lizzy & I went to Tafton. I finished marking out corn
ground before I started. I am going West.

During the intervening three years a fifth child, Lizzie, had been born. The citizens of Mount Hope had elected A. J. the town clerk for a second term.[13] Though seemingly fully integrated into the community, A. J. decided to leave his Wisconsin farm for what he hoped would be better opportunities elsewhere. It seems the Smiths' financial woes had continued unabated. After fifteen years in Wisconsin, A. J. was "going West."

His destination was Dakota Territory. Why A. J. elected to go there seems clear: A. J. had had the opportunity to see Dakota firsthand during his service at Fort Rice and on his trips up and down the Missouri River. Congress had organized it as a territory in March 1861. Settlement began soon after, a result of the Homestead Act of 1862, which encouraged people to stake claims by making land virtually free. A. J.'s cousin Byron Smith and his brother Harvey both had settled there.[14] The two previous years had had good crop seasons. A railroad line extended as far west as Sioux City, Iowa, making the territory more easily accessible from the east. Seven more railroad companies planned to begin service through the area within five years.[15] Four-horse stagecoaches were already offering mail and passenger service between Sioux City and Yankton. Steamboats carrying passengers and freight ran up and down the Missouri River after the yearly March breakup of ice. Settlers had built a gristmill on the Vermillion River and had several more in the works. Newcomers in the area believed themselves to be finally free of conflict with Indian peoples, as the last significant difficulty had occurred in the area in the summer of 1865.[16] On top of all this good news was an unusually mild winter in 1868–69. Hence, the reports from settlers to people back east were so encouraging that 1869 saw an especially large number of migrants arriving.[17] The year 1869 was full of promise for southeastern Dakota and for the Smiths.

Like many new settlers, A. J. went west without his wife and children to find land and build a temporary shelter. He left with his two brothers-in-law, Charles and Oliver Wells, heading more or less due west, on May 25, 1869. The three walked to the Mississippi River and crossed it by steam ferry to Iowa. Traveling with just one horse to carry supplies, they made most of the four-hundred-mile trip on foot. Their route took them across northern Iowa. It rained frequently. There were many "bad sloughs" to cross. They got lost. They camped along the way, fishing and duck-hunting for food. On Sundays, they remained in camp, read the Bible, and had prayer meetings. On June 10, A. J. observed, "We crossed a prairie 27 miles that we never saw a house or a fence or tree." There were some people in the area, however; realizing he had left his gun at their last campsite, he backtracked to discover that someone had taken it.

Mindful that he planned to make this same trip later with his family, A. J. carefully noted in his diary six good camping places between Sioux City and his final destination, and included the distances between each stop. On June 18, the three men arrived in Vermillion, described that year by one historian as a "lively village" of four hundred residents.[18] The next day, they found land and staked their claims, each taking 160-acre adjacent quarter-sections fifteen miles north of town. A. J. paid two dollars at the US Land Office in Vermillion for his claim. He then made a ninety-five-mile trip, much of it on foot, to the Yankton Indian Agency to visit his brother. A. J. must have been in financial need, because Harvey gave him ten dollars and loaned him another sixty-five. Harvey also sold him a buffalo robe and a pony.

Returning to his claim, A. J. had his quarter-section surveyed and built a claim cabin. For A. J. this land seemed to hold great possibilities. What lay before him actually looked ideal. Unlike Wisconsin, there were no trees and roots to contend with, no steep ledges and deep valleys to avoid—just flat, open country awaiting the plow.

The essential homesteading tasks completed, A. J. returned to Wisconsin on July 11, 1869. On September 6, he sold the remaining 150 acres of his Wisconsin property to a neighbor in exchange for a three-year-old cow, a yearling steer, $105 that he owed another neighbor, and $94.50 in cash that he pocketed.

Many of the Smiths' friends and neighbors turned out on the day of their departure to bid them farewell. One friend gave them a rooster and some apples. The family of seven had one covered wagon loaded with food, water, clothing, and crates containing seventeen chickens. The five children at this point ranged in age from one to fourteen years. Hattie had just turned nine. Mary Jane was pregnant with their sixth. Also traveling with them were six oxen, one horse, and fifteen cattle, including Nellie, their milk cow.

After crossing the Mississippi by ferry, they gathered provisions including: "27 lbs bacon at 20 cts $5.40, 1 box herring .70, 1 box lubrication .25, 1 lb coffee .40, 3 box matches .25, 1 lb crackers .15, 1 kerosene lantern 1.75, 1 lb powder .60, lubrication for wagon .40." [September 7, 1869] Additional supplies purchased later in the trip included more than three dozen loaves of bread, twelve peaches, one cake, one and a half bushels of potatoes, five pounds of beef, raisins, codfish, more crackers, oats, butter, flour, salt, molasses, twenty-five stamped envelopes, a cookstove, shoes for Lizzie, and knitting needles for Hattie. Acquiring additional provisions as they traveled necessitated, halfway through the trip, shipping to Dakota four hundred pounds of their belongings to lighten their load. They were among the fortunate ones, for many without the means to pay for shipping who made similar journeys had no choice but to leave their belongings along the side of the trail.

The four-hundred-mile journey, heading toward the setting sun along the same route A. J. had taken five months earlier, took thirty-six days. They traveled every day but Sunday, which gave both people and cattle a chance to rest. On the best of days, they made just twenty miles. Sloughs were a recurring problem, and one that at times added considerable extra mileage to skirt around. Sometimes they couldn't be avoided. One diary entry reads simply, "Sloughs, Sloughs, Sloughs." [September 14, 1869] Getting stuck in a particularly bad one required the brute strength of seven oxen to pull the emptied wagon out of the mud.

When Nellie ran off and their other cattle disappeared, they spent valuable time looking for them. They lost a sheepskin. After breaking a wagon wheel, A. J. had to travel eight miles with a team and a sled to have the wheel repaired. They ended up trading wagons with another traveler, with A. J.'s ten dollars thrown in to sweeten the deal. Later, the new wagon's tongue broke and needed to be replaced. It was cold enough for frost on occasion. Some areas lacked any grass for the cattle, and that meant going out of the way by at least five miles to find some. When they came upon a bridge that was out, they had to unload the wagon, remove the wheels, float it across, and swim the cattle to the other side. They then paid a fee and boarded little boats with their belongings to cross the river. A. J. lost his pocketbook or wallet. They left a kettle at a campsite. After one stormy night A. J. wrote, "A drunkard came in the night—lost his way—hard rain—he got under our wagon for shelter—set our chicken box out—it got water enough to drown 17 chickens." [September 20, 1869]

At last, in early October 1869, they passed Vermillion and headed north toward their new home. A. J.'s next-to-final trip entry reads, "We started for home, only got 13 miles. Din[ner] with Mr. J P Williams. [H]e gave me one sack of corn & one sack of turnips." [October 10, 1869] A. J. noted that they had missed the road. The crescent moon would not have helped as it was but a sliver that night.[19] Unable to locate the claim cabin in the dark, they slept in the covered wagon. When dawn broke, they found they were right next to their new home. "We unloaded our wagon," he noted on October 11. After their arrival, fifteen days went by before A. J. wrote again. The family was busy settling in and preparing for the harsh prairie winter that would soon be upon them.

Chapter Three

Dakota 1869–1877

When young Hattie climbed down from the creaky, mud-caked, ox-drawn covered wagon that had brought her four hundred miles from her home in Wisconsin, she saw before her a boundless, nearly flat expanse, covered in golden, shimmering prairie grass as tall as her father. The skyline was naked, and above was an immense blue and white dome. The huge sky meant she could watch cloud banks roll in for hours, or minutes—depending on the wind—and track a storm moving overhead from horizon to horizon. When a stiff breeze blew, the grass rustled and rippled like water in a big lake, reminding Hattie of the ones she'd left behind in Wisconsin. Otherwise, it was quiet . . . so quiet.

In every direction, the vista varied little. No valleys, no bluffs, no ridges, no hills, no buildings, except for the little wooden claim cabins her father and uncles had built. The landscape looked level, but there were shallow hollows, unseen in the distant prairie grass. In certain directions, the landscape was treeless. In others, there were a few trees here and there, signaling a creek bottom. Water was on their land; her father had made sure of that. But what water there was, was meager.

Before they left Wisconsin and during their journey to Dakota, Hattie probably heard talk of the quarter-section her father had claimed, and how thousands of other families were doing the same. So this place, once inhabited by American Indians, was her new home, the northeast quarter of Section 31 in Township 95, Range 52, Clay County, Dakota Territory, on the eastern edge of the Great Plains—only there was not much here. Soon Hattie and her family would learn that the Dakota prairie was not

3.1. A South Dakota farm in 2013 on the land that was once the Smiths' homestead PHOTOGRAPH BY THE AUTHOR

just impressive and quickly filling up with new arrivals, but also harsh and demanding of well-honed survival skills.

THICK RIBBONS OF PRAIRIE SOD

On October 11, 1869, the Smiths unloaded their belongings and set up temporary living quarters in their covered wagon and claim cabin. A. J. went to work on a sod house with the help of his two brothers-in-law and a neighbor. They arranged thick ribbons of prairie sod—a dense mass of soil, roots, and living grass—cut with a plow, sliced into hefty building blocks, and placed on top of each other like oversize bricks, grass side down. The structure was probably about twelve by twenty feet on the inside, with walls two feet thick. Banking the sides of houses with additional earth was common practice. A. J. wrote on November 2 that he and his neighbor "broke a strip west of the house to get sod to sod the N &

W side of the house more." The cold, unforgiving Dakota winter would soon set in.

Wood was scarce on the prairie, but cottonwood and willow trees grew near rivers and creeks. Two weeks after their arrival, A. J. went to an island in the Missouri River and cut young trees to make poles. He constructed the roof of the house with these saplings, a layer of straw, and a double layer of prairie sod, with the top layer grass side up. The floor was dirt or wooden boards. A. J. bought glass, window sash, and putty for two windows. The walls inside may or may not have been coated with a layer of milled timber or plaster and whitewashed or covered with paper or fabric. In spite of cosmetic embellishments, the place would have been leaky and dirty. Another settler recounted her time living in a sod house, an experience no doubt similar to the Smiths':

I lived in a sod house from when I was two and a half until I was four. It was just a one-room house made of blocks of sod cut from the prairie. I remember it—bugs and snakes and mice were always dropping down from the ceiling. The ceiling was made of brush, branches from the creek, fodder—you know what fodder is?—like cornstalks, weeds, anything. Mama used to hang sheets over the tables and beds so that things wouldn't fall on them. Then we got the idea of putting a big piece of muslin across the whole ceiling. We'd keep it up there for a year or so until it got too filthy and rain-stained and then take it down, tear it into strips, wash it, dry it, sew it back together, and put it back up.[1]

In addition to building the sod house, during the first few weeks in Dakota A. J. set posts for a clothesline, dug a pig trough, and covered their root cellar. He agreed to care for a neighbor's oxen for the winter to settle a debt, and to let a neighbor borrow his milk cow, Nellie, until spring in exchange for some hay. He also sold and traded some of the cattle the family had brought with them from Wisconsin for a reaper and hay rake. His prodigious networking skills paved the way not only for negotiating loans and bartering goods and services but also for setting up a Sunday school class in his house. It brought fourteen attendees during the Smiths' first week in Dakota.

In December, A. J. took on work for a neighbor, feeding his oxen one pail of bran each day for eighteen dollars a month. He also finished the sod house, built a cattle shed, and did other tasks to prepare for winter. Mary Jane was five months pregnant. Hattie was surely helping her mother prepare meals, wash clothes, and mind young David and Lizzie, born in 1864 and 1868, respectively, and at the same time, learning valuable lessons in how to be creative with meager resources.

After a short gap in the diary, when A. J. resumed writing on January 19, 1870, it was to note that he had left home, walking twenty-five miles through "deep snow, badly drifted." Supplementing the family income with jobs that took him away from home was still a necessity, just as it had been in Wisconsin. His destination was a cattle camp thirty-five miles west of Yankton where he went to work for $50 a month. His job was tending a herd of eleven hundred cattle, raised and sold to the federal government for meat distribution to Indian groups now living on reservations. In addition to providing meat, the government also offered instruction in agricultural pursuits, with the hope that it would transition the Indian peoples from a nomadic existence to farming or ranching.

A. J. returned home the first week of April 1870, stopping in Yankton to deposit one hundred dollars in the bank and to buy a map, a compass, and some candy. During his absence, he had placed an order for "lumber for a house 18 by 24 ft." [February 3, 1870] The Smiths' soddie had served as a shelter at least through their first winter. Throughout April, A. J. dug up rocks on his property, probably for a foundation for a new house. He continued to write in another volume, now missing, but during this four-year gap in the existing record, the family moved into the new house. A. J.'s 1874 final proof document, completing the homesteading process, stated that their one-and-a-half-story, eighteen-by-twenty-four-foot house had "8 doors & 15 windows. Pine siding and Shingles."[2] Their lives were improving rapidly.

THE FUTURE HELD GOOD THINGS

The Smiths had arrived in Dakota Territory in 1869 in the midst of the settlement boom brought on by several years of good weather, bountiful harvests, and the promise of expanded rail service. The sod house and the initially sparsely settled neighborhood notwithstanding, there must have been a sense of a growing economy, an emergent social network, and better days ahead. Institutions such as a territorial legislature, churches, and schools, always signs of a developing community, had been growing since the early 1860s.

The superintendent of public instruction in his 1866 annual letter to the territorial legislature stated that the benefits of public schools would soon reach every neighborhood in the territory.[3] In Clay County in 1867, of the two hundred children ages five to twenty-one, half were attending school.[4] Given the Smith family's commitment to education, evidenced in A. J.'s teaching in Wisconsin and in decisions he made in the ensuing years, it is almost certain that Hattie and her brothers were among those attending school. In fact, in 1871, the community started a school in the quarter-section adjacent to theirs.

A. J. and his fellow Brethren began meeting for worship in people's homes and in local schoolhouses.[5] The United Brethren organized a formal church in the area in 1871, undoubtedly with A. J.'s involvement. There were several congregations with rotating pastors in the area.[6] A. J. worshipped with all of them, usually attending services at different places on Sunday mornings and evenings, with classes in between. Occasionally he taught a Bible or a Sunday school class, and never missed a United Brethren quarterly meeting.

Evidence of the booming economy was everywhere. An emigrant guidebook said of Yankton, then a town of fifteen hundred, "[A]t present writing (May 1, 1870) the sound of the carpenters' hammers are heard in every direction, and new buildings are going up in every portion of the town."[7] The author also observed that Yankton County and Clay County, where the Smiths lived, were taking the lead in settlement in southeastern Dakota. He went so far as to predict that new settlers would claim most of the last available land in the two counties during the summer of 1870.[8]

The Smiths had arrived in time to have their choice of property. According to the 1870 census, A. J.'s real estate was valued at five hundred dollars and his personal wealth at six hundred, placing his economic status in the lower range of land-owning men in Clay County.[9] At this point, he had every reason to trust that the future held good things for him and his family.

A. J.'s diary paints a vivid picture of what farming life in Dakota was like. He mentions planting a broad array of vegetables, and describes setting out plum and buffalo berry trees, strawberry plants, and a "pie plant" (rhubarb). [May 8, 1875] He grew wheat, corn, oats, barley, and broomcorn, and raised livestock. He exchanged threshing and husking services with his neighbors during harvest time and hired men with a reaper to cut his wheat. When the team arrived, A. J. moved a stove to the field so some of the women could cook for the men. He even at times produced enough grain to sell, noting in June 1874 that he had sold four hundred pounds of flour.

In the early summer of 1875, A. J. and a neighbor decided to invest in their own harvesting machine, a Haines header. This four-horse-driven machine represented a substantial investment and offered farmers a cutting swath of fourteen feet, nearly three times the width of older harvesting machines. It could cut forty acres in a day.[10] Now comfortable in his farming life in Dakota and well integrated into his local community, A. J. was elected grange treasurer in April 1875. To supplement the family farm income, A. J. continued to take jobs during the winter months, including working as secretary for Dakota Territory surveyor-general William Henry Harrison Beadle for several years.[11]

We learn of the births of his daughter Jennie in 1870 and his son Harvey Beadle Smith in 1874, the latter an occasion marked by the insertion of a commercial calendar page for Wednesday, October 7, torn out and placed in the diary like a bookmark with the words "9½ lbs" and "2:20 AM." added by hand. Shortly thereafter, A. J. went to work for wages for his brother Harvey in Yankton, leaving the family on the Clay County homestead. By this time, Harvey H. Smith owned a hotel, the Smithsonian, and other properties in Yankton. One month into A. J.'s stay, his brother agreed to board him in his hotel basement in exchange for additional work. One of Harvey's building projects was under construction, and A. J. hauled thousands of bricks and sifted many loads of sand. In the evenings, he made stencils to number hotel doors, lettered signs such as "Baggage Room" and "Dining Hall," made key checks for another hotel, and occasionally worked in the Smithsonian Hotel office.

Socially engaged and gregarious, A. J. enjoyed the lively town, perhaps a location better suited to his temperament than his isolated, rural homestead. In his spare time, he attended prayer meetings through which he felt "revived in religion." [December 3, 1874] He also taught Sunday school, preached occasionally, and attended meetings of the

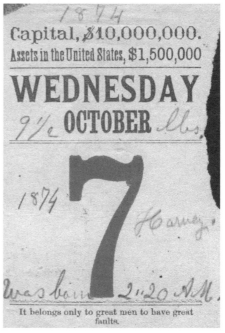

3.2. An insert from A. J. Smith's diary, October 7, 1874, the day of son Harvey Beadle Smith's birth. WASHINGTON STATE LIBRARY MANUSCRIPTS COLLECTION, A. WESLEY SMITH PAPERS, 1853–1935, M.S. 172

International Order of Good Templars (IOGT), an international temperance organization. After listening to a temperance lecture, he signed a petition for establishing an order of the Sons of Temperance in Yankton, and then joined it when it came into existence. On January 30, 1875, the chapter installed him as chaplain. A. J. worked for Harvey until April 1875, returning to the farm in time for planting.

During the summer of 1875, Hattie, age fourteen, spent a month with her uncle Harvey in Yankton. Her cousin Martha, Harvey's daughter, stayed with Hattie's family for the same period. The custom of young women living with and working for relatives or neighbors for a time was common practice—a way of broadening their horizons within safe confines. At nearly twenty-one, Wesley began working for other people. A. J., proud of his oldest son, wrote, "He did well. So did they all" [September 1, 1875], when Wesley delivered his first public speech at a Sunday school picnic.

By the winter of 1875–76, A. J. was teaching again, this time in the nearby village of Lodi. Because it was winter and the school was five miles from home, he decided to board during the two-month session. A five-mile walk would not have been a big challenge for A. J., but again, for him, being in a village might have been more appealing than living at home.

PUBLIC LAND SURVEY SYSTEM (PLSS)

Originally envisioned by Thomas Jefferson, the United States Public Land Survey began when the Continental Congress passed the Land Ordinance of 1785, which called for the survey of land in uniformly sized squares before the government sold it.[12] The Survey and its heir, the Public Land Survey System (PLSS), replaced the metes and bounds method of surveying land, still used in the original thirteen colonies and a handful of other states, including Maine, Vermont, Tennessee, and parts of Ohio. The metes and bounds method uses physical characteristics of the terrain, both natural and man-made, such as rivers, rocks, trees, and stone walls, to measure and describe property. Needless to say, many of these markers are subject to change or are altogether ephemeral, given enough time. Land surveyed this way is a conflict waiting to happen.

The PLSS, on the other hand, is utterly rational and consistent. It comprises six-mile-square townships created from a series of carefully surveyed north–south lines called Principal Meridians. As westward expansion proceeded and new lands opened up for sale, the government added new meridians. Using a Principal Meridian as a starting line, surveyors laid out more north–south lines at six-mile intervals and east–west baselines at right angles to mark the area of each township. The number given to a township is a measure of the distance north or south from a baseline; a range number is a measure of the distance east or west from a particular Principal Meridian. A township contains thirty-six sections, each 640 acres or one mile square. Quartering created subdivisions; hence, the typical quarter-section homestead of 160 acres.

Even though government surveyors surveyed Wisconsin using the PLSS, in South Dakota where it is nearly flat, the system created a completely different landscape appearance, as remarkable at ground level as it is from the sky. From an airplane, one sees a grid, a definitive pattern of 160-acre, adjacent squares that vary in color from square to square depending on the crop, the season, and the direction of the plow. Roads and trees delineate some of the boundaries. Overall, the farmland looks like a green, yellow, tan, and brown checkerboard, the outcome of the Public Land Survey System.

From a car, one encounters curious jogs that occasionally interrupt the regularity of the section-determined roads. Instead of proceeding northward, as a driver would expect, the road suddenly stops at a crossroad and then starts up its northward path again a few yards to the left. These section-line deviations are correction lines. They are the result of survey errors, the use of inferior instruments, challenging terrain, or the curvature of the Earth, which causes the meridians to converge as they go toward the North Pole.[13]

After the American Revolution, the US government was deeply in debt. One way to raise funds was to sell land in the public domain west of Ohio. In order to accomplish that efficiently, land had to be easy to sell. Surveyors were often lacking sophisticated math skills and equipment, but given the circumstances, needed to work quickly. The grid system accomplished what was required, and in the process left its indelible mark on the landscape.

The beauty of the PLSS is its simplicity and consistency. It allowed settlers to make land claims easily. They could even claim a section sight unseen from the Local Land Office, which at times some of them did. The system also kept people from "cherry-picking" the land, choosing the best of this and the best of that and shaping the property to their personal requirements.[14] A section or quarter-section, on the other hand, came as a totality, the good with the bad. This practical, democratic, straightforward system suited the rapid settlement of the American West. It also promoted community-based development because the system reserved at least one section in each township for a school.

When the Smiths arrived in Dakota, they would have encountered a landscape of seemingly endless tallgrass prairie with few roads and no tree-lined boundaries. There would have been, however, mounds of dirt marking the corners of the townships—the work of the surveyors. Rather than using the traditional surveyor's mark of a blaze on a tree, the surveyors working in the treeless prairie built mounds to mark the intersections of the north–south and east–west lines of the townships. With not much more than an occasional mound to guide the way, for settlers, getting lost was easy. A. J. noted on two occasions that he had been unable to find his claim.

But once settlers claimed the land, quarter-section by quarter-section, the landscape began to take on its linear, grid-like appearance. The land was cultivated by each owner, who sometimes planted trees as a wind barrier along section lines and constructed new roads that also followed section lines. The terrain's appearance today developed through the efforts of settlers like the Smiths. The straight roads, ones A. J. reported having worked on in lieu of paying property taxes, follow the township and section lines almost without exception, making the area easy to navigate.

"SAFE TO BORROW MONEY TO INVEST IN LAND"

The year the Smiths arrived in Dakota, property values began increasing rapidly. In an emigrant guidebook chapter titled "Who Should Emigrate to the West," the author declares that if a man were to buy a quarter-section at $5.00 per acre, in one year's time it could be worth twice that. He goes on to assert "the rapid increase in the value of real estate makes it safe to borrow money to invest in land," even though the standard interest rate was 10 percent.[15] A. J. subscribed to this line of thinking and dabbled in what had become a time-honored practice of land speculation. In the nineteenth century, land was the leading creator of wealth in America primarily because of its rapidly increasing value.[16] In August 1874, A. J. bought timberland from a neighbor for forty dollars and noted that he had "sold Peggy & calf to pay" for it. [August 3, 1874]

On September 16, 1874, A. J. went to Sioux Falls to prove up on his homestead claim. The land A. J. had claimed in Wisconsin was under the Preemption Act of 1841. In Dakota, his claim was under the Homestead Act of 1862. To receive legal title to his Dakota claim through a process known as "proving up," A. J. had to follow a lengthy process, one slightly different from the one he had followed for the Preemption claim.

He had begun his Homestead process during the summer of 1869 when he staked his claim. In December 1870, at the Local Land Office, he paid a fourteen-dollar filing fee with an affidavit stating that he was a US citizen, was the head of a family, and intended the land to be for his own use. To prove up four years later he paid a four-dollar fee and submitted a Final Proof signed by two witnesses, "persons of respectability," attesting to his having made the required improvements to the property. In addition to having built a house, the Final Proof notes that he had "plowed, (fenced 40 acres) and cultivated about 70 acres" and had "built a stable and Grainary, dug a well and set out over ten Acres of forrest trees which have been cultivated from 2 years & 5 months to 4 years."[17] A. J. signed an affidavit that he had lived on his claim for five consecutive years, had not sold any part of it, and would bear allegiance to the United States of America. Added by hand on the affidavit was a statement that he had served in the Union Army for at least ninety days, which allowed him to deduct some of his time serviced from the residency requirements. The completion of all of this entitled him to receive a Final Certificate and then a patent from the federal government, which made the land legally his.

A. J.'s Final Certificate under the Homestead Act reads: "Andrew J. Smith has made payment in full for North East ¼ of section No. 31 in township No. 95 of range No. 52 containing 160 acres. Now, therefore, be it known, That on presentation of the Certificate to the COMMIS-SIONER OF THE GENERAL LAND OFFICE, the said Andrew J. Smith shall be entitled to a Patent for the Tract of Land above described."[18] Shorthand ways of describing this parcel of land would be: NE ¼, Section 31, in Township 95N, Range 52W, in Clay County, Dakota Territory, or NE ¼, Sec. 31, T.95N, R.52W, 5th P[rincipal] M[eridian]. If written today, a description of the same property says South Dakota instead of Dakota Territory. Otherwise, it is the same.

With this certificate, A. J. achieved one of his goals in migrating to Dakota—to acquire a Homestead claim. He was also free to stake other claims under the Preemption Act or the Timber Culture Act of 1873. The very day he proved up on the Homestead claim in Sioux Falls in 1874, A. J. began a Preemption claim on another quarter-section, this one in Section 17, two miles north of his house.

A. J. must have known that the occupant of this Section 17 quarter-section, Jerome Welch, had disappeared, abandoning his Homestead claim and his sod house. The process for taking over an abandoned Homestead claim involved posting for several consecutive weeks a legal complaint in a newspaper. This A. J. did. If, after one month, Welch did not appear in the Sioux Falls Land Office at the designated time to answer the complaint, the claim became A. J.'s. Welch did not appear, so A. J. believed the claim was his. A. J., however, failed to take the next required step in the Preemption claim process. He should have done it right away. Instead, he delayed.

A. J. continued to acquire more land as he had done in Wisconsin. As an investment, he bought a lot in Yankton. In March 1875, he made a timber claim. This land, twenty-two miles north of his farm, cost him fifteen dollars. The Timber Culture Act 1873 was a follow-up to the Homestead Act. Intended to address the problem of a lack of trees on the prairie, the law allowed a settler to claim 160 acres in addition to his Homestead claim as long as he maintained trees on at least one-fourth of the acreage. After ten years, he could obtain a patent to the land.

Also in March 1875, A. J. sold the eastern half of his 160-acre homestead to Mary Jane for one hundred dollars. I learned this information through a deed search, for there is no mention of it in the diary.[19] Was he protecting his investment against some legal action, or perhaps giving his wife her half of their asset? There is no way to know why he did this.

In April 1875, just after returning from the winter working in Yankton, A. J. began repairing the floor of the sod house on the land in Section 17 that he had claimed the year before. He had a plan. The family would relocate there, and he would then rent the western half of their 160-acre homestead, a way to bring in needed income. At the new place, A. J. planted a garden, dug out the well, and lined the inside of the sod house with boards.

A. J. was in the midst of all this when he received a letter from a neighboring farmer, Levi Barton, ordering him not to trespass on the

Section 17 property. The letter must have surprised A. J., for he left the same day, May 18, 1875, walking in the rain to Sioux Falls, to take the step in the claim process that he had postponed the previous year. He also filed a complaint against Barton, a new rival. Uncertain of the outcome, A. J. went ahead and moved his family into the sod house on the Section 17 claim, commenced building an addition, and lived and farmed there for the next year.

In June 1875, A. J. noted in his diary that he had sold the lot in Yankton. At the end of the 1875 harvest season, A. J. rented to another farmer the western half of the 160-acre homestead—eighty acres that included the wooden house he had built a few years earlier. The Smiths had gone back to living in a sod house, but at least their land holdings were growing and their income increasing.

Alexis de Tocqueville in 1840 in *Democracy in America* observed, "It is rare that an American cultivator settles forever on the soil he occupies. In the new provinces of the West especially, a field is cleared to be resold and not to be harvested; a farm is built in the anticipation that, as the state of the country will soon change as a consequence of an increase of inhabitants, one can obtain a good price for it."[20] Perhaps A. J. was becoming that kind of farmer. Acquiring and selling land, however, was one thing, but managing the finances and keeping it productive was another. The Smiths' land-claim issue with Barton remained unresolved for another fifteen months. They stayed in their Section 17 sod house while dealing with unanticipated challenges of biblical proportions.

Chapter Four

"Looking for Better Times"

AT THEIR WORST, WINTER STORMS IN DAKOTA TERRITORY PACKED swirling winds of over seventy miles an hour with blowing, blinding, stinging snow, near-zero visibility, and rapidly falling temperatures. They came without much warning, sometimes several times each winter, and lasted about three days. When snow was already on the ground, it was lifted into the air in furious eddies, coming from all directions, making breathing difficult. Finely pulverized blizzard snow finds its way through any crevice, including animals' nostrils. During one blizzard on March 13, 1870, a man in Yankton County lost fifty head of cattle. The animals suffocated, the snow on their faces alternately melting and freezing until blocks of solid ice encased their heads.[1]

In one late-nineteenth-century Dakota blizzard, the temperature dropped from 20 degrees at noon to 28 below zero that night. One hundred seventy-eight people died.[2] A survivor of this particular blizzard described his experience in a schoolyard. On that relatively warm day, he and his schoolmates were outdoors without hats or mittens. "Suddenly we looked up and saw something coming rolling toward us with great fury from the northwest, and making a loud noise. It looked like a long string of big bales of cotton, each one bound tightly with . . . great silvery ropes. . . . It hit the building with such force that it nearly moved it off its cobblestone foundation. And the roar of the wind was indescribable, . . . [so loud] the teacher had to scream into each child's ear . . . [to be heard]."[3]

The Smiths endured one blizzard just three months after their arrival in Dakota. Mary Jane recalled in an interview for a newspaper article that the family's sod house was stormproof, but the shed they had constructed to house their pony was open at one end. The animal, encrusted in ice, had to be brought into the house until the storm subsided.[4] During another blizzard, Hattie was cooped up in their house with a hired man, a horse, and her mother, who was about to give birth, an ordeal her mother barely survived.[5]

Experienced settlers knew when they went out into a blizzard to track a fence with their hands or tie a rope to their front doors so that they could follow it back, hand over hand, through the blinding snow. Hattie and Mary Jane apparently did not heed the common wisdom during one blizzard. The two went out to the cattle shed to feed the stock. During their return to the house, Hattie, a young teen with courage and a good sense of direction, dragged her disoriented mother to safety.[6] The winter of 1874–75 was unusually severe in southeastern Dakota.[7]

SAVED HER FAMILY'S STOCK

Blizzards weren't the only weather-related challenges the Smiths faced in Dakota. The Vermillion River bottomlands flooded twice, once in 1875, right on the heels of the blizzards of the recent winter. When the ice broke up in the Missouri River in late March, a number of blockages backed up the water upstream and flooded the lowlands. The high water created considerable damage to homes, barns, and cultivated land.[8] A. J. referred to the problems in his diary: "Hardest rain for six years. . . . The bridge at the gulch mouth went off. . . . The country is very wet. Standing water. . . . The ground as wet as mortar. . . . Dug 1½ bush Potatoes from 15 bush[es] planted. They were drowned out. . . . Bailed water out of the cellar." [May 31, June 23, July 2, October 12, 21, 1875]

The heavy rain and floods notwithstanding, there were recurring prairie fires near the Smiths' homestead. At the end of dry summers, the prairie grasses turned brown and crisp, a blaze waiting to happen. Sometimes one could see and smell a prairie fire coming for three days. The sky blackened. Rabbits ran and snakes slithered in every direction. Forty-mile-an-hour winds brought the flames closer at an alarming rate. Cattle refused to lie down. "They sniffed and mooed, and occasionally pawed. The horses in the sod barn were also visibly nervous. They held their heads high in their stalls, and scented trouble," one man recalled.[9] The savvy settler might be able to save his family's sod house and barn, but afterwards "all was utter blackness as far as the eye could reach."[10]

During the month the Smiths arrived in Dakota, A. J. described a fire: "Yesterday & today the prairie burnt over. [I]t was a terriffic fire. It roared like the [railroad] cars—the flames rolled from 10 to 20 ft. The grandest fire I ever saw. [C]ame near loosing my wood. I tried to stop it by backfiring, but I might as well try to stop the whirl wind." [October 26, 1869]

One fire in the Smiths' neighborhood seemed to come from nowhere, sweeping over acres with frightful speed. Rivers and roads, normally barriers to a prairie fire, were not able to hold back the flames; they leapt great distances in the high winds. Firefighting with buckets and mops was useless because, according to George W. Kingsbury, South Dakota resident and author of a five-volume history of South Dakota published in 1915, the "blistering heat moved along like a wall far in advance of the devouring flames."[11] During various prairie fires, the Smiths' neighbors lost their stables, hogs, and chickens.

Taking precautions against fire was routine on the prairie. In September 1875, A. J. cut grass and then set a fire to create a firebreak, a burned-out barrier between the prairie and his fields and buildings. Hattie's family survived their worst prairie fire with A. J.'s preparation and Hattie's wherewithal. At the age of eleven, she saved her family's stock by driving them into a nearby creek.[12]

"RAIN FOLLOWS THE PLOW"

Droughts occurred regularly in Dakota, but some believed farmers could change the climate. Prominent among them was George D. Hill, the Dakota surveyor general from 1861 to 1869. Hill made his beliefs widely known that the late and early frosts and the drought conditions would moderate as farmers cultivated the land. According to one observer, Hill "stood manfully for Dakota's natural advantages as a farming country, and advocated it on the platform and through leading newspapers...."[13] His now-discredited theory of climatology, widely accepted in the 1870s and '80s and popularly referred to as "rain follows the plow," promoted the idea that cultivation of the land in dry regions would lead to a permanent change to a climate with more frequent rains.

As Charles Dana Wilber wrote in *The Great Valleys and Prairies of Nebraska and the Northwest*, published in 1881:

> *Suppose now that a new army of frontier farmers—as many as could occupy another belt of 50 miles, in width, from Manitoba to Texas, could, acting in concert, turn over the prairie sod, and after deep plowing and receiving the rain and moisture, present a new surface of green, growing crops instead of dry, hard-baked earth covered with sparse buffalo grass. No one can question or doubt the inevitable effect of this cool condensing surface upon the moisture in the atmosphere as it moves over by the Western winds. A reduction of temperature must at once occur, accompanied by the usual phenomena of showers. The chief agency in this transformation is agriculture. To be more concise.* Rain follows the plow.[14]

Wilber supported this idea using the elaborate arguments of Samuel Aughey, a so-called scientist, who, along with others, provided substantial data showing an increase in rain during the previous decade. Subsequent observers have called Aughey a "'charlatan'" and Wilber an "amateur."[15] Their ideas turned out to be little more than wishful thinking at best, and, at worst, self-serving malarkey. By the 1890s, it was perfectly clear that the increase in rain had been merely the result of a cyclical pattern. In the 1860s and '70s, however, "rain follows the plow" was a compelling idea, endorsed by many, particularly those bent on settling the West. It might have been this line of thinking that induced A. J. to stay in Dakota Territory for as long as he did.

"Visited upon Pharaoh"

Of all the challenges of farming on the Dakota prairie in the 1870s—blizzards, floods, fires, and droughts—the grasshopper scourges seemed to take the heaviest toll. In July of 1874, grasshoppers invaded the Smiths' farm for the first time. "Smoked grasshoppers. . . . Grasshoppers came so thick that I spent the day trying to keep them off of our potatoe. . . .

Grasshoppers thicker than ever. . . . Grasshoppers came in clouds to darken the sky. [T]he air was filled with living flying hoppers. . . . Grasshoppers very plentiful in the sky." These remarks were among A. J.'s diary entries for the month of July. [July 10, 22, 23, 24, 26, 1874]

On those summer days in 1874, thirteen-year-old Hattie surely saw and heard rivers of glittering darkness moving high above, dense enough to blot out the sun and make a shadow on the land. Hattie's sister Jennie, who was four at the time of the first grasshopper scourge, recalled, "They were so thick that we couldn't see the sun. My brother would swing a pail around and around his head and get it half full of grasshoppers."[16]

Kingsbury described one of the Dakota grasshopper scourges: "A mass of life [descended], . . . covering the bushes and trees and the grass, the fences and the walls of buildings so completely as to effectually conceal them from view and in as brief time as it is required to tell it, stripping the tree of its foliage and devouring the grass and gardens. . . . Woe to the careful and cleanly housewife who has left her household linen on the clothesline or a fine garment out to air. The pest has a peculiar relish for dainties of this kind."[17] He concluded, "To witness such a phenomenon is to have brought to mind the biblical account of the plagues visited upon Pharaoh, the Egyptian ruler, when he refused the Hebrews permission to leave his domains."[18]

After a time, the grasshoppers would leave, having deposited their eggs an inch below the soil surface during their stay. Their progeny would emerge, the color of grass, the next spring. In an eerie but dissimilar replay of the previous summer, during the time it took them to turn brown and grow wings, they would eat young crops before moving on to prepare for their next midsummer migratory visitation as adults.

Four times the pests came down to earth at the Smiths' homestead. A. J. reported in 1875, "The hoppers went over in swarms. Some dropped." [June 28, 1875] In late July 1876, they came in even greater numbers than ever before. They consumed the grain, corn, and most of the potato crop, and then had the audacity to remain in some areas for another two weeks, laying eggs.[19] At the time, A. J. was away, having gone to Wisconsin that summer. Mary Jane, seven months pregnant, and six of her seven children managed to keep the grasshoppers off their vegetable garden by shooing them away with tree boughs. She recalled years later that after two weeks of constant vigilance, the wind shifted, "usually a signal for the grasshoppers to move on," and she granted the children's wish to go to Sunday school. They returned to find the grasshoppers still there and the garden "a desolation."[20]

The insects were an inch or so long, hard, brown, with amber-colored wings, and could hop as well as fly. When they settled to earth, they came down like hail, making the ground a mass of crawling creatures as deep as three inches. They crunched under foot, flew into eyes, grabbed onto bare skin, and clung to skirts and petticoats. Their chewing whirred relentlessly for weeks on end. According to a US topographical engineer sent to report on the noise created by a grasshopper attack, from a distance the sound was like a train rushing by two or three hundred yards away.[21] Up close, the noise of their jaws attacking a field was, according to newspaper coverage, "like that of a prairie fire, crackling and rasping."[22] The grasshoppers not only darkened the sky and then devoured the crops but also ate dry wood, dead animals, even the wool from the backs of sheep.[23]

Attempts to destroy the grasshoppers, which were actually Rocky Mountain locusts, a species extinct today, were numerous and inventive. Methods included crushing them with rollers, catching them in bags during mating season when they were stationary, harrowing the ground where they had laid their eggs, or smoking them out, as A. J. reported trying. Farmers also drove them like sheep into stacks of straw and burned them at night in great bonfires or dug ditches around fields with deep pits placed at intervals and then poured tar and oil on the collected insects. Some tried poisoned bait or creating loud noises to frighten them away. Most efforts were for naught.[24]

The grasshopper attacks usually came in July or August, and frost could come as early as September, leaving insufficient time to plant another crop. After the worst of the grasshopper plagues, crop failures left farmers impoverished. For many, cornbread became the staple food, and burnt peas or wheat replaced coffee. Meat, sugar, tea, lard, and wheat flour were luxuries.[25] Times were desperate enough to warrant the US government sending a commission to Dakota Territory to examine the situation in the fall of 1874. That winter the federal government appropriated

4.1. Rocky Mountain locusts (*Melanoplus spretus*), otherwise known as grasshoppers, in an 1870s *carte de visite* (Jacoby's Art Gallery, photographer). MINNESOTA HISTORICAL SOCIETY, SA4.9R132

$150,000 to buy food for destitute farmers; residents who were able to help established relief societies as well.[26] After the 1876 grasshopper scourge, the governors of Iowa, Missouri, Nebraska, and Dakota Territory met in Omaha to find solutions to the recurring problem. Their answer was to plan a day of prayer for the following spring.[27]

When the grasshoppers came the first time to the Smiths' farm they were undoubtedly surprised, because the emigrant guidebook stated that the grasshopper raid of 1866 was the last in Dakota. "These pests of the farmer had passed farther East each year since their first appearance, this year [1869] reaching into Iowa, Minnesota and Missouri. . . . Dakota is now free from these pests and we have no more reason to fear their return than the people of any other section."[28] Clearly, the author was mistaken.

People at the time understood little about grasshoppers. A June 1875 newspaper article declared, "We do not expect to have another visitation of them for years to come, Dakota being entirely out of their latitude."[29] Even a professor and Missouri State entomologist delivering a lecture in 1875, after a convoluted and illogical argument concerning their migratory habits, concluded that "in 1876 we will see nothing of them."[30] Looking on the bright side, he went on to discuss his experience as a "grasshopper-eater." He had eaten a large number of them, noting:

> *When a basket of the mangled hoppers, all covered with dust, was brought in, it did not look very tempting. The brown fluid which they excrete, too, makes their odor anything but savory. But when they have been rinsed they look much better, and their odor entirely forsakes them. When they have been scalded they assume a reddish hue, not unlike a lobster, and look quite palatable. They make a soup of such excellent flavor . . . and can be preserved, too, either by drying in lumps or masses, or by pounding them into a powder which serves to make a very nice bread.[31]*

He concluded his gastronomic remarks by suggesting "the manufacture of this kind of flour would be a good industry for the people in the afflicted sections."[32]

The residents of Dakota Territory were unlikely to have agreed. And had they adhered to his suggestion that they plant only crops the grasshoppers did not favor—"castor beans, broom corn, sorghum, sweet potatoes and tomatoes," they could barely have fed themselves.[33] A. J. was beginning to have second thoughts about his decision to homestead in Dakota Territory when he wrote on September 22, 1875, "We are looking for better times."

BLACK HILLS

In the spring of 1868, the US government and the Lakota tribe, part of the Great Sioux Nation, signed a treaty at Fort Laramie, Wyoming, establishing a reservation for the exclusive use of the Lakota people in the Black Hills in western Dakota Territory. Almost all treaties with Indian peoples were primarily about the transfer of land ownership, but the treaties disguised what was really an offer the Indians could not refuse. As they lost both territory and the buffalo, their primary means of survival, they depended more and more upon federal government subsidies.[34]

The lives of Indian peoples became increasingly difficult as the US government pushed them farther and farther west and onto reservations. In December 1868, an eyewitness, unnamed correspondent for the *Chicago Tribune* reported on the state of the Yankton Sioux:

> *I refer you to the condition of the Yankton Sioux, among whom there has been an agency for the past ten years. Then they were the richest, happiest and most comfortably situated Indians on the Missouri slope; but, now, all that remains of that once powerful tribe is a miserable remnant of walking skeletons. And how shall I attempt to explain the condition of those three thousand human beings. Once they subsisted upon game; but now they have none. The buffalo range is from four to six hundred miles distant; they have raised no crops this year, the grasshoppers having destroyed what little they had planted; and the annuity they receive from government amounts to but very little by the time it reaches them. They were expected to live on what the treaty called for; but it is a well-known fact throughout the territory that they have been most shamefully treated.[35]*

With many Indian groups in this weakened condition, most violence between settlers and Indians had ended in Dakota Territory by 1869, the year the Smith family arrived. However, on occasion, bands of marauding Indians or small war parties—whose purpose it was to plunder the settlers' goods and livestock—continued to attack steamboats and emigrant trains.[36]

The newcomers believed that the land they were settling rightly belonged to them. A statement appearing in the *Yankton Daily Press and Dakotan* on June 5, 1875, reflects the prevailing attitude of many of the Euro-American settlers:

> *That portion of Dakota occupied by the various bands of Sioux belongs not to them, but to the representatives of an advancing civilization. The romance of the Indian right to hereditary possession of all or portions of the domain over which the United States now claims jurisdiction is the veriest bosh. . . . The American continent should be given over to the progress of enlightenment and the temporal advancement of those who are willing to make use of God's best gifts while they are on earth.*[37]

The Sioux had moved into what would become Dakota Territory by around 1826, and within two generations had come to think of the Black Hills as their sacred land. After the signing of the 1868 Treaty of Fort Laramie, the US Army had the task of keeping non-Indians out of the area.[38] But gold had been discovered in the Black Hills, and the news of it spread like wildfire in 1874. Prospectors entered the Indian lands in the Black Hills in droves, violating the terms of the treaty. This provoked assaults by the Sioux, also a breach of the treaty.

In addition to the prevailing attitude about the rights of white settlers to the land, there was now greed at work. Recognition of the valuable mineral resources in the Black Hills led to mounting political pressure on President Grant's administration to take back the Black Hills from the Sioux. As had so often happened in the past, the US government broke its promise and issued the Sioux a deadline to leave the Black Hills by the end of January 1876. On February 1, the government gave the army the go-ahead to drive them out of the region, and the Great War (or Black Hills War) of 1876 began.[39] The Great Sioux Nation, in the end, lost to the gold diggers.

Meanwhile, a surveying party set out for the Black Hills from Yankton in late winter of 1876. Their mission was to find the best routes from Yankton for the growing numbers of gold seekers headed to the Black Hills.[40] According to an obituary, Wesley, A. J.'s oldest son, was working with a party of surveyors in the region at the time of the June 1876 Battle of the Little Bighorn, or Custer's Last Stand, the most famous battle in the Black Hills. Indeed, A. J. mentioned in his diary that Wesley had started for the Black Hills on May 20. According to the newspaper, Wesley "recalled standing guard against surprise attacks of the Indians."[41]

Whether Wesley was actually part of a surveying party that was in close proximity to Custer's Last Stand, I was not able to confirm. Even though most of the battles that year between the US Cavalry and the Lakota, the Northern Cheyenne, and the Arapaho peoples took place in Montana and Wyoming, and the Black Hills were some four hundred miles west of where the Smiths lived, the conflict—and what Wesley may have witnessed—most likely contributed to a pivotal decision A. J. would soon make for his family.

"NEXT-YEAR COUNTRY"

The late 1870s and early '80s were what historians call "the Great Dakota Boom"—good crop years that brought in loads of settlers.[42] The grasshoppers left and the rain returned. By 1883, the onslaught of migrants from Iowa, Illinois, Wisconsin, Minnesota, and elsewhere had claimed almost every acre in the territory east of the Missouri River.[43] The Smiths, however, could not have known of these good years ahead. They just happened to have been in Dakota for a particularly challenging seven-year stretch.

In the spring of 1876, having endured a move back to a sod house, three years of one climate-related calamity after another, vague threats of conflict with Indian groups, and a national economic depression triggered by the financial panic of 1873, A. J. and Mary Jane experienced yet another setback. On April 28, 1876, just as the new planting season was getting under way, A. J. entered in his diary a disconsolate comment: "I sold out my trouble with Levi Barton for his buggy. Consideration $75. The Lord helped me." The details of the conflict with Barton remain a mystery. What we do know is that the Smiths lost the Section 17 Pre-emption claim. With their old house rented to their tenant, they had no place to live. A. J. seemed once again at loose ends, noting in his diary that he was selling and delivering pictures and maps.

Even though his family's first four years in the territory had been bountiful, they still owned some land, and life in southeastern Dakota offered many positive things, the past three years had proven to be horrific, and the grasshopper visitation of summer 1876 was the proverbial last straw. The Smiths faced a difficult decision: Should they leave or stick it out?

Leaving was not an option for all settlers in the Dakotas. As one popular 1883 song (with lyrics that varied according to location) put it:

> We've reached the land of drought and heat,
> Where nothing grows for man to eat;
> For winds that blow with scorching heat,
> Dakota Land is hard to beat.
>
> . . . .
>
> We do not live, we only stay,
> We are too poor to get away.[44]
> (Unattributed, "Dakota Land Is Hard to Beat")

O. E. Rølvaag aptly described the situation in his classic 1924 novel, *Giants in the Earth: A Saga of the Prairie.* People stayed where they were because poverty, he wrote, "that most supreme of masters, had deprived them of the liberty to rise up and go away."[45]

Even today, farmers and ranchers in the Dakotas refer to the place as "next-year country," a mind-set in which hope springs eternal. Rain will come; next year things will improve. Better to stay put than to pull up stakes. The inclination to stay put in the late nineteenth century might have been encouraged by the tendency at the time to denigrate farmers who complained about the difficult conditions despite the government's growing acknowledgment that 160 acres was not enough land to sustain a family farm in the harsh climate of the Dakotas. Some viewed the farmers' situation as the result of shiftlessness or ineptitude. The commissioner of agriculture for the state of Nebraska (just across the Missouri River from Vermillion) wrote in 1887, "It is the crop of the bad cultivator that is burned with drought, eaten by insects, or caught by the frost."[46] The chancellor of the University of Nebraska wrote in 1894 that farmers who appealed for aid revealed a "want of spirit that leads some men to forget their manliness."[47]

A. J., however, had a choice. As a native and literate English speaker, he had been able to find a variety of jobs to earn money to supplement his farm income. Unlike many of the immigrant farmers in the area, he had proved up on his homestead to gain a patent to his land. Should he choose to move on, he had enough resources to sell to enable him to buy a train ticket. Thankfully, he would not have to repeat the overland, covered-wagon journey, as the transcontinental railroad line had opened in 1869. Many settlers were leaving, and most of the homesteaders who had the means to move on were, like A. J. Smith, native-born Americans of European heritage.[48]

"The Pacific Slope"

A. J. was accustomed to moving. His was a family of seasoned settlers. His father and grandfather before him had migrated to new states— from Connecticut to New York to Pennsylvania. The family was a part of the Anglo Diaspora. In fact, all three of A. J.'s younger brothers also left Pennsylvania to find their fortunes in the West. A. J. and Mary Jane's migrations—from Pennsylvania and Ohio to Wisconsin, then Dakota, and now somewhere new—undoubtedly solidified for Hattie the idea that if one place isn't suitable, try another.

On June 24, A. J. left for Wisconsin, perhaps to see whether it was worth trying to return there. But he soon made his decision. Upon his arrival home in Dakota on August 17, 1876, he noted having been "sick over one month." One month later, he wrote, "Soon as I was able I commenced to settle up my business. . . . The grasshoppers have taken all our Oats & Wheat & vegetables. We had a little corn & barley & a few potatoes. I felt discouraged and made my arrangements to see the Pacific Slope." [September 20, 1876]

Mary Jane gave birth to their eighth and last child, Mina, on October 4, 1876. Two weeks later, A. J. sold his eighty-acre half of their original homestead to his brother Harvey for five hundred dollars. Mary Jane retained the other half of the homestead, still leased to a tenant.

There is a certain sad irony in the fact that A. J.'s patent to his first Dakota homestead was delivered to him on May 15, 1876.[49] It was just at this time that he was beginning to wrestle with his decision in response to his wearisome, four-year struggle against nature and the facts that the family had no house of their own and not enough land on which to survive. The harsh demands of farming on the prairie had taken their toll. Looking back in 1879, he wrote, "Drouth one year, floods 2 years and grasshoppers 4 years called so loud on my financial affairs, I felt it a necessity to leave while I had yet means left to get away."[50]

On November 3, 1876, A. J.'s brother-in-law drove him to Yankton where, with his brother Frank, he exchanged his stenciling tools for a watch, an important amenity for train travel. A. J. must have delighted in the fact that oxen and a covered wagon were no longer necessary to journey west. This time he would take the Iron Horse. A. J. boarded the Dakota Southern Railway bound for Omaha. From there the Union Pacific and Central Pacific Railroads took him across the continent to San Francisco. The trip took nine days, including stops and changeovers. He left the rest of the family—Mary Jane, two nearly grown sons, Hattie at sixteen, three young children, a toddler, and the newborn—in Dakota to fend for themselves.

In San Francisco, A. J. boarded the SS *Dakota* and headed for Seattle and Port Townsend on Puget Sound, where his brother David, a teacher, lawyer, and judge, lived. In leaving Dakota Territory, A. J. was looking for a place where he and his children could find land—land that would be worthy of their efforts, land that would not require a daily battle with the elements. What he found upon his arrival in Washington in November 1876 looked promising. Water fell gently from the sky with surprising regularity. Everywhere he looked was water, welcome after his seven years in drought-plagued and fire-prone Dakota Territory.

CHAPTER FIVE

Washington 1877–1881

THE TRAIN PULLED INTO THE STATION IN SAN FRANCISCO AFTER THE long, westward journey. Hattie, her mother, and seven siblings had been cooped up in the jam-packed, smelly train car for a week. As they left the crowded train platform and headed for the dock to board a steamship, Hattie's two-year-old brother Harvey disappeared. He was nowhere to be found. The family was frantic. Hattie rushed into the street and asked three small boys if they had seen him. None had, but they said they knew where lost boys might be found. She grabbed one of the boys and insisted he take her to the police station, where she found Harvey unharmed.[1]

"EMIGRANT CAR"

Hattie and her family had traveled to San Francisco from Dakota Territory over the first transcontinental railroad track—opened for business on May 10, 1869—just as A. J. had done six months earlier. In 1877, the year Hattie and her family made their overland trip, journalist Frank Leslie made the same one and reported in *Frank Leslie's Illustrated Newspaper*: "A journey over the plains was [once] a formidable undertaking, that required great patience and endurance. Now all is changed. . . . The six months' journey is reduced to less than a week. The prairie schooner has passed away, and is replaced by the railway coach with all its modern conveniences."[2]

The trains carried all kinds of passengers on a single track. People of means on summer excursions enjoyed many modern conveniences. A May 1873 article in *Scribner's Monthly*, "A Few Hints on the California Journey," with a header, "A Practical Guide for Ladies Taking Summer Excursions from the East to San Francisco and Northern California via the Pacific Railroad," included advice on what and how to pack, how to obtain the best seating, where to eat during stops, the scenery to expect, and interesting side trips. The article described the luxurious accommodations available in "Pullman's Palace Sleeping Cars":

> *These rooms occupy the whole width of the car, with the exception of a narrow passage-way on one side. There are six ventilators in each, and four windows, two of which look out-doors, and two into the passageway, which has corresponding windows opening outward. On one side of the room is a long sofa, on the other two arm-chairs, whose backs are movable and can be tipped back to a convenient angle. There are looking glasses on the walls. There is plenty of room above and below for your bags, bundles, and baskets. Between the two drawing-rooms is a dressing-closet, which is used by nobody in the car except the drawing-room occupants. At bed-time the porter enters, pulls the sofa out into a roomy bed, manipulates the arm-chairs in some mysterious way so that they form another bed, produces sheets, blankets, pillows from repositories overhead, hangs curtains over doors and windows, presents you with a handful of clean towels, and departs, leaving you shut into as snug and secluded a bed-room as any one could desire.[3]*

What Mary Jane and the eight children experienced, however, was very different from the excursion version of the trip. They made their journey in an "emigrant car,"[4] those very words often painted in large yellow letters on the exterior to distinguish it from "mixed" or first-class cars.[5] Some passengers would book an entire car if they were transporting animals and household goods. The Smiths, however, were traveling light, adhering to the modest baggage weight limit.

Robert Louis Stevenson made the cross-country trip in an emigrant car in 1879, just two years after the Smiths. His descriptions of the experience, first published in a magazine, offer a picture of what the journey must have been like for them. After traveling from New York City, Stevenson arrived at Council Bluffs, Iowa, just across the Mississippi River from Omaha, and found himself *in front of the Emigrant House, with more than a hundred others, to be sorted and boxed for the journey. A white-haired official, with a stick under one arm, and a list in the other hand, stood apart in front of us, and called name after name in the tone of a command. At each name you would see a family gather up its brats and bundles and run for the hindmost of the three cars that stood awaiting us, and I soon concluded that this was to be set apart for the women and children. The second or central car, it turned out, was devoted to men travelling alone, and the third to the Chinese. . . . I suppose the reader has some notion of an American railroad-car, that long, narrow wooden box, like a flat-roofed Noah's ark, with a stove and a convenience, one at either end, a passage down the middle, and transverse benches upon either hand. Those destined for emigrants on the Union Pacific are only remarkable for their extreme plainness, nothing but wood entering in any part into their constitution, and for the usual inefficacy of the lamps, which often went out and shed but a dying glimmer even while they burned. The benches are too short for anything but a young child.*[6]

Stevenson described the periodic arrival in his car of the newsboy who on the emigrant journey sold "soap, towels, tin washing dishes, tin coffee pitchers, coffee, tea, sugar, and tinned eatables, mostly hash or beans and bacon."[7] He mentioned that his train had to move frequently to a side-track to allow the other trains, those without emigrants on them, to pass by. His fellow passengers, he wrote, were mostly American-born, repre-sented a broad cross section of the country, and "were fleeing in quest of a better land and better wages. The talk in the train, like the talk I heard on the steamer, ran upon hard times, short commons, and hope that moves ever westward."[8]

After traveling across the plains—described by Stevenson as "a world almost without a feature; an empty sky, an empty earth; front and back, the line of railway stretched from horizon to horizon, like a cue across a billiard-board; on either hand, the green plain ran till it touched the skirts of heaven"—he arrived at Ogden, Utah, where he changed cars to the Central Pacific line. Here the cars had higher ceilings and thus, more fresh air. Leaving the Union Pacific was a welcome relief, for the cars in which they "had been cooped for more than ninety hours had begun to stink abominably. . . . I have stood on a platform . . . and as the dwelling-cars drew near, there would come a whiff of pure menagerie, only a little sourer, as from men instead of monkeys. I think we are human only in virtue of open windows."⁹ A week after leaving Council Bluffs, he arrived in San Francisco just as the Smiths did.

"WHITE CAPS ROLL ON THE SOUND"

When A. J. landed in Washington in mid-November 1876, the local newspaper reported, "Mr. Smith is a practical farmer, . . . tired of that grasshopper region and cannot longer afford to put up with their ravages."¹⁰ He had arrived in the Pacific Northwest with no specific plan for what was next. He knew he would have to work for wages at least for a time, even though his long-term goal was to own land and farm again. He briefly worked at odd jobs in Seattle. Always a good networker, he met Reverend Charles A. Huntington, an Indian agent, who offered him a job as an assistant teacher at the Makah Indian Agency. As the New Year approached and the school term was to begin, A. J. made his way to the coastal village of Neah Bay in Clallam County, near Cape Flattery, at the far northwestern tip of the Olympic Peninsula, about as far west in the continental United States as one could go.

A. J. was particularly well suited to his new teaching job. In the late eighteenth century, the US government had begun appointing agents to live among Indian peoples to protect them from non-Indians, negotiate treaties, distribute annuities from the government, and guide or force them into adopting mainstream, Euro-American social patterns. The government acculturation policy at Indian agencies focused on speaking, reading, and writing English, on Christianity, and on agriculture, all areas in which A. J. was experienced.¹¹ He also had some familiarity with working among Indian groups from his time in the army. What he believed about the Lakota people he brought to the Makah people: If they were educated and given knowledge of God, they would be happy, "smart & intelligent." [January 19, 1866]

The situation, however, was complicated. US government policies for Indian Agency schools removed children from their parents, placed them in boarding schools, insisted that they speak English only, and extinguished their tribal customs and traditions. Deviating from the schools' expectations could result in harsh punishment.[12] A. J.'s diary comment, "I heard the children in the dining hall. They still improve," a remark he made early in his time in Neah Bay, and would repeat in his diary in months to come, might be viewed as code words for the results of this policy aimed at destroying the language and culture of the Makah people. [January 25, 1877]

As in the past, A. J. attended Sunday school and religious services every week. He noted that a large percentage of the attendees at the observances were Makahs. A. J. resumed the peripatetic habit he had adopted in Dakota of attending services at one place and Sunday school at another—in this case, services at what he referred to as "Bohada" (undoubtedly Ba'adah Point), where he was living at the school, and Sunday school at Neah Bay, the village two miles away. His worship choices were limited, but he must have enjoyed the diversity of the company and the opportunity to do more proselytizing.

Living on the seacoast seemed to hold particular interest for A. J. "Graveyard of the Pacific" is a name often given to the rugged and weather-beaten stretch of coast from the mouth of the Columbia River north to Vancouver Island. He remarked on the wreck of the *Commodore*, a commercial sailing vessel that went aground in a strong gale near Cape Flattery during his first month there. When Reverend Huntington learned of the accident, he offered the shipwrecked mariners shelter at the Neah Bay Agency.[13] A few months later, A. J. had the opportunity to assist Reverend Huntington in taking photographs of the dangerous, rocky coastline. Twice in his first few weeks on the Olympic Peninsula, A. J. noted gale-force winds and seas high enough to cause ships to turn back to port.

A. J.'s new surroundings whetted his appetite for exploration and observation. His heightened awareness brought frequent comments on nature: "White caps roll on the sound. . . . I took a walk on the rocks. I found 5 different colored star fish." [March 9, 28, 1877] He seemed particularly mindful of not only the sea but also the maritime climate, regularly commenting on the weather. He marveled at the comparatively early onset of spring, remarking on February 4, "The birds of spring sang sweetly," and in March, "The frogs in the creek held their first Praise meeting—with songs of joy that summer is here," and "All nature seems to praise the Lord. I too would join in praise." [March 13, 26, 1877] His deep appreciation of the mild climate and ample rainfall would grow as he began planting crops with the Makahs. This place represented a fresh start to A. J., but he needed to find his own land.

The agency put to good use A. J.'s multiple skills. In addition to teaching, he worked on a road and in the garden. He washed windows. By March, he was cooking for the children at the school, noting in his diary, "I baked 43 loaves of bread," reviving the skills he had developed at Fort Rice. [April 3, 1877] Soon the agency would name him the blacksmith. Most days he found time to make notes in his diary. On March 5, 1877, he noted, "Ruthford B. Hays Inaugerated Pres't. of the United Stated for 4 Years. . . . in Washington City. D.C." Though geographically isolated, A. J. kept up with significant events nationwide.

One day in early April 1877, A. J. watched the side-wheeler steamship *Dakota* pass by the Makah School and expressed the hope that his family was aboard. The *Dakota* was on its way east to Port Townsend, and the family would have to backtrack west by mail boat to get to where he was. A. J. had to make two trips to Neah Bay to meet the mail boat to see if they might be on it. Mary Jane and the children finally did arrive four days later on April 7, 1877. A newspaper reported that A. J. "was made happy this week by the arrival of his wife and eight children, among whom are some stalwart boys. . . . What is Dakota's loss is our gain."[14]

"WESTWARD I GO FREE"

In nineteenth-century America, what was known as the frontier, which A. J. chased as he moved ever-farther west, presented adversity, diversity, and opportunity to migrating Euro-Americans. The frontier wasn't stationary. It was both a moving target and a process. The Old Northwest—today Ohio, Indiana, Illinois, Michigan, Wisconsin, and part of Minnesota—was an early frontier. After 1820, the frontier began rolling westward as the federal government opened new lands for homesteading and settlers migrated. Wherever the frontier found itself, it was characterized by collision, conquest, and human diversity, creating sometimes violence and always a nexus of cultural and economic exchange among various immigrant groups and American Indian peoples. Other characteristics of the frontier included the use of land resources in new ways and economic opportunity, particularly for the newcomers. Migrating settlers, by necessity, were resourceful and ready for new challenges. As Willa Cather wrote in *O Pioneers!*, a novel based on her own early years on the Midwestern prairie in the 1880s, "A pioneer should have imagination, should be able to enjoy the idea of things more than the things themselves."[15]

The idea of the West, the mythical West, fueled the imaginations of pioneers. Viewed as a place to flee to, a place where one could be free from whatever held one back, it was a place that many people perceived as better than where they were, a repository of hope. Even though he had never actually been west of the Missouri River, Henry David Thoreau observed in his 1862 essay, "Walking":

> *Eastward I go only by force; but westward I go free. . . . I should not lay so much stress on this fact, if I did not believe that something like this is the prevailing tendency of my countrymen. I must walk toward Oregon, and not toward Europe. And that way the nation is moving, and I may say that mankind progress from east to west. We go eastward to realize history and study the works of art and literature, retracing the steps of the race; we go westward as into the future, with a spirit of enterprise and adventure.*[16]

The US government reinforced this mythical West and aided the reality by making cheap land available to settlers. The Preemption Act of 1841 allowed "squatters" living on public land to buy up to 160 acres at a low price, as long as they resided on the land and worked to improve it. As one US senator said during congressional debates over the law in 1841:

> *It is in the very philosophy of things, in a country like ours, whose free institutions awaken and bear up the spirit of aspiration from a humble hut, as well as the lofty palace, that the poor man, surrounded by his wife and his children, and animated by a holy love of those endeared objects, with a pure conscience and a resolved purpose, relying*

upon his own unassisted arm, should go forth to the wilds of the far West to improve his fortunes, and confirm his personal independence. He meets, there, men like himself, who have entered upon that new experiment with the same ardent hopes and lively expectations.[17]

The connection between family, independence, hope, hard work, and westward expansion was clear in the minds of nineteenth-century Americans.

Twenty-one years later, the Homestead Act of 1862 took the idea of land development a step further and made acquiring land even more affordable. As Dakota historian Kingsbury wrote in 1915, "Uncle Sam was rich enough to give all of his children a farm."[18]

Westward migration seems to have been a family affair, something that reoccurred generationally and often took place in familial networks. Mary Jane's half-brother and the Smiths' close neighbor in Wisconsin and Dakota, Oliver W. Wells, also migrated to Washington with his family. The rural, usually large, Euro-American family strategy for ensuring the livelihoods of the next generation included moving with the frontier. The Smiths decided to leave Dakota not only because of their environmental and financial challenges but also because they believed it prudent to reinvest what resources they had on new land in the West—the Far West. Their oldest children were coming of age. This decision would allow all of them to eventually stake land claims near each other. A. J. believed something better lay ahead and beyond. It was time to pull up stakes and move on again—time to find new land.

A. J. had acquired his 320 acres in Wisconsin under the Preemption Act of 1841 and his 160 acres in Dakota under the Homestead Act of 1862. Since the law restricted settlers from owning more than one Homestead Act property at a time and Mary Jane still owned part of theirs in Dakota, if he was to acquire land in Washington, he would have to find a way to do it other than through the Homestead Act.

LIFE BEYOND A SOD HOUSE

With the ten of them now back together, what would be for the last time, the Smiths found a place to stay in Neah Bay. A. J. noted that Wesley "fixed 2 bed steads." [April 10, 1877] They got two free cows to milk. Reverend Huntington butchered a hog and gave them the head. A Makah fisherman, Cuchubsub, caught a thirty-three-pound salmon for them. Olly planted a garden and Wesley did some whitewashing. It seems that the accommodations and food were simple but adequate. A. J. continued to be away much of the time working at the Makah School, but he was able to go back and forth to their new home with relative ease.

The older children found work to earn money. Within a month, Wesley had secured a position teaching at the Makah School, a line of work he was to continue for years to come. Olly found work at the nearby US government Life Station. Hattie cooked in the agency kitchen alongside her father. In August, having just turned seventeen, she accompanied Reverend and Mrs. Huntington and their children to Olympia, where she would attend school through the eighth grade. She worked, probably doing child care or housework, in exchange for room and board.[19] Her cross-country train journey, the sea voyage along the Pacific coast, working at the Neah Bay Agency, and now attending school in a relatively large town would have opened her eyes to the possibilities of a life beyond a sod house on the prairie.

Toward the end of 1877, Reverend Huntington left his position as Indian agent and another agent replaced him. On December 4, A. J. learned that his services at the agency would no longer be needed after December 31, 1877.

"WE CONTINUED TO CARE FOR LIZZIE DAY AND NIGHT"

An unexpected turn of events interrupted any thoughts A. J. may have had about his next step. On December 11, he wrote in his diary, "My [daughter] Lizzie is sick. I went to see her," and four days later, "I am at home helping to take care of Lizzie," and the next day, "We watch day & night with Lizzie. We hope for her recovery, yet the Lord knoweth best. We would she might live, Gods will be done." Her condition was grave. It was typhoid fever. The following day, "Wesley & Oliver came & set up with Lizzie." The expression "set up with" in A. J.'s diary usually suggested a "death watch." His last entry that year was, "We continued to care for Lizzie day & night." [December 19, 1877] The diary goes silent at this point, with two pages torn out. Using a different pen and darker ink, he went back later and added the words "till 2:30 AM. Dec 25." Though he does not say it explicitly, that was when nine-year-old Lizzie died, on Christmas.

This seems to have been the sole instance in which someone removed pages from one of A. J.'s four diary volumes. If A. J. tore out the pages himself, the missing ones could simply have been a consequence of an accident of pen and ink or a spilled beverage. On the other hand, they might suggest that whatever anger A. J. may have expressed at the death of his young daughter, perhaps even toward God, was something he did not want to be preserved in the written word.

When A. J. resumed writing, it was, for him, in a highly unusual retrospective mode. On February 11, he recounted in some detail what had transpired during the previous six weeks.

I got some cold Dec 27 & 28 washing. I was taken with diareah 29. [C]ontinued a week. [N]ot very well the week following to Jan 5th. Was taken with Typhoid fever about that time. Jan 10. I could not eat any thing for about 2 weeks. I drank a little beef broth. [F]ever left me about Jan. 24. I began to amend & my apetite came & I felt like a wolf. I gained in strength a little every day. I can now walk round & help a little tho I am very weak. The Baby was taken sick soon after I was. Was not so sick as she might have been—better now. Jennie was taken sick before I was. She did not get so sick as Lizzie. She began to get better about Jan 10. She is nearly well. My wife was taken sick about Jan 10. She has been very sick. [T]wice we thought she was dying. She still survives & the fever left her Feb. 9th. Her pulse fell from 165 to 130. We now think she may recover. [February 11, 1878]

The whole family except three-year-old Harvey contracted typhoid. The bacterial disease, caused by ingesting contaminated food or water or through close contact with an infected person, follows a characteristic four-week (or longer) pattern. Early symptoms include high fever, weakness, fatigue, and intestinal problems. Continuing high fever, weight loss, exhaustion, and delirium follow. Full recovery can take months, and temporary hair loss can be a consequence as the body gradually restores itself.[20]

Of the surviving family members, only Mary Jane suffered a bout that was life-threatening. She recovered after being bedridden for forty-nine days. The older boys had less-serious cases of the disease. Hattie lost all of her hair.[21] Jennie, Hattie's sister, in her 1938 interview, recalled, "When we arrived at the Neah Bay reservation, our whole family was taken ill with typhoid fever. Dirty water had been thrown about the house."[22] A. J.'s note that they had spent December 27 and 28 "washing" suggests an effort to rid the premises of the lethal bacteria.

The Smiths had left Dakota under duress, without any apparent specific plan for the future. After the harsh and unforgiving Dakota climate, A. J. found the Olympic Peninsula gentle and cheering. When he found work at the Neah Bay Agency and his family joined him, his optimism returned. But then, he lost his job. One of his eight children died on Christmas Day. The rest of the family was gravely ill for weeks. With no income, no land, and no clear picture of what the next step should be, it was a disheartening picture.

That is, until someone entered their lives, a man who would continue to shape the future of the Smith family in ways yet unknown. The fortuitous meeting of A. J. and Dan Pullen came during the siege of typhoid fever. Dan Pullen was a fur trader who had come up the coast around Cape Flattery in his schooner, plying his trade, and had stopped at Neah Bay. "Mr. Dan Pullen came here Feb. 23rd," A. J. wrote in his diary. "He has set up 4 nights with our sick, gave 4 cans of stuff. Peaches, Pineapples, Beef, & Mutton, kind." [March 1, 1878] Not only did Pullen give selfless care to a family in need, a family he'd only just met, but he also gave A. J. some good advice. Within one month, A. J. was preparing to go south, where Pullen had told him land was available for the taking.

CHAPTER SIX

Quillayute Country

DANIEL WEBSTER PULLEN, THE SECOND SON AND FIFTH OF NINE CHILdren, was born in Maine in 1842 to millwright Daniel Pullen and his wife, Mary Ann Dudley. The two sides of his family, both originally from England, went back six and eight generations in America. When Dan was a boy of seven, his father contracted scarlet fever and died at age thirty-six. The disease tore through the household. Dan's older sister died of it, and the disease left two of his siblings completely deaf and Dan with a serious hearing loss. The 1889 Washington territorial census listed him, at age forty-seven some twenty-five years after his arrival in the Pacific Northwest, as "deaf."[1]

Widowed with eight children under the age of thirteen, Dan's mother managed to make ends meet for another twenty-three years in a house surrounded by sawmills,[2] an environment that would have helped Dan feel right at home in the Pacific Northwest. Family lore had Dan leaving home at fourteen, but the 1860 US Census lists him as being in Maine and having attended school that year. It is more likely that he left home after the age of eighteen, probably around 1861.[3] In doing so, he became part of the Yankee Diaspora, like A. J. before him. The Pullens' stressed financial situation and the lack of available land in Maine prompted most of them to migrate west.

There are two versions of the family story as to how Dan landed in Washington. In one, a self-published story by a Smith descendant, young Dan sails all the way around South America's Cape Horn on his way to the Olympic Peninsula—a fourteen-thousand-mile, six-month voyage.[4] In the other version, he signed on as a crewmember on a vessel bound for Panama, crossed the isthmus by railroad (completed in 1855), and continued by ship to San Francisco.[5] Given that he left home sometime after 1860, the more likely story is the latter. By that time, steam-powered ships were making regular runs between New York and San Francisco, with the isthmus railroad trip in between the two ocean voyages.

In the early 1860s, the reputation of the Atlantic leg was particularly bad. A Panama newspaper reporter wrote of one 1860 trip, "We are assured that a more filthy, nasty pigstie could not be found anywhere than the whole ship is from one end to the other. The dirty, greasy tablecloths were rendered still more disgusting by being used at night as pillows . . . ; in fact everything a perfect disgrace to both captain and owners."[6] The uncomfortable, tripartite journey took three to four weeks.[7]

The family stories always suggested that Dan's whereabouts in the late 1850s and '60s were unknown. The mystery may have simply emerged from his reluctance to be too specific about when he had left Maine. If he left after passage of the Civil War Military Draft Act of 1863, he and his brother Marquis, known as "Mart," at ages twenty-one and twenty-five, may have been resisting conscription. The law's passage triggered riots in several New England towns and a demonstration of fifteen thousand people in a town a few dozen miles from where the Pullens lived.[8] Draft dodging was widespread. In later years, when Civil War service was an enormous badge of honor, Dan may have felt shame at not having served his country. One way or another, Dan made it to the Olympic Peninsula, out of the reach of the Union Army.

Landing near Seattle, Dan hunted on Whidbey Island and worked as a "bull puncher" at a Port Gamble logging camp in an industry that had burgeoned around Puget Sound in the mid-1850s. He drove teams of oxen pulling logs and, as a newspaper article put it, "had the reputation of being able to get more 'pull' out of a team than any man in the business."[9] Dan and Mart joined forces around 1865 and acquired a pilot schooner. Working out of Neah Bay, Mart boarded large ships of captains unfamiliar with the intricate network of coastal channels to pilot them through the Strait of Juan de Fuca to and from the Salish Sea and Puget Sound. Dan skippered the transfer boat that took Mart back and forth to the ships.[10] Known for its storms, rough seas, and fog, the area was a dangerous and challenging place to sail. At times Dan's youthful daring proved to be risky. The same newspaper article that described his prowess with the ox teams told of his actions during one particularly rough storm:

> *Dan was at the cape and wanted to make Port Townsend. It blew a terrific gale and all kinds of craft were huddling in the bays waiting for good weather. But Dan was not made of that kind of stuff, and all alone in the little schooner pointed his bowsprit for Point Wilson. He afterwards confessed that it was foolhardy. . . . When his little sail hove in sight there was a great wonder expressed as to what crazy or intoxicated mariner had ventured out in such weather, but one old salt solved the problem by exclaiming: "Why, that's Dan Pullen; he's the only man that dare do it, and he's neither crazy nor drunk."[11]*

Sometime late in the 1860s, Dan began trading with the Quileute people, an Indian group living on the Pacific coast forty miles south of Cape Flattery. He traded for elk horn and sealskins and probably the skins of martin, mink, muskrat, cougar, deer, and bear. Dealing in sealskins and other furs was a very profitable business at the time. The mobility of his schooner allowed him to get top dollar for his goods. On his rounds along the Strait of Juan de Fuca and Puget Sound, he sold the furs and bought items he later exchanged with the Quileutes—sugar, tobacco, matches, brightly colored cloth, and other manufactured goods.

In 1871 or 1872, Dan, his brother Mart, and two other families became the first Euro-American people to settle on the Quillayute Prairie, a few miles inland from Dan's trading-business landing spot, in effect intruding on Quileute territory. Their small settlement, which grew slowly, became known as Quillayute, one of several anglicized spellings of *Quileute*, which later came to be written *Kwo'liyot'* in the Quileute language.[12] Dan built a house and barn and, although he continued fur trading, by the end of the decade, he was raising and selling cattle with his brother as well.

The rugged country was rife with wolves, which proved to be destructive to the Pullens' livestock. A newspaper article described the challenges Dan and Mart faced: "It was of no use to shoot them as it did not materially lessen their number, so they resorted to poison. For instance, on one occasion, when they had been obliged to drive in the stock in the daytime, Dan shot a pig, salted him with strychnine, tied a lariat to him, mounted his horse and dragged the pork out into the prairie. The next morning the bones of that pig were surrounded by a band of dead wolves."[13] Such extreme measures brought the wolves in the area close to extinction twenty years later.

A few years after settling, Dan and Mart invited their siblings back in Maine to join them in Washington Territory. Their younger brother Ephraim took them up on the offer, probably after dropping off their mother and sister Sarah in Iowa, where a fourth brother had settled. Abbie, another sister, also moved to Quillayute country with her husband in the early 1870s. Sarah would leave Iowa and join her siblings in Washington later.

Burning Fern

In early 1878, following the Smiths' typhoid fever episode, Dan invited A. J. to stay with him and his brother, both bachelors, so A. J. could find land, stake a claim, and begin homesteading.[14] On April 1, as he prepared for his journey to Quillayute, A. J. put his family on board a steamer bound for Olympia, where the younger children would attend school. There were no schools in Quillayute, nor would the settlers build any for years to come. With the family headed to Olympia where they could continue their recovery from typhoid, A. J. paid four Makahs eight dollars to take him to Quillayute. The Makahs were skilled mariners with seaworthy canoes as long as fifty feet, carved of western red cedar, and designed specifically for transporting cargo. Over centuries of living on the sea, they had developed sophisticated ways of navigating, and had added sails to their canoes to take advantage of the maritime winds.[15] From the beach where the Makahs left him, A. J. traveled up the Dicko-dochtedar ("Dickey" to the settlers) River six miles to Pullens' Prairie. A. J. would stay with the Pullen brothers for more than six months while he found his own claim and began homesteading near the Pullens' place.

The US government had not yet surveyed the land in the Quillayute area, so A. J. was a squatter, as were the other newcomers. He started preparing the land by burning the dense cover of fern that grew as high as ten feet. The land was flat and the soil fine-grained and fertile.[16] Best of all, the prairies lacked the gigantic trees common across most of the region, freeing a farmer from having to fell them and remove roots before cultivating the soil—an extraordinary boon. In less than one week, A. J. had planted 450 apple trees, 300 plum sprouts, and 15 cherry sprouts. He then planted wheat and a kitchen garden and began investing in livestock. Even with no proper barn, his Washington Territory farm was looking more prosperous than the ones he had invested years in building in both Wisconsin and Dakota. On August 2, A. J. and three neighbors began constructing an eighteen-by-twenty-four-foot log house, eleven logs high.

A letter delivered by "Quileut Jimmy" arrived on September 7, bringing the news that Mary Jane and the children were back in Neah Bay. Given the village's inaccessibility by land, to join A. J., the family would have to travel by sea around Cape Flattery and down the coast to the beach near Quillayute. A. J. arranged for Dan Pullen to fetch them and their household goods in his schooner.

Dan's schooner trip must have also been a trading mission to Port Townsend, a major sealing port, because it was another six weeks before he returned with the Smiths. When the family arrived, Jennie, then seven, recalled, "[T]he Indians met us. They were very friendly."[17] The day after their arrival, October 29, 1878, the family moved into the new house. Initially, the accommodations were a bit rough, although after living in a covered wagon, a claim cabin, and two sod houses, to the Smiths it must have seemed luxurious. Three weeks later, the house was finished and suitably furnished to become part of the housing rotation for A. J.'s Sunday school classes.

"IN THE NEAR FUTURE VAST WEALTH WILL FLOW"

The year 1879 confirmed that A. J.'s 1876 decision to migrate west once more had been a good one. The family was all together save for the comings and goings of the oldest three children, who were now adults with ventures of their own. Wesley periodically visited from Neah Bay, where he continued to teach at the Makah School. Olly returned to live with his parents and began clearing and planting his own Quillayute homestead. Hattie, after attending school in Olympia, at age nineteen cooked at the Makah agency again and visited her family on occasion. In January 1880, she came home to live with her parents. David, at fifteen, was a bit of an adolescent rebel and later self-described as "wild."[18] He packed his trunk and left home, only to return three days later, and was inexplicably uncooperative on occasion. Mary Jane and A. J. taught the youngest three children at home.

In October 1879, A. J. wrote a one-page, autobiographical statement in which he gave an account of his life and his current surroundings. The following excerpt is a good sketch of where he saw himself and his community at the time, and what he believed the future held. It also provides a window into his optimism at this moment.

> *At present writing Oct 1879 I am in a log house 18 x 24 ft, have a barn 50 x 68 ft, 10 acres enclosed in a good rail fence, 200 plumb trees set 300 apple trees and other fruit. There are 20 claims taken and 44 men, women and children. No county Organization, roads, bridges, mills, school (except Sunday School), Post Office, no officials—every man does what is right in his own eyes. The neighbourhood is as quiet as any I ever lived in. There are no frame buildings, or lumber except such as is split. All the present settlers are located on Fern Prairies. Soil rich black vegetable mould. The first settlers came here in 1870. Jacob Balch and family. Pullen Bros. The principle business at present is stock raising, the farming is carried on to some extent. In the near future vast wealth will flow from the Quileut valley. Lumber, coal, fish, fruit, cattle, sheep, and hogs, butter, oats, barley and wheat, potatoes.*[19]

COME AND SEE!

In Quillayute, the Smiths were isolated. So remote was this place that nearly thirty years later, one of A. J.'s granddaughters wrote vividly of her concerns about her father, Wesley, living alone in such a place: "Yes alone and I repeat it with almost a choaking sob, <u>alone</u>, shut in on one side by the roaring ocean and, on the other by the deep forest and hills."[20] Nonetheless, A. J. found ways to make contact with the outside world. He took the matter of unreliable mail delivery into his own hands by submitting a petition to the US Postmaster General to establish a postal route from Clallam Bay to Quillayute. The position would give him control of the situation and bring him some much-needed income. A. J.'s efforts to secure the contract for the postal route took a number of months and involved multiple steps, including making maps of the proposed route and taking "Bonds as Post Master $1000" to Neah Bay. [January 26, 1880] With Dan Pullen's help, he fashioned a special mail sack with lock and key. Finally, on March 18, 1880, he received his commission as postmaster, along with a copy of the laws he was to follow.

A. J. began writing for a local newspaper soon after his arrival in Quillayute. His nearly monthly reports gave him another link with the outside world. He functioned as a one-man chamber of commerce for the growing Quillayute settlement. In one report he wrote:

> *I frequently get letters of inquiry about the country. . . . I would earnestly say to those seeking homes, COME AND SEE. If you want good land, where soil is rich and deep, come and see; good water, good timber, free soil, free homes, COME AND SEE! Our mail route is established, and we expect service soon. Cattle, sheep and hogs do well here. Fish and game are abundant. 1,400 fruit trees have been set in the valley this Spring. . . . I do not like telling any man what he had better do, but if any one who is willing to work wants a home let him come. If there is nothing here to satisfy, the world is wide; but they can't go much farther west without crossing the "pond."*[21]

A. J. worked to combat the notion that it rained all the time on the Olympic Peninsula. "We have been haying for the past three weeks," he wrote in August 1879. "I never saw better weather for the business, in any state. No rain, bright warm sun. . . . For two weeks past the nights have been so clear that the Alhambra by moonlight can't compare with our Mt. Olympus, for beautiful scenery."[22] Wildlife, as both a threat and a source of sustenance, required attention too. "Bears have injured the oat crop of the Pullen Bros. . . . A few sheep have been killed by the panthers. . . . The lake abounds with a new species of fish resembling salmon. . . . Grouse are plentiful. Salmon will be abundant in October; also geese and ducks," he reported.[23]

In addition to the mail and the local print media, the proximity of the river and the ocean provided another means for Hattie and her family to connect with the outside world. By steamship, they could travel to more-populated places such as Port Townsend and Seattle. The multipurpose *Dispatch* made runs every week, bringing supplies and passengers, and on one occasion, sixty-three sheep for Dan Pullen. With no harbor or wharf available, however, the boats had to anchor offshore with canoes used for unloading. There were sailing schooner trips as well, but they could only anchor in calm seas, their arrivals and departures not adhering to any regular schedule.

The family traveled the Dickey and Quillayute Rivers in canoes to "the beach," which, beginning in May 1879, A. J. would refer to as La Push. The settlement near the beach had probably acquired its name—a corruption of *la bouche*, French for "mouth"—from the crew of a French paddle steamer that had wrecked at the mouth of the river.[24] The distance from Quillayute to La Push by water was about seven miles, so Quillayute residents some-times spent the night at La Push. At least some of the time they slept on the beach. On one occasion A. J. reported, "Olly climbed a tree & staid there till morning to get out of water. He was camping on the river near the beach." [March 1, 1880] Born and raised on the Midwestern prairies, the young man found novelty in the beach, the sea, and the giant trees.

The large canoes of the Quileutes provided long-distance transporta-tion by sea. At least twice, A. J. traveled to Neah Bay in a canoe rowed by Howeattle, the husband of Mamma, who on occasion dug potatoes for the Smiths. The trips to Neah Bay were for visiting Wesley and friends, for buying A. J.'s clothing, fabric for Mary Jane's sewing, and shoes for the family, and for restocking provisions. A. J. piggybacked his mail-route deliveries onto many of these trips.

The livestock also offered access to travel. Jennie remembered that the family rode horses over the trails, particularly to and from the neigh-bors' farms. Horses and oxen could pull carts and sleds as needed. Hattie became a capable horsewoman. If she hadn't already honed her riding skills to expert level in Dakota, she did so in Washington.[25]

HATTIE

Hattie's decision to leave her job as a cook at the Neah Bay agency was, according to Wesley's diary, a disappointment to then Indian agent Charles Willoughby. He wrote that she felt unwelcome by the agent's wife and decided to return to live with her parents in Quillayute.[26] Hattie's own letter to Wesley six months later tells a different story. In it, she warned her brother that she had heard Willoughby planned to fire Wesley from his position as teacher at Neah Bay. She referenced her own work for Willoughby the previous year as an episode that had ended badly. She feared the same fate would befall Wesley. There was a touch of paranoia in her tone.[27]

Her decision made, on November 24, 1879, Hattie expected to board the schooner *Champion* to go to La Push. Bad weather prevented the ship from sailing for more than a week. On December 2, it was finally able to set sail. A storm came up suddenly, and for six days Wesley did not know where the schooner was and feared for his sister's safety. He eventually learned that the ship had anchored in the lee of Tatoosh Island near the tip of Cape Flattery to wait out the storm, but not until December 11 was Hattie able to make her way back to Neah Bay. Wesley brought her belongings ashore and there she stayed until December 29, when her brothers Olly and David came to get her, probably on horseback. What should have been a two-day trip ended up taking over five weeks because transportation alternatives there were so limited and challenging.[28]

After Hattie returned to live at home in early 1880, A. J.'s few diary mentions of her suggest that her time was spent doing the mundane tasks one would expect a farm family's oldest daughter to perform—helping her mother run the household and caring for her youngest siblings, who were now three, five, and almost ten. A. J. did mention that twice she made five-day visits to stay with neighboring families to care for their children. Hattie also, on the other hand, went hunting with A. J. and her brother David.

Shortly after Hattie arrived in Quillayute, even though it was already the middle of January, she put together a Christmas tree party to which she invited a number of the neighbors to make a gathering of fourteen. "Spent a pleasant evening," A. J. commented. [January 16, 1880] This event may well have been the beginning of the family tradition, recalled by Jennie, who would have been ten in 1880, of including a tree in every Christmas celebration:

> On Christmas we always had a tree. Once the Indians sent me a hundred little dolls. They had bought them from a store at Neah Bay. We divided them among all the neighbors for Christmas. We made all our presents. Covered cardboard with bright cloth was used for the boxes and the little dolls were dressed. We had a fine Christmas dinner with all kinds of meat, ducks, geese, chickens, plenty of eggs and lots of cream, with cakes and strawberry pie. We lived high. We had elk meat and venison often. Then in the evening we had dancing in one of the larger houses and brother played the violin.[29]

A. J. noted in his diary that Hattie had also hosted a party to celebrate her parents' twenty-sixth wedding anniversary. Honing her hostess skills, which she would perfect in later years, she invited three couples and "got up a good supper &. . . . they staid in the eve. We had a good visit," A. J. wrote. [February 26, 1880]

In February, Hattie set about constructing a bedroom for herself on the second floor of the house. She must have been looking for more privacy than she found living in a four-room house with two parents and five siblings. She planed the wood for the wall, and Dan Pullen "jointed the boards" for her and then put up the "partition & made & hung the bedroom door." [February 16, 19, 1880]

Dan Pullen continued to be present in the Smith family's life throughout that spring. He owned much more land than any of the other settlers did, and was perhaps the most prominent Euro-American man in the community. A. J. mentioned him in the diary much more than he did any other neighbor. Dan did some plowing for the family. A. J., in turn, bought beef from Dan, planted his seeds, delivered his sheared wool to the river landing, and sought his help with making the mail sack. Dan was the first of several neighbors and family members to deliver mail for A. J. During the summer and fall of 1880, A. J. mowed and hauled hay with his sled—one load to his barn for every three to Dan's. He milked Dan and

Mart Pullen's cows when they were away on cattle drives and helped them cut windfalls on their new cattle-driving road from Quillayute to Clallam Bay.[30] Dan attended A. J.'s Sunday school classes and socialized with the Smiths. That summer Hattie was among the guests at the second annual two-day Independence Day celebration at the Pullen brothers' house.

Dan had been a big part of the Smith family's life in Washington from the start. They undoubtedly felt indebted to him for all he had done for them. In March 1880, Hattie's father remarked that Dan Pullen had come calling with his brother and two friends. This and the work Dan did on Hattie's bedroom were the only hints that a relationship might be developing between the two.

During 1880, Hattie made a couple of trips to the beach, which would have put her near Dan's trading activities. Where Hattie might have stayed is unknown, but the Makah Indian agent at Neah Bay reported in 1879 that the Quileutes living there were hospitable and "several families have erected very neat houses. . . . The settlers, as they come and go, invariably occupy one or other of them; the Indians, proud of the opportunity to vacate for the time being in their favor, giving the whites, particularly the ladies, sole possession, with an abundance of new blankets. All this is very gratifying, and shows the good feeling existing."[31] On another visit to La Push, Hattie accompanied her mother to the steamer. Mary Jane was making an overnight trip to Neah Bay, something she was now able to do with her grown daughter in the house.

On October 13, after three days of diary entries in which A. J. noted that he went to Sunday school, churned butter, fixed a spring, and cut posts for a woodshed, he wrote, "I packed my trunk," with no mention of where he was going, or why. The next day he cut and peeled more poles for his woodshed, ordered five hundred three-cent stamps and 250 envelopes, and unofficially turned over to Mary Jane responsibility for the postal service.

Then two days later, leaving David at home to care for four-year-old Mina, the rest of the family went to La Push. All traveled in Wesley's canoe but Mary Jane and Hattie, who went on horseback. The next day, everyone except Hattie, her father, and her older brothers returned to their homestead. Wesley and Olly left with Howeattle in his canoe to go to Neah Bay so Wesley could return to work at the Makah School. Olly would return to La Push with Howeattle two days later. Hattie and A. J., however, remained at the beach because they were departing on a schooner.

Unsure of when it would appear, they awaited the ship's arrival. During this interval, A. J. moved lumber for Dan's new trading post and visited James Island, a sea stack near the beach. According to A. J., it was five acres and surrounded by water only at high tide. From its 150-foot height, he could see the Quillayute River and its tributaries and a snow-dusted Mount Olympus in the distance. Their wait in La Push turned out to be eight days, long enough to kindle Hattie's relationship with Dan.

Finally, the schooner anchored near the beach. Hattie and A. J. boarded and sailed away. Arriving in Neah Bay on October 23, they had a daylong layover. A. J. dropped off the mail at the post office and visited with the ship's captain. The schooner set sail again. When A. J. disembarked in Seattle, he immediately attended a prayer meeting and began looking for work. A newspaper report and a letter from Hattie's uncle tell us she was in Seattle to attend school.[32]

"God Is Good to Me"

While in Seattle, several people entertained A. J. He bought a pair of glasses and attended a Republican Party meeting in the opera house, where he heard the governor speak. Two days after his arrival, he began work for a newspaper owner who had hired him to do various tasks.

It seems that the man was starting an agricultural endeavor, because A. J. spent three weeks burning huge trees and logs to clear the land. This laborious process involved boring into the trees, placing embers into the boreholes, and then tending the fire. Once the burned trees fell, A. J. cut them into logs and set fire to them again. With trees so plentiful, it was more cost-effective to burn them—some as thick as boxcars—than to transport and sell the wood to a lumber mill. What people called "saplings" in the Pacific Northwest were what A. J. would have called "trees" back in Pennsylvania, Wisconsin, and Dakota. Clearing the land in this way was surely unlike anything he'd done before landing in Washington. Having learned the wisdom and ways of the land in three different places, he now was learning them in a fourth. The land cleared, he then planted more than three hundred blackberry bushes and nearly one thousand strawberry plants.

A. J. had some respite from his work in Seattle. He enjoyed Thanksgiving dinner at the home of a new acquaintance and went shopping "down town." He bought "a hat 1.50. Oil coat 1.50," and, mindful of his children at home, "some books for Jennie, Harvey & Mina $1.25." [December 10, 11, 1880] He continued to find day work with various people. Reconnecting with his United Brethren in Christ fellowship, he attended regular prayer meetings, Sunday school classes, Bible readings, and occasional temperance lectures. On December 31, 1880, he "set up with" Elder Atwood's son, who was sick. "I kept up fire & gave medacine every hour." That night he "watched the old year out & the new year in. God is good to me." [December 31, 1880]

A. J. must have felt a sense of satisfaction at having built a new homestead for his family. His modest forty acres with good soil and ample timber would be manageable. In the climate of the Olympic Peninsula, drought, blizzards, grasshoppers, and prairie fires would not be issues. A. J. and Mary Jane's children all could look forward to building their own homesteads, as there was still plenty of cultivatable land available for homesteading in their neighborhood. And the growing metropolis of Seattle offered A. J. opportunities to earn the money he needed and the companionability and activity he so desired.

CHAPTER SEVEN

The Pullen Family 1881–1889

ON FEBRUARY 26, 1881, A. J. SMITH AND DAN PULLEN WENT SHOPPING in Seattle. Over the course of two days, the men bought items for an upcoming event that would join the two families and set the course of Hattie's future—Dan and Hattie's wedding. For his daughter, A. J. bought six place settings of silver flatware and two napkin rings, all monogrammed "H.S.P.," an outlay of $20.25—what A. J. would have earned in twenty days of work—and a "Gilt locket pocket Bible with clasp." [February 26, 1881] And Dan, envisioning the grand house he planned to build for his bride, bought bedroom furniture, an extension table, a lounge, a large rocking chair, a dozen napkins, glassware, china, and more silverware.

Three days earlier, Dan and Hattie had been in Clallam County, where they obtained their marriage license.[1] In recent months, they had each sat for their portraits at Seattle photographers' studios. Hattie wears a buttoned, tight-bodiced, dark-hued dress with a narrow standing collar, edged in lace and adorned with a large brooch. Intricate gathering of a shiny fabric drapes over her shoulders and across her chest, the central part giving the effect of multiple strings of beads. On top of all of this is a necklace and pendant. If her hair had fallen out during her bout with typhoid fever three years earlier, it had grown back enough so that she could wear it elaborately arranged into a pulled-back cluster of long sausage ringlets that flow over one shoulder. They show off her flower-shaped earrings and contrast with her short frizzled bangs and crimped crown hair. Her blue-gray eyes convey a steely determination.[2] On the back of an original print of the photograph she inscribed, "Miss Harriet Smith Afterwards Mrs. H. S. Pullen."[3] Dan, light-eyed and balding, his

Left: 7.1. "Miss Harriet Smith, Afterwards Mrs. H. S. Pullen," in Hattie's hand-writing on the back of the photograph, ca. 1881 (Peterson & Bro., photographer). Right: 7.2. Daniel Webster Pullen in February 1880 (McClaire & Quirk, photographer). BOTH: AUTHOR'S COLLECTION

mouth and chin obscured in a mustache and long goatee, sports his dress clothes—cravat, vest, and jacket.

According to Annie Dillard in *The Living*, her historical and thoroughly researched novel about pioneers in Washington Territory, women in the Pacific Northwest in the nineteenth century advised younger women to marry men from New England because they treated women right. A girl also fared best, she wrote, with an older man who had already established himself and done the arduous work of improving his claim.[4]

Twenty-year-old Hattie had attended school and worked since her family's arrival in Washington, but in an isolated place like western Clallam County, her marriage prospects were few. Assuming what Dillard wrote is true, Hattie not only found a man from New England who embodied all the aspects of a perfect husband but was also heroic in the eyes of her family. Moreover, he was the wealthiest man in what people call the West End of Clallam County. He offered her the security that came with large land holdings. The precariousness of the Smith family's

89

financial situation, something Hattie had experienced her entire life, made the prospect of owning and working a large tract of land appealing. Land was something she had watched her parents seek with limited success her whole life. With Dan she could have it immediately, or so it seemed. Dan and Hattie's eighteen-year age difference may have felt like an advantage to them both at the time, but it would become an issue for Hattie in years to come.

As plans for the Seattle wedding proceeded in February 1881, A. J. waited at the wharf all of one day and then did the same a few days later. He was looking for Mary Jane. The mother of the bride finally did arrive in time for the wedding, which A. J. described in his diary in a paragraph that reads like a newspaper announcement:

> *Dan Pullen & Hattie M. Smith*
> > *Were Married*
> *In the M.E. Church at 10:30 PM.*
> *By Rev. A. Atwood. P. E. Feb. 28th, 1881.*
> *About 60 persons were present.*
> > *Seattle Wash.*
> *A reception was given at Eld. Atwoods.*
> *A few friends accompanied them to the wharf—where Mr Pullen &*
> *Lady & Miss Tillie Atwood took state rooms on board the Str.* North
> Pacific *to Port Townsend. [T]hence they will go to their home in*
> *Quileut [Quillayute], on the str.* Dispatch *March 7th.*

Stepping out of his newspaper voice at the end, A. J. added, "Tickets $12.50." [February 28, 1881]

An article about the wedding appeared in a newspaper a week later. It tells us that the International Order of Good Templars Lodge, of which Hattie was a member, not only gave the couple a glass and silver pickle holder but also came en masse to the ceremony. The temperance organization admitted men and woman equally by 1852 and was in the vanguard of women's suffrage.[5] After the reception, the article concludes, Dan and Hattie embarked on their weeklong honeymoon in Port Townsend. After another two weeks at Neah Bay, they would be at home in La Push.[6]

7.3. Tillie Atwood and Hattie Smith in a tintype, ca. 1880. CLALLAM COUNTY
HISTORICAL SOCIETY

"The Pullen Mansion"

In February 1880, a year before the wedding, a local newspaper published an article by A. J. in which he reported on an Indian village of some thirty houses and thirty-eight families at the mouth of the Quillayute River. "I think a man with $2,000 capital could do a good business to set up a trading post, to buy furs, fish, elk and deer skins. . . . If some man would keep goods, groceries, &c. to sell, and let the Indians understand that they had a sure market for all their furs and fish it would stimulate industry," he noted.[7]

Within two months, a merchant had responded to A. J.'s suggestion. Sutcliffe Baxter of Seattle made Dan Pullen a proposal: He would build a store, which Dan could manage and at the same time act as his agent in sealskin trading with the Quileutes. Baxter would deliver groceries, dry goods, and hardware to La Push by schooner and pick up Dan's sealskins at the same time. Among the items the settlers would have wanted were tools, grain, seeds, muslin, calico, gingham, sugar, flour, spices, and candy. The boat would anchor in the shelter of James Island; Dan could pay Quileutes to unload goods into their canoes. In this scenario, Dan would no longer need to make lengthy trading trips in his schooner and could think about taking a wife.

By the end of July 1880, Baxter had sent for a load of lumber to begin construction of the store. He ran a railroad line of a few hundred feet across the beach to transport the lumber and other goods to the site. By October, the building was ready for business. It proved to be "a great convenience to the settlers," as well as to the Quileutes and other Indian peoples living in the area, A. J. reported.[8]

When Hattie and Dan arrived in La Push in March 1881 after their wedding, Dan's residence was in a wing of the store. There the newlyweds made their first home. As soon as he could, after the US government completed its township survey in 1882, Dan made a Homestead claim of 160 acres on the Quillayute Prairie near A. J.'s claim, several miles inland from La Push. According to Dan's Homestead proof questionnaire, he built a house on the claim and lived in it with Hattie from August 1883 to January 1885, long enough to legitimize the claim.[9]

Dan also made Preemption and Timber claims at La Push. Gradually, over the next eight years, he increased his acreage by buying 160-acre

Homestead claims from his sister, Hattie's uncle and brother, as well as property from at least four neighbors, a total value of $3,360. In today's dollars, this would be the equivalent of more than four million dollars measured in economic power or influence.[10] As did most homesteaders, Dan went about accumulating land for himself and Hattie without regard for the rights of the Quileute people, whose ancestors had been there for centuries. Altogether, he owned more than fifteen hundred acres in Quillayute country by 1891, significantly more land than any of his Euro-American neighbors.[11]

Hattie assisted Dan with the store and trading post. The Pullens continued to raise sheep and cattle on their land at Quillayute. Having grown up in a homesteading family, Hattie was also a valued partner in farming and ranching matters. She was physically strong, had great stamina, and was a skilled horse handler.

Dan and Mart drove the cattle to market in Port Townsend twice a year. [August 27, 1880] They hired Quileutes to dig their potato crop in exchange for half the harvest. One of Dan's granddaughters recalled hearing that because the potato loads were a challenge to carry down the trail to the river, Dan suggested that if the Quileutes cleared a path wide enough for the wagons to pass, he would haul the potatoes to their canoes for them. The Indians agreed, and thus the first path, later a road, from the Quillayute Prairie to the river came to be.[12]

Before long, the La Push house Dan had dreamed of became a reality. He filed a notice of intention to make final proof on his Preemption claim of 153 acres of oceanfront land at La Push in April 1883 and began the process of proving up on this claim a couple of years later.[13] In 1886, with his ownership seemingly secure, Dan went ahead with plans for the house's construction.

He and Hattie selected a site near the store on high ground just south of the mouth of the Quillayute River, about forty feet above sea level. The spot was on a point of land that juts into the ocean, allowing a commanding, breathtaking, 180-degree ocean view. Dotting the sea just offshore were several sea stacks, making a picturesque view the Pullens would enjoy from most windows of the house.

Hattie and Dan could have seen a number of houses in Seattle, Olympia, or Port Townsend to inspire their own plans. Port Townsend,

7.4. Aerial view of La Push, Washington, taken between 1945 and 1970 (Clifford B. Ellis, photographer). UNIVERSITY OF WASHINGTON LIBRARIES, SPECIAL COLLECTIONS, ELLIS 5321

in its heyday in the 1870s, had been their honeymoon destination. Today it is renowned for its large number of ornate Victorian houses. The Pullens probably acquired a mail-order house plan from an architectural pattern book, a resource that had grown in popularity since the Civil War. It would have included not only the floor plan, elevations, and building instructions but also patterns for millwork cross sections.

Dan brought in by schooner the lumber for the grand house and began construction with the help of his brother Mart, Hattie's brother Harvey, A. J.'s brother Harvey, and another man.[14] The wood had been precut and framed in Seattle, enabling the crew to quickly assemble the structure in the fall of 1886. The house included a parlor, dining room, kitchen, pantry, office, and lavatory—ten rooms in all. It was unlike anything La Push, or even all of Quillayute country, had ever seen. Ostentatious might have been the word for it, especially considering its location looming above the Quileute village, which was strung out along the shoreline less than fifty yards from the house.[15]

Referred to locally as "the Pullen mansion,"[16] it was a Queen Anne Victorian type, which was popular in the Puget Sound area after the

7.5. A Quileute police officer, another Quileute, Chester and Royal, seated, and Dee Pullen, standing, near the back of the Pullens' house, with the water tank, ca. 1893. WASHINGTON STATE LIBRARY MANUSCRIPTS COLLECTION, A. WESLEY SMITH PAPERS, 1853–1935, M.S. 172

railroads made it possible to obtain factory-made woodwork. The house had a cruciform floor plan, a front-facing gable, a complex roofline, two-story bay windows above inset wooden panels, meticulously detailed trim painted in contrasting tones, corbelled chimneys, and one-story porches with bracketed supports. A photograph of the side of the house shows a water tank, an indication of indoor running water. The Pullens paid twenty-five cents a day to members of the Quileute tribe to haul water from the Dickey River, keeping the tank full.[17]

By the winter of 1886–87, the Pullens were able to move into the new house. The following year, they added a barn and a woodshed to the back of the house. Five years after that, Dan hired a carpenter to build an addition. Not the kind of dwelling one would expect to find on land that had been claimed from the wilderness a mere decade before, it must have been astonishing for the neighbors to watch it go up and continue to be expanded. It was the house of a family with financial resources and a sense of its own importance. For Hattie, life in La Push was seemingly secure.[18]

7.6. The Pullens' La Push house and woodshed from the northwest in February 1888, before the tower and addition were built (David T. Smith, photographer). (See figure 9.3 for an image of the house after the construction of the additions.) WASHINGTON STATE LIBRARY MANUSCRIPTS COLLECTION, A. WESLEY SMITH PAPERS, 1853–1935, M.S. 172

THE PULLENS LIVED COMFORTABLY

In addition to working alongside Dan in the store and trading post (now the Washington Fur Company), helping with the farm, and managing the house, Hattie looked after the children. Mildred, called Dolly, had been born in 1882 above the store, one year after the wedding. Three sons followed—Daniel Dee, called Dee, in 1885, Royal in 1887, and Chester in 1889. The Pullen children's first playmates were Quileutes and several Smith cousins, one of whom Harriet nursed along with her own child to save the baby's life when the mother became ill.[19] The family cook, a Quileute named Sam, also served as a caregiver for the Pullen children and taught them his native tongue, which they spoke before they could speak English.[20] There was no school nearby except an Indian Agency school. It was probably not open to the children of settlers, and the Pullens

7.7. Sam and his son Buster (*Kā'-ă-'lish*) in about 1895, on the porch of the Pullens' house at La Push. In Hattie's handwriting on the back was written: "Cooked for me 15 years. Sam my Indian Cook & his little boy, who was born on the same day as my Dan was, April 27, in 1892. H. Pullen." CLALLAM COUNTY HISTORICAL SOCIETY

7.8. Dee and Royal Pullen in the yard of the Pullens' La Push house in about 1890; note the antlers decorating the porch (David T. Smith, photographer).
COLLECTION WALTER R. AND MARY E. PATTERSON, SEATTLE, WASHINGTON

would have considered it an inappropriate place to educate their children anyway, so Hattie and Dan hired an English governess for a time. When asked about his governess in an interview, Royal recalled school lessons with his siblings in the house.[21]

The Pullens lived comfortably after moving into their new dwelling. They had disposable income to hire regular household help—Sam as the cook and his wife as the maid. Several other Quileute women did laundry, and other members of the tribe worked on and off helping in the garden as well. On at least two occasions, the Pullens hired dressmakers to make clothes for Hattie and the children with a sewing machine the Pullens had ordered from Seattle. While Dan was plain in his attire, Hattie seemed to have dressed herself and the children handsomely. The two dressmakers reported that between 1890 and 1892, they made a blue corduroy suit for Dee, seven dresses and a jacket for Mildred, and at least nine flannel, velvet, lawn, or gingham dresses and a princess wrap for Hattie, all either white, black, or one of three shades of blue—cadet, Dutch, or "American."[22]

The family's income came from a variety of sources. Dan was a notary public for the State of Washington and postmaster at Quillayute following A. J.'s tenure. Two years later, the US government decided that La Push needed its own post office. Hattie—referred to as *Hatty S. Pullen* and *him* on the Post Office Department appointment document—became its postmaster.[23] (Hattie spelled her name with a "y" in letters of the 1880s; her mother, father, and others usually spelled it with an "ie," although Wesley wrote "Hatty" and "Hattie" in the same 1879 diary entry, and Olly did the same in an 1898 letter.[24]) The Pullens dedicated a ten-by-ten-foot room in their house to serve as the post office. When schooners and sailing vessels were unavailable, serving as postmaster for remote, coastal Clallam County sometimes involved transporting the mail by walking along the beach and through the woods and using canoes to portage across the rivers. The Pullens' horses and a network of family members made the job easier for them than it might have been for others.[25]

Hattie housed and fed a steady stream of boarders in their house. They rented small parcels of land to Baxter for the trading post and to the Neah Bay Agency for the new Quileute School, where Hattie's brother Wesley had become the teacher. Hattie accepted a twenty-dollar gold piece from a neighbor who wanted to bury his son on the Pullens' land claim. They pastured horses for other people, rented out horses, and Hattie sold colts on occasion. Her fifty chickens brought in income from the sale of eggs and poultry. She and Dan sold some beef, mutton, wool, milk, and butter. Their garden supplied their own produce needs and that of their boarders and netted a little surplus, which yielded additional money. Altogether, they had an ample income.[26]

WEST END

The Pullens' busy lives as parents, storekeepers, ranchers, and postal workers still allowed time for socializing. On Christmas 1883, Mart Pullen invited friends for a "free supper" followed by another gathering at a neighbor's house. "A beautiful Christmas tree, well laden, was stripped [of presents] at Mr. Maxfield's the same evening to a house full of all ages, who were happy. It was a grand success. Some speaking and singing. The presents to the loved ones spoke volumes for their loving hearts," A. J. reported in a newspaper article.[27]

7.9. Gold Digger and Sunday, Hattie's horses, on the Pullens' Quillayute homestead in 1890. CLALLAM COUNTY HISTORICAL SOCIETY

There was also time for outdoor activity in the surrounding wild country. Hattie's expertise with horses had developed on her parents' Wisconsin and Dakota homesteads. When she learned to ride, she was so small that she had had to mount her horse by leaning on its neck while it ate and then kicking it until it raised its head so she could slide onto its back. A skilled rider, "she never rode astride; she just wasn't raised that way," as her son put it.[28] She kept two saddle horses at La Push and rode along the beach regularly. Hattie annotated a photograph taken by her brother David, who had become a professional photographer with a studio in Seattle, "These are my two thoroughbred horses. Uncle Eph gave me one for a saddle horse & Uncle Mart [on horseback] gave me the coalt for a cart horse. He sayes she will be so gentle & nice for the children & me. I call her Sunday. 1890 Hatty Pullen."[29] The uncles she refers to were Dan's brothers.

An autobiographical statement by Hattie's Dakota cousin, Martha Smith Cutts, recalled a cattle drive and other trips that she and Hattie made on horseback during Martha's six-month sojourn in Quillayute in 1886:

While in Quillayute, Hattie and I went with the cattle drive to Pyscht [Pysht] on the Straits. It was customary for the neighbors to drive their beef cattle to market each fall. It took two days. There were no wagon roads, just a trail. We rode horseback single file. When the way was steep, we held on to our horses and he pulled us over the hump.

We heard the elk whistle but saw none. The men sang to the cattle and they followed the trail single file. At night we slept in the hay in a barn. The men cooked their sourdough pancakes over an open fire in a long handled frying pan. They were expert in turning the cakes by a flip of the pan. We saw no women on the way. All were bachelors.

When the tide was out, the beach was a lovely place for horseback riding that we often enjoyed.[30]

Hattie frequently took her children on horseback to visit her parents and siblings at Quillayute Prairie. Royal recalled his mother carrying him wearing a long baby dress, suitable for showing him off to her parents. When he was old enough to ride his own horse, Hattie would take its bridle at the river crossing and tell Royal to stretch out with his feet up along the animal's back and hang onto the saddle horn while she swam the horses. The forest was so dense that they could not see daylight above or anything beyond the impenetrable green wall on either side of the trail. Returning at night after visits, Hattie always carried an oil lantern and sang songs as they rode. Their dog Heck kept close to the horses, staying almost underneath them. When Royal was older, his mother told him there had been wolves and cougars following them on those rides. Her singing had kept them at bay. "A cougar cry," Royal remarked, "is a terrible thing to hear when you are alone in the woods at night."[31]

For a time the Pullens kept a bear cub chained to a stump in front of their house. Considered by the locals to be pests, bears had on at least one occasion destroyed part of the Pullens' oat crop.[32] Nevertheless, the Pullens kept a bear as a pet. As the months rolled by, it grew to formidable proportions. One day it pulled the staple at the end of its chain out of the stump where it had been tethered and started rambling around the yard. Hattie got a rope and lassoed it from one of the windows of the house. Then she handed the rope to one of the Quileute boys who worked for them and told him to keep the bear from chasing her while she grabbed hold of the loose end of the chain. The plan was to entice the bear back to the stump.

At first the plan worked. The bear edged closer to the stump, but then it lunged toward the boy, who dropped the rope and ran for a nearby fence, leaving the bear free to go after Hattie. She let go of the chain and ran behind the stump, then around and around the stump they went, the bear in hot pursuit. Finally, the end of the chain caught and wound around the stump, allowing Hattie to drive the staple through a link in the chain. When Dan got home that night and heard the story, he went out to see if the bear was secure. When he got close to the stump, the bear moved toward him. An experienced hunter, Dan knew with bears it was better to stand his ground than to run. Without moving, he waited for the bear to get within reach and then hit him above the eye with a hammer. The bear didn't bother him anymore, but it had to live with just one eye. Dan eventually decided it was getting too big to keep and gave it to a zoo.[33]

NEIGHBORS

When asked in an interview if he and his brother Dee had played with the Quileute children, Royal replied, "All the time. That's all we had to play with. They'd come up there on the hill. [Dee] and I would take up sides, see, . . . I had my Indian kids . . . [Dee] had his . . . both cliques. We'd go down on the beach and have a fort and have a fight. . . . We used to have a lot of fun that way."[34] The forts they built were made of huge pieces of driftwood, tons of which washed up on the beach in front of their house. They skipped rocks in the surf. The Quileute children taught Royal to speak their language. Their only English words were swear words, which they also taught Royal. He recalled watching the Quileute mothers comb lice from their children's hair and then eat the lice from the comb. When the community landed a whale, the Quileute children would walk around chewing on blubber cut into slippery, licorice-size strips.[35]

On occasion, Hattie and her children went out to a flat island known as "Bird Rocks," north of La Push, where the Quileutes regularly went to gather seagull eggs. The nests were so numerous that one could hardly move without stepping on one. Royal recalled watching the Quileutes place the eggs in big baskets, enough to fill several canoes. They would then boil them in large copper kettles set over a fire, scoop them up with dippers, and eat them with horn spoons right there on the beach.[36]

At times, the Pullens worked closely with their neighbors to address emergencies. In the nineteenth century, there was no US Coast Guard. The sea had her way with mariners, and whatever remained after a ship wrecked was left to those who happened to be nearby. The treacherous waters that lay just offshore in front of the Pullens' house and the Quileute village meant shipwrecks were a repeated occurrence for the community. In 1880, Hattie's father had recommended in a newspaper article that La Push needed a "wreckmaster . . . to take charge of these things," and that Dan Pullen would be the best choice for such an appointment.[37]

No one ever officially appointed Dan to such a post, but in 1893, he had an opportunity to act in that capacity. In the dark of early morning on October 4, the bark *Leonor* from the major port at Valparaiso, Chile, wrecked on the beach just above the mouth of the Quillayute River. Nine on board survived; six were lost. The bodies, however, didn't just remain at sea. They washed ashore one by one over the next ten days. Dan, Hattie, several other settlers, and three Quileutes retrieved the remains, cleaned them up, dug graves, and arranged for burial services. Wesley Smith kept a diary describing each detail:

Fri. 6th Sebastian & Dan & Fred Baxter and one or two others buried one man who came ashore near the wreck. Dan P., Fred B., Sebastian (Petersen), Indians Joe, Carl and Luke and myself brought the Captain's wife, from where the sailors left her among the logs near the wreck, to the old school house.

Sat. 7th Mrs. P[ullen] & Mrs. Thompson washed and dressed her and Dan went to the prairie for Mr. Fletcher to hold services, and to get his children.

Sat. 7th [W]e found one man about 5 ft. 8 or 9 in. tall, a Jap I think, head crushed on top and brains protruding. A cut over one eye. Light

*goatee, flag (German I think) tattooed on left arm, light crop of hair
and whiskers short and scattering, though may have been worn off.
Light mustache. Fred B. and Sebastian dug the grave. Sebastian, Sal-
stad and myself buried him, by the Frenchman. . . . Mr. Fletcher came
down and gave a short address and we buried the capts wife in Dan's
field. She looked well and had kept remarkably well.*[38]

A judge and his wife visited Hattie and Dan some weeks after the
wreck and took a walk on the beach with their hosts. A newspaper article
quoted the judge:

*"The debris was strewn along the beach for a half mile on either side
of the wrecked vessel, and it would seem that there was enough lumber
to build three or four good sized houses. . . . Heavy timbers two and
three feet in diameter were snapped square off seemingly as easy as a
person could break a twig. . . . The captain was swept from his vessel
by a tremendous wave just as she struck the rocks and that was the
last seen of him, but the sailors had almost succeeded in getting ashore
with his wife when a wave dashed over the raft and when it had
passed the lady was gone. Her body was found the next morning by
an Indian who had started up the beach to Neah Bay and he at once
notified the settlers. . . . One of the sailors . . . in departing from the
doomed vessel . . . took a block of matches, and rolling them in his hair,
tied an oil cloth tightly over his head. As he boarded a piece of wreck-
age, he remarked, 'Boys, I will have a fire for you when you land,' and
he did."*[39]

No 911, no ambulances, no hospitals, no doctors, no coroner, no
funeral home, not even a cemetery. Such was life in Quillayute country
in the late nineteenth century. Hattie's sister Jennie told of being sick one
winter and being hauled on a sled from Quillayute over the trail through
the snow-filled forest, forty miles to Clallam.[40] Under whatever circumstances came their way, the multitasking Pullens and their Quileute
neighbors did what had to be done.

Now perched at the edge of the continent, as far as their respective westward migrations could take them, and apparently prosperous in the big house with substantial land acreage and four healthy children, Dan and Hattie, a strong and resilient pair, seemed to have a promising future ahead of them. In just ten years, Hattie had gone from living in a sod house on the prairie to a Victorian Queen Anne mansion overlooking the Pacific Ocean. Dan, poor and fatherless at the age of seven, had set out on his own as a young man and, via a circuitous, two-decade journey, had found his way to the same place. Their respective families of origin, all part of the Yankee Diaspora, had been largely reunited after challenging westward journeys. And they were living peacefully with the "other" in their midst. Their story was a triumph over nineteenth-century adversity and diversity and, seemingly, a realization of Hattie's father's optimistic forecast just two decades earlier—"vast wealth will flow from the Quileut [Quillayute] valley."[41]

CHAPTER EIGHT

The Quileutes

THE LAND THAT DAN PULLEN, AND LATER THE SMITH FAMILY, SETTLED upon had been the homeland of the Quileute people for centuries. Their territory was a rough square, beginning about thirty miles south of Cape Flattery and running another thirty miles along the Pacific shore and then thirty miles inland. In the nineteenth century, the Quileute people numbered between two and three hundred. They had lived for thousands of years near the beach at the mouth of the Quillayute River, scattered inland along several tributaries, and on the fern prairies. Although their territory eventually became much smaller, unlike most Native American peoples today, they still live within sight of their ancestors' graves.[1]

Before contact with settlers, the Quileutes subsisted on the vast bounty of the sea and the rivers, utilizing land-based resources as well. In addition to whaling and fishing in the ocean, they fished for salmon in the river, foraged for fern roots and camas (a nutritious potato-like perennial bulb that grows wild on the prairies), and hunted mammals. Accessible only by water because of the mountains to the east and the density of the forests, their part of the Olympic Peninsula was difficult territory to negotiate, even by those familiar with it. Early surveyors noted that the area was among the densest forestland in the United States, nearly impenetrable. What trails existed were too rugged even for horses. There was no safe harbor along the rocky, treacherous coast. As a result, the region had escaped settlement by Euro-Americans for decades.[2]

The first non-Indian people to arrive came by boat, usually the consequence of a shipwreck. They were maritime fur traders from Spain, Russia, Great Britain, and America. A British seaman, John Meares, described the coastline in 1788 after a trip south from Cape Flattery: "The appearance of the land was wild in the extreme—immense forest covered the whole of it within our sight, down to the very beach, which was lofty and cragged, and against which the sea dashed with fearful rage. The shore was lined with rocks and rocky inlets, nor could we perceive any bay or inlet that seemed to promise the least security to the smallest vessel."[3]

The native peoples of the Olympic Peninsula called these outlanders *ho'kwat*, meaning "drifting house people" or wanderers.[4] The wanderers would come and go, although in one instance the crew of a shipwrecked Russian trading vessel, the *Sv. Nikolai*, spent more than a year struggling with the environment and variously fighting with, hiding from, and finally living with the Makah, Hoh, or Quileute peoples as captives or slaves. In 1810, an American sea captain rescued thirteen survivors of the original crew of twenty-two. Even after this event, these Indian peoples managed to live for several more decades in peaceful isolation from the assault of Euro-American culture and commercialism.[5]

James G. Swan, the teacher of the Makahs at the Neah Bay Agency, visited the Quileutes in 1855 and 1861. He wrote after his second visit, "Ours was certainly the first trading vessel ever there and the actions of the Indians showed how unaccustomed they were to a stock of goods." He mentioned the Quileute village at the mouth of the river and their head chief, Howeatl, who had been friendly and "of great service to the whites" at the time of an earlier shipwreck.[6]

AN AFTERTHOUGHT, AN OUTPOST

Meanwhile, during the mid-nineteenth century, the US government was making efforts to "civilize" the Indian groups living in the region. The Quileutes were party to an 1856 treaty signed by their leaders and those of the nearby Quinaults and Isaac I. Stevens, the governor of Washington Territory. In signing it, the Quileute people ceded their ancestral lands to the United States and agreed to settle on a yet-to-be-determined reservation within one year of congressional ratification of the treaty, which took place in 1859. In exchange, they received the right to continue fishing and hunting on unclaimed lands, payments of twenty-five thousand dollars over twenty years, and an additional twenty-five hundred dollars for clearing land for agricultural purposes. The terms of the treaty gave the US president the right to relocate them if deemed necessary, and required them to remain friendly toward all US citizens. The federal government agreed to establish an agency with an agricultural and industrial school and to provide the services of a blacksmith, a carpenter, and a physician.[7]

From the beginning, there were misunderstandings on both sides. The US representatives failed to understand the relationships among the various Indian peoples living on the Olympic Peninsula, evidenced by the government's assumption for two decades that the Quileutes would eventually, either by choice or by force, live within the territory of the Quinaults, another Indian nation living to the south. The US president's executive orders establishing the reservations of *both* the Makahs, in 1872, and the Quinaults, in 1873, cited the Quileutes as if they were simply a subdivision of either, or both groups, when, in fact, the Quileute people were an entity unto themselves, with their own language and customs.[8]

By the time the Quileute people had appeared on the radar of the US Office of Indian Affairs, its agents were recognizing that the Quileutes had misunderstood the treaty they had signed, and that they had no intention of giving up their land to move onto the Quinault reservation. The agent writing the 1867 Quinault Agency annual report noted that the Quileutes "still inhabit their old place of abode, and nothing of an ordinary character would induce them to leave the scenes of their childhood and old hunting grounds, . . . and, until the lands they now occupy are needed for settlement, it will be their home still."[9] Note the agent's caveat: "until the lands they now occupy are needed for settlement"—a reflection of an attitude widely held among Indian agents and settlers at the time.

R. H. Milroy, superintendent of Indian Affairs for Washington Territory, reported in 1872 that the Quileutes "say they never agreed to sell their country," and agreed only "to keep the peace with citizens of the United States," and thus refuse "to leave their homes."[10] Milroy made this report at about the same time Dan Pullen and his brother settled in the area. Milroy stated that the area was "almost wholly unexplored . . . and, from the quality of the country . . ., is likely to remain so for many years to come."[11]

Because of the region's isolation and the prevailing belief that the area was only marginally fit for agricultural purposes, and thus not likely to be heavily settled by Euro-Americans anytime soon, the government did not force the Quileutes to leave their homeland and settle on a reservation. Nonetheless, some settlers assumed the government eventually would do so.[12] The US government had been shoving Native American peoples aside for decades, so it is not surprising that the settlers of Quillayute, including Dan Pullen, might have assumed the same would happen in their area.

In an effort to clarify the situation, in 1877, without the knowledge of the Quileute people, the Office of Indian Affairs transferred them to the jurisdiction of the Neah Bay Agency, which oversaw the Makah people living to the north. The Makahs had no affiliation with the Quileutes except for a trading relationship. This development only further confused the Quileutes as to their status.[13] The agent in charge of the Neah Bay Agency, Charles Willoughby, wrote in regard to the Quileute people in 1881:

> *In concluding my report of the Indians, I should neglect to do my duty did I not make special mention of this band, numbering 300, which has never availed itself of the advantages offered at the [Makah] industrial school [at Neah Bay, where A. J. had taught and Wesley continued to teach], except in a very limited way. This is accounted for from the fact that the band is located 30 miles distant and [has] no communication by road or trail, and the continued severe storms on this coast make it extremely hazardous for canoes, their only method of traveling, to make the trip except in the most favorable seasons, to which add the strong prejudice existing among them against letting their children go to any great distance from home. In view of these circumstances, and the repeated application of the leading men of the tribe, for a school in their village, there being by last census 50 children of school age, I would suggest the establishing of a branch school at Quillehute.[14]*

Overall, the Quileute people had been an afterthought, an outpost, first of the Quinault Agency, then the Makah Neah Bay Agency, and, in effect, were largely left out of the agency and reservation systems established by the US government. Even as late as 1885, the Indian agent for the Makahs at Neah Bay admitted that it was "a difficult matter to reach these Indians, as the only mode of travel is on foot, over a trail too rough for horses, or by sea in a canoe, and for this reason I do not visit them as often as I would like to."[15]

Meanwhile, the Quileutes lived peacefully and seemed to accept the intruders who had begun settling within their territory around 1870. The agent in charge of the Quinault Agency reported in 1874 that the Quileutes were "very peaceable, and . . . letters [from the few settlers in their midst] assure me that the Indians are not troublesome, but in many ways are of assistance to them."[16] However, the messages were mixed. Two years later the same agent reported that "it is the desire of . . . [the] settlers to have them [the Quileutes] placed upon the reserve."[17]

The Quileutes themselves seemed to be of two minds. On one hand, they had become accustomed to receiving the payments from the US government and the goods that traders like Dan Pullen brought them in exchange for furs. Yet, at the same time, they began to recognize that the settlers were taking their homeland. Even though a major part of their subsistence came from the sea, they also depended on hunting and foraging on the fern prairies, where most of the settlers were homesteading. As one Indian agent noted, "As the settlers are taking up the land most favorable for the growth of . . . [camas], a substitute is looked for."[18]

The same agent reported in 1879 that the Quileutes were loyal to the US government and held the settlers in friendly regard. Should the US government decide to move them onto the Makah reservation, he continued, "I am satisfied no force will be needed . . . and although they are naturally endeared to the homes of their forefathers, and express constantly strong fears in this respect, yet I am certain . . . they would be sadly obedient. And the day will come when this removal will be necessary, for the country they occupy is fast bedotted with the homes of several families of whites."[19]

It was becoming clear that Euro-American people would indeed continue to settle the area despite its inaccessibility. The idea that the removal of the Quileute people to the Makah reservation was inevitable was a position that would soon begin to change within the Office of Indian Affairs.

The fact that conflicts between the Quileutes and the settlers had not yet come to a dangerous breaking point was partly because relatively little of the homesteaded land could be cultivated, and thus continued to be held for timber. With the area not densely settled nor cultivated, the Quileutes were able to continue hunting and foraging until their own tastes began to change in favor of potatoes and other root vegetables the settlers had introduced.[20] What they needed from the sea continued to be readily available. The intrusion on the Quileute homeland was slow and subtle, but insidious.

THE QUILEUTE VILLAGE

By the time the Smith family settled at Quillayute, the Quileute village at La Push was well established. If they were nomadic, as some people claimed, it was only for part of the year, because they spent long periods living near the beach.[21] In January 1880, one year before Hattie and Dan married, A. J. described the village thus:

> At the mouth of the Quileut river is an Indian village, it contains 14 siwash houses, and 15 siwash Boston houses. They have seven stoves and several fire-places and chimneys. Thirty-eight heads of families two of whom keep two wives each. There are 45 boys 61 girls and 66 tilicums, composed of men, women and children, some of whom are grandfathers, grandmothers, and a few families. The tribe numbers about 250. They have several horses, and one man has a place [as opposed to a house shared by several families]; also raspberries, gooseberries, and currant bushes set out. Most all cultivate small patches of potatoes, and a few turnips. They have some useful utensils and tools. The men have canoes and catch a great many seal and fish. . . . I saw them take a salmon that would weigh about 40 or 50 pounds, Jan. 20, 1880.[22]

The unfamiliar terms are from the Chinook Jargon, a trade language of limited vocabulary used to communicate among settlers and various

Indian groups of the Pacific Northwest. "Siwash house" referred to traditional Indian houses, *siwash* a term meaning "Indian," with some derogatory connotations suggesting "worthless." "Boston houses" meant those in the style of the settlers' houses, the term having derived from references to the early traders in the area, many of whom came from New England. "Tillicum" meant friend or common person as opposed to a "tyee," or chief.[23]

At the core of Quileute culture was fishing and whaling. During seasonal salmon runs, they set up weirs across the rivers to catch them. According to Royal, from the sea they brought in boatloads of red snapper. Occasionally they would harpoon a whale and bring it ashore in front of the Pullens' house. The raw strips of blubber were their "candy." They used a particular gristle to make balls that would bounce like rubber. The whale oil they sold to the Pullens and others.[24] In July 1888, they shipped off by schooner 760 gallons of it, their take from three whales.[25]

Once Royal watched them harpoon a whale, the men struggling with the massive animal while it towed their boat out to sea. They lost all of their gear and eventually had to cut loose from it.[26] Even successful attempts to land a whale involved the efforts of several canoes of men laboring for hours. One young Quileute described what it was like when a thrashing whale broke their canoe into pieces and his group of whalers landed in the ocean. All of the men survived when they were picked up by fellow Quileutes in another canoe. Eventually, they succeeded in killing the whale.[27] During the summer of 1888, the Quileutes killed seven whales, three of them landed on the beach at La Push, apparently a high number for one season.[28]

The fern prairies were located a few miles inland from the village. They were a vital resource for the Quileute people, and also where A. J., Dan, and other settlers had homesteaded. So important was this land to the Quileute people that when agent Willoughby and agency teacher Swan met the Quileute chiefs Xawishat'a, Tlakishka, and Taxa'wil at the mouth of the Quillayute River in 1879, the three chiefs signed an affidavit claiming the treaty negotiators had misled them in 1856. They specifically mentioned "prairie land where the camas grows," which they said they would have never given up voluntarily. They proposed to keep one-half of the prairie land and offered to sell the other half.[29]

What made the prairies so attractive to a settler planning to farm was the absence of the enormous fir trees that grew nearby. The centuries-long Quileute practice of maintaining the prairies by burning them regularly, section by section, allowed the ferns to regenerate and kept the timber at bay. The prairies drew elk and deer, animals they hunted, and encouraged the growth of certain plants they foraged, particularly camas,[30] which they cooked over heated rocks placed in pits covered with wet leaves and mounds of earth.[31] The Quileute women pounded the fern roots into a pulp, dried it, and made it into dough for fern-paste bread.[32]

Quileute families moved regularly from their homes near the sea to summer campsites on the fern prairies, where the men hunted and the women foraged. The Quileutes viewed the prairies as belonging to the tribe collectively, with heritable use-ownership rights of separate sections accorded to specific families as long as they continued to use the land.[33] The ongoing maintenance that the Quileutes provided made the prairies a convenient, if intrusive, place for settlers to clear and cultivate.

Over time, the settlers objected to the Quileute burning of the prairies. At the same time, the dietary preferences of the Quileutes changed in favor of cultivated vegetables; they gradually ceased foraging and hunting. By the 1890s, they had stopped burning, and essentially had given up their claim to the fern-prairie lands.[34]

Among other traditions that died out or changed with the coming of settlers were slavery, polygyny (the practice of one man having more than one wife), head flattening, potlatching, and certain burial customs. For centuries, Indian peoples living along the Pacific in the Northwest had sporadically practiced slavery, a status symbol, usually a consequence of capturing members of rival tribes. Polygyny, reserved for high-status men, took place as well. Both practices quickly faded away as the Indian agents discouraged them.

A number of Pacific Northwest Indians practiced head flattening. Soon after babies were born, families bound their infants into cradles where they stayed, except for washing and replacement of the bark padding, until they could walk. According to anthropologist George Pettitt,

"A pad of cedarbark fiber and a band of the same material were used to bind the infant's head to the bottom of the cradle to give it the much desired wedge shape."[35]

The intertribal potlatch, practiced by a number of Indian groups in the Pacific Northwest, was a massive, competitive, gift-giving festival, central to a gift economy at the time. Potlatches marked major celebratory, transitional events such as marriages, births, and deaths. Gifts distributed served as payment for the obligation of remembering changes.[36] The US government fought the practice for years, nominally because the result was the temporary impoverishment of the host tribe or family, which would result in the government having to support the family in need. More broadly, it was contrary to the norms of white America and thus something to be stamped out.

The Indian agent at Neah Bay wrote to Wesley Smith sometime around 1890, "You can inform Quillayute Indians in general and Jim Black in particular that I am decidedly opposed to potlaching and that the government has forbidden the practice. . . . If they want to give to the very poor and the very old of their own tribe I have no objection. You can inform Jim Black that if he gives $200 in a potlach that he need not expect any help from the government."[37] The US government was of the opinion that its payments would go to waste if given away in potlatches.

In their strong desire to continue the practice, an occasion to party as well as to give gifts, Indians flummoxed the agents by calling the gatherings birthday parties or bartering meetings, thus concealing what was really going on. A. J. wrote in one of his 1880 newspaper articles, "The Quileutes are having a grand 'pot latch.' All the Neah Bay [Makah] and Ozett Indians [a small group that was a part of the Makah people] are here."[38] Anthropologist Pettitt described a vital aspect of potlatches: "Drinking whale oil in prodigious quantities, and spewing it on the fires, was an important supplementary means of impressing visitors with the wealth and profligacy of the host."[39] Central to the practice was the strongly held value that wealth and status were measured by what one could give away rather than by what one possessed. A potlatch cost resources, but those who practiced it deemed it a worthwhile investment, bringing prestige that a family could only acquire in this way.[40]

Another striking difference between the Quileute people and the settlers were customs surrounding death. The Quileutes traditionally removed bodies of the dead through an opening in the back of the house to keep other souls from following it. They wrapped the remains of high-status men in blankets and placed them with their tools and weapons in their canoes, elevated among the branches of treetops, most often red alders, and secured them with ropes made of spruce roots.

Pettitt published his findings in 1950. As he put it, "For the people of La Push, acculturation is not an academic question but a current reality which has produced considerable confusion and left some of them living rather dazedly in the ruins of the culture they knew best, like the victims of a fire or a flood."[41] Pettitt based his writings on the observations he made while living among the Quileute people, and on his interviews with those who remembered the early years of Euro-American settlement.

WESLEY

Pettitt attributed many of the changes that took place in the Quileute culture to the presence of Hattie's brother Wesley Smith, their first school-teacher, who was also a lay preacher, justice of the peace, postmaster, surrogate dentist, and the Quileutes' only representative to the supervising Neah Bay Indian Agency. Pettitt commented, "Under his determined leadership all Indian children went to school, and in the interests of their conversion into citizens, he vigorously opposed all traditional practices of the older Indians. In many ways, his success was phenomenal. Head-flattening was forbidden, tattooing was condemned, potlatching was rigorously limited, gambling became a crime, healing rituals by shamans were banned, the awe in which shamans were held was ridiculed, children were prevented from attending night ceremonies, and the tribe was constantly exhorted to live a good life."[42] The cultural bias of Wesley Smith—and of Pettitt, some fifty years later—is evident in these observations.

The Quileutes understandably had resisted sending their children to the schools at the Neah Bay and Quinault Agencies as the US government initially expected them to do. The children would have had to board at the schools, rarely seeing their parents. The Quileutes also feared that schooling might be a form of deception, leading to the sale of their

8.1. A. Wesley Smith, his assistant teacher, and thirty-four Quileute students in front of their La Push school in about 1890 (David T. Smith, photographer). WASHINGTON STATE LIBRARY MANUSCRIPTS COLLECTION, A. WESLEY SMITH PAPERS, 1853–1935, M.S. 172

children into slavery. After Neah Bay agent Willoughby recognized their reluctance, he recommended in 1881 that a branch school be established for the Quileute people. The government did just that. In 1883, Wesley left his teaching job at the Neah Bay Agency to run the agency-sponsored Quileute School at La Push.

Wesley had maintained his family ties to Quillayute, and had even already homesteaded 160 acres there by the time he became the teacher at La Push. To establish the new school, Wesley repaired an abandoned house that an early trader had built near the beach. Dan Pullen had claimed it and charged the agency a monthly rent for use of the building. The school opened on December 1, 1883, with twenty-six students.[43]

One of Wesley Smith's first tasks as teacher was to give English-language names to all of his students. In his Indian census of 1884, there were 250 Quileutes, none listed with surnames. About one-quarter of them had Anglicized first names. By 1890, more than one-third had surnames, and many had Anglicized first names listed in a column alongside their Quileute names. For source material on names, Wesley turned to the

US history books and the Bible he had brought with him from Neah Bay. Some of the names he selected included Hudson, Lee, Cleveland, Taft, Penn, Washington, and Jefferson. From the Bible he borrowed Jacob, Joseph, Esau, Isaac, Rebecca, Daniel, Mary, Martha, and Mark. From local people he took Bright (Wesley's assistant teacher and, later, his wife) and Pullen (the name of his brother-in-law).

Here I found the explanation for the name of tribal elder Lillian Pullen, whose legacy I encountered on my visit to La Push in 2004. Her grandfather had been one of the students of Wesley Smith, who had given him the name Joseph Pullen. Some Quileute names had already been phonetically Anglicized, such as Buckety Mason, California Hobucket, Benjamin Sailto, and Arthur Howeattle. Wesley deemed those names acceptable.[44]

In 1890, six years into Wesley's tenure at the Quileute School, the Office of Indian Affairs issued a directive amending the policy of giving English-language names to Native Americans. It reads:

> *There seems . . . to be no good reason for continuing a custom which has prevailed to a considerable extent of substituting English for Indian names. . . . Doubtless, in many cases, the Indian name is difficult to pronounce and to remember; but in many other cases the Indian word is as short and as euphonious as the English word that is substituted, while other things being equal, the fact that it is an Indian name makes it a better one. For convenience, an English "christian name" may be given and the Indian name be retained as a surname. If the Indian word is unusually long and difficult, it may perhaps be arbitrarily shortened.[45]*

The practice continued despite the new policy. In the 1900 census, the Quileute Pullen family, for example, included three generations, all but the youngest with Indian names as well. Harry Pullen, age sixty-one, was also How-with-pace. His wife, Anna Pullen, fifty-nine, was also Bear hitz-h. Their son Joseph (Joe), who would have been eight years old when Wesley Smith began teaching at the Quileute School, was also known as Tse-uc-tse-la-thln, and his wife, Cecil, was Da-i-a-pus as well. Their three-year-old daughter, Dewey, on the other hand, had no Indian name. By 1916, in this family, only Harry and Anna Pullen were still using their Indian names.[46] Three decades later, all living Quileutes had English-language names, although many had Indian names as well, a way of supporting the old traditions.[47]

Less than one year after the Quileute School opened, the Neah Bay agent reported, "None of the children had ever been inside a school-room before, and now all know the alphabet. Others spell in words of one and two syllables, and some of the brighter ones read very well in words of two syllables, and have learned to sing several pieces quite creditably. The short history of this school completely refutes the statement made by honorable gentlemen in the last session of Congress, that it is a useless expenditure of money to attempt educating Indian children in a day school."[48]

At least one Quileute concurred that Wesley's teaching and guidance had been a positive influence. W. H. Hudson edited and published a short-lived newspaper in La Push between 1908 and 1910. In describing the education that Joe Pullen, his fellow Quileute—who Hudson considered to be among the most "progressive type of Indians in the Pacific Northwest"—he wrote of "the good influence Mr. Smith had over the Indians."[49] The curriculum included reading, writing, spelling, arithmetic, geography, Bible studies, and, for the boys, gardening and "ordinary chores," and for the girls, "household duties," sewing, and cooking.[50]

Several dozen student drawings from 1904–05, collected and saved by Wesley near the end of his tenure as teacher, show subject matter that includes birds, flowers, world maps, masted schooners, and elegantly attired white women. Many of them are finely rendered in colored pencil, but only one includes an image—a seal—that might be considered reflective of the Quileute traditional culture. If this is an indication of the students' drawing assignments, their own choices of what to draw, or the decision of what to keep on Wesley's part is impossible to know. Regardless of whether or not one supports all of the changes that Wesley Smith encouraged or required, his influence was considerable and lasting.

WHITE MAN'S LAW

Although the Quileute people during the first decades of Euro-American settlement might seem on the surface to have been passively accepting of the newcomers' presence, there was another compelling reason why widespread conflict remained minimal. Between 1864 and 1866, the Quileutes had their first encounter with the long arm of the white man's law. In August 1864, the superintendent of Indian Affairs for Washington Territory reported to the commissioner of Indian Affairs in Washington, DC:

Nearly a year ago three Indians of this [Quileute] band murdered a white man near the Straits of San Juan de Fuca. In the discharge of my duty, I directed the person in charge . . . to demand the murderers. . . . The tribe refused to accede to the demand, and made threats of an attack upon the Agency and the destruction of government property. . . . These Indians are untamed, know but little of the whites, and suppose they can easily set at defiance the authority of the government. . . . The band to which the murderers belong is not numerous, does not perhaps exceed seventy-five or one hundred warriors, but their advantage consists in the fact of their village being surrounded, for many miles, with an almost impenetrable forest of gigantic growth. . . . Nothing can be done, either by sea or by land, until another year.[51]

The US government finally took action in the matter two years later by sending soldiers, who apprehended not only the accused murderers but also ten others, on various charges. According to the Indian agent, the Quileute prisoners admitted their guilt and even boasted about it. Although jailed, they never stood trial, because the following spring they escaped from prison at Fort Steilacoom, near what is now Tacoma, and made their way back to La Push.[52] The Quileute people, however, had learned a lesson: The law of the US government could, and would, be brought down upon them.

Minor conflicts simmered between the Pullens and their neighbors during the 1880s. Not long after Hattie and Dan married, Dan clashed with a powerful Quileute shaman named Doctor Obi, feared by Quileutes and settlers alike. On July 27, 1882, all thirty-two settlers in the area signed a petition, forwarded to the commissioner of Indian Affairs, requesting that he remove Doctor Obi from the area because he was a constant menace. Charles Willoughby, formerly the Indian agent at Neah Bay, assembled a hearing at which Clakishka, a Quileute sub-chief, testified that Obi was guilty of tearing down a fence that ran between his garden and the Pullens' pigpen. When Dan Pullen went to Obi's house to discuss the matter, the doctor attacked him with a club. Clakishka intervened to save Dan's life.

Doctor Obi's daughter, however, told another side of the story. She claimed that Dan had come to her family to insist that they remove their house from "his property." She also maintained that Pullen had forced their neighbors to move their dwelling down to the beach so it would not be so close to where the Pullens intended to build their house. Obi refused Dan's request, Dan grabbed him, and they began to fight. Obi hit Dan over the head with a club. Obi's son, Yakalada, the Quileute village police officer, arrested his father and took him to Neah Bay for a hearing. For nearly a year, he was in jail.[53]

The government investigation that followed revealed that Doctor Obi was among those arrested after the 1863 murder of the white man, a crime to which Obi admitted. The details of the murder, based on Quileute witnesses, were put into the record. However, too much time had passed and the identity of the victim was unknown, so Obi did not stand trial. Still, in 1879, suspected of a long series of cattle shootings, he continued to be a threat to the settlers. Perhaps as confirmation of his power, in about 1897, he was the last Quileute to have the old-fashioned burial that began with the removal of the body through the back of the house.[54]

Another time, Hattie's brother Wesley angered some Quileutes by punishing one of his students. The Quileutes surrounded Wesley and his female assistant teacher and threatened them while they were on their way home from school. Wesley proposed to his assailants that he be permitted to take his assistant home and then he would talk to them. At home, he was able to arm himself and hold his attackers at bay for a time, but the confrontation erupted again. According to Royal, Doc Last, another shaman, was about to strike Wesley with a "fatal" blow when Hattie stepped out on the trading post balcony. Leaning a shotgun and rifle against the railing and holding another rifle in her hands, she shouted to the Quileutes in their own language that she would shoot anyone who laid a hand on her brother. "They knew she was a crack shot and had the drop on them," Royal recalled.[55] The angry mob backed off and let her brother go, but Hattie stood guard until Dan returned. As Royal put it during an interview, "She stood the tribe alone." Such was Hattie's reputation.[56]

Dan gathered the settlers. They sent word to authorities in Port Townsend, who sent an armed revenue cutter. Its officers apprehended five of the ringleaders. According to Hattie's sister, "The Indians had planned to kill my brother for whipping a boy."[57] Later, the authorities, probably from the Indian Agency, held a hearing to interview Wesley and a number of his assailants, all of whom denied any intention to harm Wesley. One participant, identified only as "Robertson," interrogated Ka-kis-ka, the Quileute chief, who stated that none of the Indians was holding a stick during the encounter. Asked if he was afraid of soldiers, he responded he was not. The interrogator continued, "Do you know the consequences of harming A[lanson] W[esley] S[mith]?"

Ka-kis-ka responded, "The I[ndians] are afraid to do anything wrong to whites."

Another Quileute answered, "If he kills whiteman the soldiers would punish or kill him. I know the soldiers would take him away and he would not come back. The soldiers will hang him if he kills whites."[58]

Ka-kis-ka's reply and the actions of the sub-chief and the Quileute police officer in the Doctor Obi incident are evidence that those in tribal leadership positions sought to maintain peaceful relations with the US government authorities. Not only was this a response to their fear of law enforcement and the military, but it was also undoubtedly a way to help ensure their own power within their group.

Arguably, some of the friction may have arisen as the result of displays of arrogance on the part of the Pullens. In one example, the Pullen family maintained a gardening spot on James Island, *A-Ka-Lat* (Top of the Rock) to the Quileutes. This small but towering sea stack, today an island but at the time attached to the mainland and accessible by foot at low tide, was a part of Dan's Preemption claim. It juts out of the water just off the shore in front of where the Pullens' house once stood. Tall evergreens cover much of the top. Dan built a road up the east side of it so that he could take his plow team up to work the garden.

James Island had served for centuries as fortification, at times when the Quileute people were in conflict with other Indian groups. Its topography allowed the Quileutes to not only see across the water for miles but also to defend themselves by rolling rocks and flinging boiling water from above. Their attachment to James Island, however, went beyond its role as a natural fortress. At 160 feet, it was ideally suited to whale sighting. It also held spiritual power for them, and had long been a burial place for high-status individuals.[59] Royal, who lived at La Push from the time he was born in 1887 until the age of ten, remembered seeing canoes containing bodies there.[60]

Seemingly unmindful that the Quileutes regarded James Island as sacred ground, the Pullen family would go there not only to garden but also to picnic. In a taped interview, Royal's daughter asked, "Did the Indians consider James Island kind of sacred?"

Royal replied, "No, we never thought it was, because Father more or less claimed it, you see. Because he owned all the property on that high ground, and the Indians lived down . . . between the beach and the edge of the hill."[61]

It is also worth noting that Royal in later years was adamant that *nomadic* Quileutes frequented the area when his father began trading with them, and that Dan had encouraged them to settle near the coast so they would have access to supplies where he landed them, the locale later known as La Push.[62] Royal Pullen's information in this instance was biased and inaccurate.

"CAMPING AT LAPUSH"

An early 1890s newspaper article by an unnamed reporter, datelined "La Push, July 29" and titled "Camping at Lapush," begins by describing an outing made by the family and friends of Frank Balch, an early settler who arrived in Quillayute country with Dan Pullen in the early 1870s. By the 1890s, he was a "leading merchant" in the area. The event included the group's three-day stay at the "popular seaside resort" at La Push (the Pullens' house) and a two-mile drive on the beach in their "light horse rig."

The article also notes that Hattie's mother had "made a pleasant call last week at the Lapush hotel," and that Hattie's youngest sister and brother and three friends had enjoyed the "beautiful table spread on Mrs. Pullen's lawn." Then abruptly, in the same paragraph, the reporter states, "The Indians were scooping smelt from the surf as it rolled in on the smooth, sandy beach." The next paragraph continues, "Indian William captured a whale. Oil is plentiful. Nelly Gray's baby died July 27th. The camp made the usual wailing. It was dressed, put in a large trunk and buried the same day. The house was torn down by friends, carried a short distance and burned." With that, the article ends.[63]

Smelt gathering was an important custom among the Quileutes. The Makahs' teacher, James Swan, visited La Push in 1879, watched them gather smelt with special curved-handled nets, and wrote about the process. The fish came in on the tide in vast numbers and were deposited and left flapping on the sand. The "Indians rush into the surf and press the outer edge of the net down firmly on the sand, ... the swash of the breaker forcing the smelts into the net. Then, as the water recedes, they turn round quickly and hold the net so that the undertow will force more smelts into it. In this way I saw them take at least a bushel at a single scoop," he wrote. Women and children waited on the beach to take the catch to their houses, where the fish were strung on strips of cedar bark and hung up to dry and, later, boiled for meals.[64]

What is remarkable and peculiar about the short newspaper article, which cites this important food-gathering event, is the odd juxtaposition of the leisure-time, society doings of the settlers and the workaday toil and tragedies of the Quileute people who lived within a stone's throw of the Pullens' seaside mansion. Perhaps watching the drama of the traditional "scooping smelt from the surf" served as enjoyable entertainment for the assembled guests at the Pullens' "popular seaside resort." The writer presents the reports on plentiful whale oil and a Quileute baby's burial as newsworthy afterthoughts. The contrast between two cultures could hardly have been starker. The article serves as a kind of allegory for the two sides of life at La Push in the 1880s and '90s.

Chapter Nine

La Push 1889–1897

It was a quiet September day in 1889. The Quileutes had left en masse on a hops-picking excursion. The annual fall event was more than just a way to earn money; it was also a junket, a vacation of sorts. Everyone looked forward to it, and all but the very oldest and infirm participated. Invited to help with the harvest by farmers along Puget Sound, they traveled well over one hundred miles on foot, camping along the way. According to the Indian agents, the expedition presented an opportunity for some members of the group to obtain alcohol, something unavailable to them at La Push. Alcohol or not, it was an adventure for all.[1]

Their La Push village, just below the Pullens' house, comprised, according to Royal, a double row of "big shacks and potlatch houses . . . built from driftwood and drift lumber" from ships that had broken up along the coast, as well as some frame houses in the style of the settlers' buildings.[2] All the houses were empty. They would be gone for weeks.[3]

On that day, probably September 9, the entire village went up in flames. The blaze consumed every bit of it, including twenty-six houses and all of the Quileute' smokehouses, whale and sealing outfits, canoes, oil, tools, baskets, and sacred ceremonial regalia. There were no witnesses to the fire—at least, no credible ones from the point of view of the US government authorities. There was, however, one likely suspect.

Dan Pullen knew the time for hops picking would come as it did every year. An empty village might have been the opportunity he had been waiting for. One Quileute, who would have been about twenty at the time of the fire, stated to anthropologist Pettitt in the 1940s that an old man unable to join the expedition had witnessed Dan Pullen and three other white men set the fire. Another Quileute, Harry Hobucket, writing in 1934, stated not only that Dan had set the fire with two accomplices—his neighbors, K. O. Erickson and Frank Balch—but also suggested, based on information passed down through Quileute families, that at least one elderly Quileute had died in the fire.[4] Neither the Indian agents' correspondence nor the Office of Indian Affairs reports, however, mentioned any deaths caused by the fire.

After the fire, three months passed before the Neah Bay Indian agent, who oversaw the Quileute people, visited La Push to investigate. During that interval, his main source of information about the incident was Hattie's brother Wesley, the de facto Neah Bay Agency representative at La Push. After his visit, the agent made clear he suspected that Dan had set the fire.[5] Hattie's brother Harvey B. Smith, on the other hand—a young man at the time of the fire, who lived on Smith family land surrounded by the reservation all of his life—told Pettitt that he did not believe Dan Pullen would have been involved in starting the fire, as the goodwill of the Quileutes was too important to his trading business.[6] The government authorities never accused anyone of the crime.

Regardless of the circumstances and who was at fault, the village burned, and apparently, it was a case of arson. Assuming it is true that Dan set the fire, what could have brought him to commit this evil deed? Why would the Indian agents consistently have suspected that he was the perpetrator? Why was he not prosecuted?

Dan's Pattern

The actions of an arsonist that day in 1889 seemed to fit Dan's pattern of aggressive behavior. As early as 1880, Dan had developed a reputation for intimidating his Quileute neighbors. In 1880, A. J. wrote in a local newspaper, "[T]he Indians fear [Dan Pullen] and will do his bidding."[7] An Indian agent writing in early 1889 commented, "Pullen would have the advantage" in any dispute over the land, "he having the Indians all afraid of him."[8] Hattie's sister Jennie years later in an interview stated, "Mrs. Dan Cullen [sic], my older sister, lived near us. Her husband had the Indians pretty well under control."[9] "Under control" seems to have been a euphemism for bullying or acts of violence.

Royal published several vivid stories of his father's prowess as an Indian fighter. How much of the stories are family lore and how much of them are historical fact are arguable. One of Royal's stories is as follows:

The Indians at LaPush had great respect for Dan Pullen's fighting ability, which was not shared by the Indians at Neah Bay and elsewhere. One Indian from Neah Bay thought he was the best fighter in the tribe. He came into the store to pick a fight over some purchases. He called Father a liar and leaned over the counter. Father grabbed him by his long hair and hit him on the side of the head with his fist, in which he had a round scale weight that he had put his hand over when the Indian began to haggle with him over prices. The Indian went out cold, and Father dragged him out of the store for the other Indians to see. The LaPush Indians ran the Neah Bay Indian out of the place for bragging and daring to think he could lick their Dan Pullen.[10]

Other accounts came from less-biased observers—officials at the Neah Bay Agency. An 1884 letter from the agency physician to Wesley, for instance, reports that he had received complaints from some members of the tribe that Dan had mistreated a tribal police officer, Parker, resulting in Parker's imprisonment. Parker "received damage with a stick somewhere about the head" from someone in La Push, the doctor wrote.[11] It was the word of a Quileute against the word of a settler. At this point, the agency staff seems to have been giving Dan the benefit of the doubt, the doctor indicating he felt he had to trust Dan's word. Soon, however, the agency's attitude toward Dan's behavior would change.

Later in 1884, Indian agent Oliver Wood wrote to Wesley, "The Quillehute Indians are complaining bitterly against the action of Mr. Pullen, which I very much regret. They inform me that he demands a rental of them for the privilege of remaining at . . . [La Push] and that he has ordered some of them to pull down their houses." Wood went on to say that he had "the most friendly feeling for Dan," but that his position as agent compelled him to take legal action against anyone known to damage the property or person of a Quileute.[12] He also asked that Wesley show his letter to Dan, which he did.

Dan responded to the agent, who then wrote again to Wesley explaining that the commissioner of the General Land Office of the Department of the Interior had issued an order in the spring of 1884 prohibiting settlers from filing claims on lands occupied by Indians. Wood's interpretation of the order was that until Dan had a patent for the land, the ownership of his property was unclear. Dan had filed his Preemption claim in July 1882, claiming to have settled there in March 1880, and submitted his Final Proof and paid for his entry in July 1883, all before the commissioner had issued his directive. Dan believed the land was his and, therefore, that he had a right to charge the Quileutes rent; however, he did not yet have his patent to the claim.[13] This fact would become central in a later conflict between Dan and the federal government.

The Preemption land-claim process at this time normally took about two years between the filing of a claim and the approval of the patent, and another year or so until the General Land Office and the President of the United States actually issued the patent. For example, A. J.'s brother, Harvey H. Smith, had traveled from Dakota Territory to Quillayute country to make a Preemption claim of 163 acres on the Quillayute River, near La Push, for investment purposes. In early 1886, he made his claim entry, built a house, and lived in it for the required fourteen months before returning to Dakota. In February 1889, he received his patent.[14]

Dan's claim was still in limbo in 1884, yet he behaved as if the land were his, as evidenced by a deed for five acres of the claim that he and Hattie wrote to the partner of trading post owner Sutcliffe Baxter for land on which the trading post stood.[15] The Pullens were selling land in 1884 that was not yet legally theirs. In response to a complaint by Indian agent Wood, the General Land Office ordered an investigation to determine what was going on at La Push.[16]

In 1885, agent Wood wrote to Wesley, "California [a Quileute] was here a few days since and complains that Dan wants to tear down his house and that he refused to allow it done whereupon Dan beat and kicked him severely. Is there any truth in the statement?"[17] His question indicates an element of disbelief and his continuing wish to give Dan the benefit of the doubt. But what California had reported must have been confirmed, because the next month, in his official annual report to the commissioner of Indian Affairs, Wood wrote:

> *Daniel Pullen made entry on the lands on which their village is located, and ever since that time he has tried to exercise full control of all the premises and endeavored to have the Indians pull down their houses for his accommodation. . . . The Indians make frequent complaints of the acts of Pullen, but as they are off the reserve I am powerless to give them such protection as they should have. They have occupied this land from before the knowledge of the oldest Indian on the coast or any of their traditions. They have built some very comfortable frame houses and have several very large buildings built in Indian style from lumber manufactured by themselves, and they feel it would be a great hardship to be driven off and lose all their buildings and improvements, and all fair-minded people will agree with me.*[18]

California stated, according to an official from the Department of the Interior:

> *"My house was removed . . . by Pullen; it was situated on the land where his house now stands. He came into my house and told me to tear it down; I said 'No, . . . I have just finished a new house.'. . . He came to my house again and sitting down by my side said 'I want you to tear your house down, I am going to build a house on this place where your house now stands. I want you to tear the house right off.' I said 'No, sir; I do not want to put my house off,' and when I said 'No,' he struck me in the face and said 'I want you to tear your house right off.' I was holding two babies when Pullen struck me and I did not want to strike him back because one of my feet was cut with an axe and I had to walk around on crutches. I tore my house down; I was afraid of Pullen. He gave me a keg of nails."*[19]

When W. L. Powell took over the Neah Bay Agency after Oliver Wood left in 1885, he wrote to his superiors, "You will find several letters, written by the former agent here, on file in your office, about this man Pullen. He gives any amount of trouble and we can never have peace among the Indians there until he is removed. . . . It is a wonder to me that they have not killed this man, and if all I hear about him is true, I think they would be justified in doing so. . . . I have a delegation of some 20 Quillchute Indians here, who have many complaints to make of their treatment."[20]

The complaints continued. In April of 1886, just as Dan and Hattie were poised to begin building their grand house, agent Powell wrote to Wesley, "The delegation of Indians complain of Pullen making them leave the hill and come down on the beach where high tide reaches them. Is this so?"[21] Quileute Jimmy reported that Dan not only had forced village residents to remove their houses but also had bribed them to do so. Some years later, Jimmy described his conversation with Dan, as reported by a government official:

"[Dan said,] 'Jimmy, you go tell Taylor to get off; to take his house off,' and said again to me 'you go tell Albert to get off.' Albert's house belong to Howeattle and when he died he gave it to Albert so he told them to pull the house down, and Albert and Taylor said, 'No, . . . I do not want to pull my house down; this is my grandfather's house.' Pullen gave me $6, and told me to give it to Taylor, which I did, and told him: 'I am afraid Dan Pullen going to kill you.' He gave me $7, to give Albert and I said to Albert 'You have to get off; I am afraid Dan Pullen will kill you; that is what he trying to do all the time.' He took the money to get off."[22]

Addie Sox, another Quileute, corroborated Jimmy's report. She also stated, "Dan came to my house and asked me if I would let him have my garden as he wanted to raise something and gave me a blanket worth $5, to pay for the fence and for work I had done and old stumps. He said he did not buy the ground, just the fence and to have lots of wood, and when he quit keeping store he would go up to the prairie and give me back the ground."[23] Addie Sox revealed that Dan was not only pushing his Quileute neighbors out of their houses but also taking over land they had already cleared for cultivation.

Wesley was probably able to corroborate what the Quileutes had told the Neah Bay agents because, as the schoolteacher, he was deeply involved with the Quileute people. The agents consistently praised his performance at the Quileute School in their annual reports.[24] Given his integrity and the expectation that he would report to his superiors at the agency on the activities of his brother-in-law Dan, Wesley found himself in an awkward position, navigating between family loyalty and what he believed was right for the Quileute people. His moral compass would not allow him to defend Dan's actions.

Dan and Hattie went ahead with building their house. Even though they knew the Land Office was planning to conduct an investigation into the legitimacy of Dan's Preemption claim, they had enough hubris to continue with their plans. Three years elapsed before the Land Office actually began its investigation, delayed by deaths and resignations at the agency and the inaccessibility of the land.[25]

It was now the summer of 1887. The house was finished and the Pullens had moved in. J. M. Carson, the special agent charged with the investigation, though unable to find any settlers who would corroborate the Quileutes' accusations that Dan Pullen had torn down some of their houses, concluded that "Pullen has bulldozed the Indians so much that they have become afraid of him. It appears that when the land survey was finally recorded in 1882, the government surveyor neglected to do as the law requires, to record on his field notes that this tract of land was occupied by an Indian village."[26] As a result, Dan had been able to file his La Push Preemption claim without any problems. So here was yet another twist in the case: The US government had failed to adhere to its own policy of prohibiting settlement claims on officially surveyed land where Indians resided.

To complicate matters further, Dan circulated a petition and, with the help of a traitorous Quileute named Jack, garnered the signatures of thirty-five members of the tribe. The petition requested, "[A]s Daniel Pullen had always been a friend to the tribe and bought their skins, they, in consideration thereof, desired that Daniel Pullen be appointed Chief of Police."[27] Dan and Jack, however, had led the Quileute people to believe that what they were signing was an agreement to help build a new road. When agent Carson took an interpreter to La Push, he learned not only that the Quileutes unequivocally did not want Dan to be their police chief but also that A. J. Smith had created the petition and forged his own son Wesley's name as its creator. Wesley pronounced the petition a forgery. Why would A. J. do this? He wanted to present Dan in the best possible light to the Land Office and dispel any notion that the Quileutes might think ill of him. His foolish effort backfired.

The pressure on Dan and Hattie began to mount. They retained a lawyer on September 5, 1887.[28] In October, the Local Land Office, based on Carson's findings, found Dan's land claims to be fraudulent and directed their cancellation. The rationales given were: 1) His Preemption claim at La Push was occupied by a village of Indians; 2) During the settlement of the Preemption claim, he was acting as agent for the Washington Fur Company, and thus using the claim for business and not for settlement; and 3) The land on his nearby Timber claim was suitable for agriculture, something not allowable under Timber claim rules.[29] Dan applied for a hearing. On December 3, 1887, the Local Land Office agreed to hold one at some time in the future.

"For the Permanent Use and Occupation of the Quillehute Indians"

During what turned out to be a second three-year hiatus while they waited for their hearing, the Pullens erected their barn and woodshed in 1887.[30] Their business with the Washington Fur Company and their family life continued. They and their children enjoyed a prosperous life at La Push, with both Dan's and Hattie's families nearby.

But then, in February 1889—the US government finally recognizing the autonomy of the Quileute people—President Grover Cleveland signed an executive order withdrawing from sale and settlement eight hundred acres of land, "set apart for the permanent use and occupation of the Quillehute Indians."[31] The new reservation encompassed both the Preemption and the Timber claims Dan Pullen had made in 1882 and 1883. The president's order, however, contained a qualification: "[T]his withdrawal shall not affect any existing valid rights of any party."[32] That gave the Pullens considerable reason for hope. The question hinged on whether or not Dan had an "existing valid" right to the land, which from Dan and Hattie's point of view, he did.

Despite the federal government's good intentions in creating a reservation for the Quileute tribe, nothing had really changed. As the Neah Bay agent put it in his 1890 annual report, "The proviso [in President Cleveland's executive order] leaves the Indians precisely as it found them, as most of the land withdrawn had been taken up previously by whites under the homestead and preemption laws. Not an acre that is worth anything to them is left. Their village, their homes and what [have] been the homes of their fathers for generations, as the immense shell mounds prove, [have] been homesteaded by a white man [Dan Pullen], who has erected his dwelling-house in the center of this village."[33]

In addition to the Pullens, two other settlers had made Homestead claims within what was now the reservation. One of them was Hattie's photographer brother, David T. Smith. The other was her sister-in-law, Wesley's wife. The only differences between their claims and Dan's were the facts that the Pullens' house sat squarely in the middle of the Quileute village, whereas the others had homesteaded about a quarter of a mile away. These homesteaders also kept themselves under the radar, and in the latter case, did not develop the land. The government never challenged their claims. Eventually the properties became part of the Quileute reservation.[34]

It may have been the presidential executive order that prompted a frustrated and angry Dan Pullen to set fire to the Quileute village, assuming he was the guilty party. The fire took place just six months after the issuance of the executive order during the first time the village was empty. The Neah Bay agent—in his reply to Wesley's letter apprising him of the fire—commented, "As you remark it is an easy matter to say or think how the fire started, but quite a different thing to prove it. Every one who knows what the state of affairs [has] been there, when they hear of the fire immediately suspect certain parties."[35]

It was Dan's behavior immediately following the fire that led John McGlinn, the Neah Bay agent who took over the agency shortly after the fire, to suspect that Dan was the culprit. McGlinn's 1890 annual report to the commissioner of Indian Affairs in Washington, DC, states: "After

9.1. The beach at La Push looking northwest toward James Island from the Pullens' house, with Quileute homes in the foreground, ca. 1890. CLALLAM COUNTY HISTORICAL SOCIETY

the fire, Mr. Pullen, the settler, sowed grass-seed on the site of the burned homes, inclosed it with a barbed-wire fence, and, not satisfied with doing this, fenced them off from every other available location by five strands of barbed wire," thus ensuring that no Quileute would attempt to rebuild right next to his house, but rather on the beach, about three hundred feet away.[36] In a symbolic replay of what the US government had done to Native Americans for decades, in moving them farther and farther west across the continent, Dan saw to it that the Quileute people were pushed right up against the lapping waves of the Pacific Ocean on a narrow strip of beach amid piles of storm-shifting driftwood.

Three months after the fire, in December 1889, agent McGlinn went to La Push. He made every effort to help the Quileute people rebuild. As to the location of the new village, he hammered out an agreement with the Pullens whereby the Quileutes would build on the beach, as Dan wished. It was an unsatisfactory solution given the tides and winter storms, but McGlinn seemed resigned to it as the best he could do given the ongoing dispute. Revealing more of his personal position on the matter, he wrote to Wesley, "If Mr. Pullen will consider a moment he will understand, that the Indians hold the land jointly with him until it is decided in the courts, and as for priority of possession, their claim is a great deal better than his for their fathers held possession before his fore fathers came over the Atlantic Ocean. However, the question will be settled some time and I hope soon." In the letter, he enclosed a sketch of the agreed-upon location for the new Quileute houses.[37]

With McGlinn's help, the

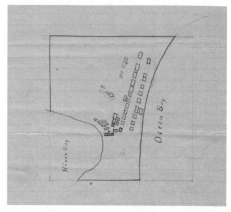

9.2. A drawing by John P. McGlinn, Neah Bay Indian agent, indicating the future location of the Quileute houses, enclosed in a letter of December 23, 1889, to A. Wesley Smith. (The large cross-like shape represents the Pullens' house, situated above the rows of small boxes, which represent the proposed houses.) WASHINGTON STATE LIBRARY MANUSCRIPTS COLLECTION, A. WESLEY SMITH PAPERS, 1853–1935, M.S. 172

Quileutes were able to voice to government authorities their objections to having to move their village to the beach, but McGlinn indicated they should not get their hopes up, because any remedy would take a long time. In the meantime, he wrote to Wesley that the Quileutes should go ahead and build on the beach. He also asked Wesley to try to see to it that they were not "molested while erecting their houses."[38] Yet Dan's aggressive behavior toward the Quileutes continued. After first increasing the rent for use of his building and then serving an eviction notice, he tore down the agency-run Quileute schoolhouse, which had been on his claim for seven years.[39] Wesley's response was to ask the Quileute men to agree to give one to five days each to help build a new one. Thirty of them agreed to help. The new school building went up quickly.[40]

Apparent Victory

The hearing at the Local Land Office, requested and granted in 1887, finally took place in November and December of 1890. Among the witnesses during three weeks of testimony was agent McGlinn, who argued that the government should remove Dan from the land. The Local Land Office concurred and once again determined to cancel Dan's claim entries.[41]

Dan appealed to a higher authority, the commissioner of the General Land Office, who, in spite of McGlinn's efforts on behalf of the Quileute people, found in Dan's favor in September 1891, reversing the 1887 and 1890 decisions of the Local Land Office and ordering that Dan's Preemption and Timber claim entries be approved for patent. The bases for his reversal were: 1) Dan was legitimately using his Preemption claim for settlement and not merely for business; 2) The government had waited too long to initiate any proceedings against his claim; and 3) The timberland was, in fact, unfit for cultivation, as Dan had stated in his entry, and was therefore a legitimate Timber claim.[42]

Spurred by this apparent victory, Dan and Hattie enlarged their house. They needed more space. They continued to house boarders, and a fourth child, Chester, had been born in 1889. By March 1892, they had added two rooms, raised the roof on part of the house, and erected an impressive, two-story, square tower crowned with a railed widow's walk, adding to its grand and impressive visual statement.[43] It was now truly the Pullen "mansion."

There was, however, a caveat in the General Land Office Commissioner's 1891 ruling in Dan's favor. In view of communications he had received from the commissioner of Indian Affairs, he ordered that the case be held open for twenty days to allow the commissioner of Indian Affairs to present the matter to the secretary of the interior in Washington, DC.[44] The final decision now rested with the Department of the Interior. But no decision would be forthcoming anytime soon. The situation remained in limbo and forced the Pullens to wait yet again.

Even though Dan had won this round, there was momentum pushing against him, spurred by the Indian agents who disapproved of his behavior and the evolving prevailing attitudes in the country. Although

9.3. Hattie and her family in 1895, with the tower addition to the house clearly visible (David T. Smith, photographer). COLLECTION WALTER R. AND MARY E. PATTERSON, SEATTLE, WASHINGTON

in the *Seattle Press-Times* pronounced the General Land Office's ruling "A Righteous Decision," Carson, the land agent who had investigated the situation back in 1887, took issue with the newspaper's position. He proclaimed in a letter to the editor that had the commissioner known all the facts, he would not have reversed the decision in Dan's favor.

Carson made a number of points. An important one was the significance of James Island (a part of Dan's Preemption claim) to the Quileute people. The agent noted that it was "a veritable fort," which explained why the Quileutes "are and always have been . . . attached to this village and locality."[45] Carson also cited the many people who had recorded that an Indian village had long stood at La Push at the site of the Pullens' house. Carson himself had observed thirty-two Quileute houses there during his 1887 investigation. Neither the press nor testimony offered during the hearings, however, noted the detailed description of the village, published in 1880, before Dan had even made his Preemption claim, by Dan's own father-in-law, A. J. Smith. His newspaper article states, "At the mouth of the Quileut river is an Indian village, it contains 14 siwash houses, and 15 siwash Boston houses."[46]

Carson even asserted that the failure of the US surveyor to note the presence of an Indian village at La Push, as he was required by law to do, may have been the result of some "unknown influence."[47] He also observed that Dan had made a Homestead claim of 160 acres at Quillayute and, at the same time, was minding his La Push trading post. Carson suggested that Dan was actually living at La Push, some six or seven miles away, during the time he was supposed to be meeting his residency requirement at Quillayute. Even if true, the Land Office often overlooked this type of rule-bending during Homestead and Preemption claim proceedings. In Dan's case, however, the Land Office and the Office of Indian Affairs would ultimately use his unconscionable behavior toward the Quileutes and his avaricious land acquisitions against him.

"THE FIRST OF ITS KIND ON THE WESTERN COAST"

In the nineteenth century, America's Manifest Destiny narrative, a belief held by many, viewed Native Americans as standing in the way of progress. US policy during the presidency of Andrew Jackson, from 1829 to 1837, was one of removal, pushing Indian peoples to lands west of the Mississippi. In 1830, Congress passed the "Indian Removal Act," culminating in the heinous 1838–39 "Trail of Tears," in which the US government forced the Cherokee Nation to migrate west. The Cherokees suffered from exposure and disease along the way, and many died before they reached their destinations.

In the mid-nineteenth century, US policy shifted away from removal toward confinement on reservations. In the 1880s and '90s, reformers who called themselves "Friends of the Indian" began to address the "Indian problem." Reformers maintained that Indian assimilation into Euro-American culture through education could improve the situation on the reservations. Thought to be the cornerstone of democracy, this brand of education did more than simply teach reading, writing, and arithmetic. It also transmitted Euro-American beliefs and worldviews, including patriotism, Christianity, capitalism, and the cultivation of foodstuffs. Many reformers viewed Native Americans as children in need of guidance. The prevailing public stance was patronizing, pervasive, and perhaps stemmed from collective guilt over what had transpired through US government policy in the past.

The case against Dan Pullen commanded a great deal of attention in the press statewide and among the locals in Quillayute country. The *Seattle Press-Times* in 1891 noted that the case was "the first of its kind on the western coast where the validity of an entry had been questioned when made on land occupied by Indians. The Indian agents have been urgently pressing the matter for a decision, and even Indian societies in the East, whose distance leads the people in Washington [DC] to believe that the 'poor Indian' is abused in the wild and woolly West, have had a great deal to say in the matter."[48] This attitude, growing across the country, ultimately influenced the outcome of the case.

At about the same time that Dan Pullen requested his hearing, the General Land Office of the Department of the Interior revealed its evolving stance on the matter of settlers' claiming land where Indian peoples lived. In 1887, the office reissued its 1884 directive to the Local Land Offices and the US Surveyor General with added emphasis: "The allowance of such entries is a violation of the instructions of this Department, an act of inhumanity to defenseless people, and provocative of violence and disturbance. . . . Surveyors General will instruct their deputies to carefully and fully note all Indian occupations in their returns of survey hereafter or reported, and the same must be expressed upon the plats of survey."[49] Perhaps the failure of the La Push surveyor to note the presence of the Quileute people in 1882 had prompted the General Land Office to issue its directive.

To summarize the government's 1891 actions in the Pullens' land contest: After hearing from the Office of Indian Affairs, the commissioner of the General Land Office decided that Dan's presence violated the rights of the Quileute people; however, because the commissioner believed the land claims themselves were legitimate, as a land officer, he lacked the authority to cancel the entries. Thus, the commissioner shifted the responsibility back to the Office of Indian Affairs, which, on November 5, 1891, took it to a higher office, the Department of the Interior, to whom both agencies reported. Dan and Hattie would have to wait another two years for its decision in the case. Waiting was something they were becoming familiar with, but during this next uncomfortable interval, they began to wrestle with the growing financial burden stemming from their legal battles. At the same time, they encountered a new and consuming distraction.

CHAPTER TEN

A Man with a Badge

ON TUESDAY, AUGUST 9, 1892, A MAN WITH A BADGE SHOWED UP AT Hattie's door—a summons, a complaint, and a writ of attachment in hand. The sight of the sheriff must have filled her with apprehension. The summons "commanded" Daniel and Hattie, both named as defendants, to appear in the Superior Court of the State of Washington for Clallam County within twenty days to answer the complaint of Sutcliffe Baxter and the Washington Fur Company.

The complaint alleged that the Pullens, over a six-year period, had "converted" to their own use $18,704.51 (equivalent to about half a million in 2014 dollars[1]) worth of property belonging to the company. Even though they were the wealthiest family in the area, eighteen thousand dollars was probably more than their net worth. Given that much of their wealth was in land, they did not have ready access to cash. If, as the complaint alleged, they owed the company that amount of money, they did not have it.[2]

The law in Washington State at the time stated that converting borrowed property to one's own use without the intent to return it was a crime. The remedy was restitution—being compelled by the court to give back what was converted or a fair dollar-value equivalent of it, if the converted property had been consumed or was not returnable. According to the law, committing conversion on this scale was grand larceny. If found guilty, upon conviction, the Pullens would be "imprisoned in the penitentiary not more than fourteen years nor less than six months."[3]

The writ of attachment was another matter—with shocking and immediate consequences. It gave the sheriff the authority to confiscate personal property and attach real property of a value equal to the dollar amount of the alleged conversion. Right then and there, the sheriff led away all of the Pullens' cows and seven of their horses, permitting them to keep just one gelding. Among the horses he took were Hattie's beloved Sunday and Gold Digger. He also confiscated an ox yoke, a wagon, a plow, and myriad other items essential to their ranching and farming operations. By taking control of the assets in dispute, the government could make sure they still existed at the end of the lawsuit so that the prevailing party could have them. Without enough of the Pullens' personal property to cover the alleged debt, the sheriff attached their real property as well. Not only that, he also attached the property of Dan's late brother Mart. The probate court had not yet settled his estate, and it owed the Pullens some money.[4]

The case was so complicated that it did not come to trial for nearly a year. The maximum time allowed by law that the court could hold personal property was two hundred days. When that time had elapsed, in March 1893, a judge authorized the return of the animals and other personal property to the Pullens. He then, however, issued attachment orders for a 393-acre farm belonging to Olly Smith, Hattie's brother, and confiscated his fourteen horses, twenty cows, three oxen, and farm equipment, under the mistaken belief that the farm belonged to the Pullens. Strapped for cash, the Pullens had sold the land and farm equipment to Olly the previous year. Through legal means, Olly got his property back quickly, but the Pullens' land remained attached.[5] That meant they had to request permission from the court to plant their garden when planting time came, a request the judge granted them.[6]

Five months before the sheriff showed up, Dan's boss, Sutcliffe Baxter, who had not set foot in La Push for eight years, sent a former business partner named E. M. Williams to La Push to investigate his suspicions that the Pullens were taking items from the store for their own use without paying for them. Williams spent three months in La Push, boarding at the Pullens' house and at the same time snooping around to gather information that would allow Baxter to build a case. In May, Baxter joined Williams in La Push and together the two surreptitiously continued the information-gathering. On one occasion when the Pullens were away, they entered their house without permission to search it for items Baxter would later claim they had stolen. On another occasion, Baxter secreted himself in a room on the store's second story where he had bored a hole in the floor so that he could spy on Dan at work below. From this activity, he determined that Dan had taken $2.40 out of the till to pay a man for shearing his sheep.[7]

Amid accusations and denials of theft, on June 1, 1892, Baxter fired Dan from his position as store and trading post manager. Dan had worked for Baxter since 1880 at a salary of $125 per month since 1886, the year Baxter incorporated as the Washington Fur Company.[8] As part of Dan's contract, Baxter agreed that Dan could take from the store items for his family's use at cost plus freight. The store sold everything from food staples to clothing to hardware to furniture, merchandise that Pullen ordered and Baxter sent to La Push by schooner. Dan believed he had served his employer well, claiming to have done the work of four men. He was, he said, "drove plum to death," working seven days a week, some days until midnight.[9]

Baxter may have been exacting revenge on Dan for his refusal to live up to an alleged 1884 agreement whereby Dan would sell his La Push land to Baxter.[10] It is not clear, however, that such an agreement ever existed. Dan claimed he'd never had any intention of selling his claim to Baxter.[11] If Baxter couldn't have a large stake in this land, then Dan wouldn't have it either. He secretly reported Dan's plan to build a house in the middle of the Quileute village to the Neah Bay Indian agent, who apprised the Local Land Office, which began its investigation in 1884.[12]

The financial stakes surrounding the matter increased during the 1880s. There was talk in the press that La Push held enormous potential as a transportation hub and harbor site, development that would become easier after the removal of the Quileute people, something many locals believed would happen. Baxter saw owning land in La Push as a future bonanza. One newspaper article from early 1893 said that the fifteen hundred acres that Dan owned in the Quillayute River valley were "bound" to "enrich his children . . . whenever that neck of the woods is annexed to civilization by means of a railroad."[13] Another article proclaimed that Quillayute country would soon be "one of the richest" areas of the state.[14] By firing Dan and gathering evidence of theft for a lawsuit, Baxter perhaps believed he could drive the Pullens into bankruptcy, and thus acquire their 153 acres at La Push, which by 1892 people believed was enormously valuable.

The Lawsuit

The lawsuit, *Washington Fur Company, a corporation, Plaintiff, vs. Daniel Pullen and Hattie S. Pullen, Defendants* in the Superior Court of Clallam County, was under way. The suit named Hattie as codefendant because she had worked alongside Dan, running all aspects of the business. The Pullens retained lawyers in addition to those they had hired for their land case. During the next ten months both sides collected evidence, found people who would sign affidavits, and hired accountants to analyze the account books that each party had kept. This necessary defense came at an immense cost of time and money to the Pullens.

Baxter and his lawyers gathered affidavits from people who agreed to sign a form, which read: "_____, of the County of Clallam, Washington, being duly sworn, on oath says: That he is now and for ___ years has been a resident of the community where defendants, Daniel and Hattie S. Pullen reside; that he is familiar with and knows the general reputation of them in the community where they reside for truth and veracity, that said reputation is bad."[15] A few people added personal observations in their own handwriting; most of the twenty-three people Baxter found simply signed the statement.

Why would so many of the Pullens' neighbors sign a statement attesting to their "bad" reputation? Envy seems to have been one motivator. Dan Pullen had amassed nearly ten times the acreage of any of the other settlers in the region. The Pullens' house was ostentatious. They housed and fed a steady stream of guests. They appeared to employ a retinue of servants. And, of course, rumor mills, in the absence of certain knowledge of the situation, can spread inaccuracies. In this case, there was ample time for the information to inflate.

Family correspondence includes hints of what people in La Push thought of the Pullens. Hattie's sister-in-law, Wesley's wife Gertie, commented on their extravagance. She asked Wesley about whether Hattie's new furniture for the Pullens' recently completed house had arrived, and then wrote, "If they keep spending they won't have anything left to pay their crew of lawyers."[16] Two months later, she wrote about Dan's plan to buy a boat: "What more is he going into. At the rate they are going, they . . . won't have enough to finish their suit, will they, if they indulge in all the good things."[17] Remarking on Hattie's presumptuousness, she wrote, "So Hatty is going or has gone up sound again, has she? Did she take the baby this time or did she leave him with grandma? I hope she hasn't the cheek to ask her to look after her young ones another month."[18] As early in the marriage as 1883, one of the Indian agents facetiously asked in a letter to Wesley, "How is the <u>Widow Dan</u> getting along. Does he behave himself," suggesting that Hattie was off on her own at times.[19]

Hattie's mother, Mary Jane, the grandma who had cared for Hattie's children, thought the Pullens indulged them, commenting that she was "sorry about Hattie's children every one spoiled."[20] She also expressed the wish that Hattie had married a Christian man. If so, the "poor girl would have been different. I think we are all influenced more or less with our surroundings, don't you."[21]

Hattie also seems to have been something of a troublemaker. Her own brother Wesley wrote in 1896 to the Indian agent at Neah Bay, his boss, that he suspected her of taking actions behind his back that undermined his authority and put his position as the Quileute agency teacher at risk. The agent in another exchange of correspondence with Wesley suggested that Hattie was guilty of talking up an abortive plan to dig a canal through the middle of the village at La Push, a plan that understandably unnerved the Quileutes. The agent asked Wesley to tell her to keep quiet about the idea until after the government settled the land issue.[22]

Other behavior on the part of the Pullens may have further alienated their neighbors. Witnesses claimed the Pullens had a governess for their children, which they did, for a time. Hattie seems to have taken particular pride in this, something no one else in Quillayute country could afford to do. "My Governess" in Hattie's handwriting annotates a photographic portrait of a young woman posed outdoors near the Pullens' house. In later years, Hattie repeatedly told people she had employed a governess

10.1. The Pullens' governess at La Push, Washington, in about 1890, with "My Governess" and "Miss Morris, Lapush, Wash," in Hattie's handwriting on the back of the photograph (David T. Smith, photographer). CLALLAM COUNTY HISTORICAL SOCIETY

when her children were young.[23] Hattie seems to have been arrogant and may have behaved in imperious ways that offended her rural, hardworking neighbors.

Among Baxter's "bad-reputation" affidavits, two in particular stand out. A dressmaker for the Pullens who had lived at their house for several months signed a lengthy affidavit and provided testimony that she had observed Hattie taking items such as bolts of fabric, buttons, and thread from the store's stock.[24] A neighboring settler, John Carnes, who seems to have been something of a ringleader in the case, stated that there was "no productive land whatever in their possession . . . that [Dan] kept 6, or 8, horses . . . and has never raised enough produce to keep said horses . . . that defendants built a large house at La Push . . . that all of the material for said house was taken from plaintiff's store at La Push. That defendants have never had any other income except the salary from plaintiff."[25] He went on to list the Pullens' servants and stated that the Pullens kept five saddle horses for pleasure only.

Baxter also had nine Quileute Indians sign affidavits. They, of course, would have had ample reason to consider Dan Pullen an enemy, given their repeated conflicts with him and the 1889 fire that destroyed their village. Yet not one of them referred to those incidents. Likewise, there was no suggestion of the conflicts with the Quileutes or the fire in the settlers' affidavits or testimonies.

To bolster his case, Baxter sought ways to demonstrate that the Pullens were extravagant. Like John Carnes, he also claimed that the Pullens' only income was from the salary he paid Dan, thus suggesting they could only have built their elegant house and maintained their lifestyle by stealing. Among the items Baxter accused the Pullens of converting were a typewriter, a safe, a sewing machine, a sink, several stoves, three mahogany tables, wallpaper, lumber, brick, lead pipe, windows, doors, a cultivator, a brush breaker, a wagon, two hay forks, barbed wire, five horses, a milk strainer, a coffeepot, rolled oats, apples, crackers, cans of apricots, onion sets, and turnip, carrot, and cucumber seeds. The picture of extravagance that Baxter painted was convincing when the attorneys questioned him on the stand, especially in light of the affidavits and corroborating testimony from other witnesses.[26]

Riding Hats and Red Hair

Among some three hundred evidentiary objects and documents, three riding hats commanded the most attention during the trial. They signified extravagance. Baxter testified, "On the 24th of June 1891 I bought from the Goldstein Company two ladies' derby riding hats and one silk bell topper riding hat of the value of $16, which were shipped to the store at La Push and taken by defendants and never accounted for." The court confiscated the hats and designated them one of the exhibits for the trial.[27]

Bought in Seattle from a fine haberdashery and part of a fashionable woman's riding habit, they were festooned with gilt monograms and were the kind of accessory only a lady with the time for horseback riding for pleasure would wear. Hattie wore the hat in part because it happened to be the perfect container for her long, red braids. She wore her vibrant red hair wrapped around her head like a crown.[28] One comment about my great-grandmother I heard repeatedly from my mother, corroborated by others, was that her hair reached "down to her ankles."[29] An old woman by the time my mother got to know her, Hattie would braid her long tresses and pin them into a thick coil atop her head, making her appear even taller than she was. Some of it was by then faded and white, but when she pulled out the hairpins, the long, heavy strands, most of the time hidden, were still red.[30]

Hattie's red hair was passed on to my grandfather, Daniel Dee, and his two younger brothers—the three nicknamed "Red," "Pink," and "Little Pink"—and then on to my sister and me. My own experience told me red hair was alternately a target of admiration and of ridicule, but for better or worse, it was unusual. Red hair, occurring in only about 2 percent of the human population, was, in my own experience, a marker of specialness. The lineage back to Hattie—a visible, undeniable link, much admired in my family—was stamped with this piece of physicality, a bridge to the past, and I live with it daily. An interesting aside: I have noticed that a high percentage of actors in television commercials have red hair. Online discussion speculates that this is because red is a high-visibility color and red hair is unusual. It is memorable, so an actor with memorable hair advances a memorable product. Red hair makes people pay attention.

In the absence of any color photographs of Hattie, I have had people ask me on more than one occasion, "How do you know her hair was red?" Hattie's son Royal reported that during her 1877 bout with typhoid fever, his mother temporarily lost all of her "beautiful fiery red hair . . . her pride and joy."[31] Writers frequently remarked on her hair color, but only to say her hair was red. I often wonder: Was it the color of chili powder, a chestnut horse, or maybe a new copper penny? In the various descriptions, it is never auburn, ginger, or carrot—just red.

Royal even suggested that Hattie's red hair might have offered her some protection in the family's conflicts with the Quileute people. He told a story in one interview: "The Indians worshipped the sun. Therefore, during an eclipse they would make a great racket—bang on pans, shoot guns, etc. to scare away the evil spirit. Then when the sun reappeared, they claimed that they had indeed scared away the evil spirit. The Indians would never harm anyone with red hair—they thought the sun, which they worshipped, had blessed that person."[32] It seems the hat that contained her remarkable red hair came to signify both the woman and the trial.

UNSCRUPULOUS CAPITALIST

Hattie, seeking every possible advantage and feeling desperate, had written her brother just before the start of the trial, "Dear Wesley, Judge Green [our lawyer] says you must be here because you are the best witness we have. You are known for your truth & you have shuch a good Reputation that your evidence will go farther than all the rest put together. Come soon as you can. <u>Come Come</u>. Hatty."[33] Although Wesley had signed a carefully worded affidavit and would have been a credible witness because of his stellar status in the community, there is no record of his testimony.

One juror, Ely Peterson, a neighbor of the Pullens—and oddly, one of the people who had signed an affidavit attesting to the Pullens' "bad" reputation, and thus a seemingly biased juror[34]—wrote a letter to his wife. "As I do not see any prospects of me coming home for a week or two, I will scribble you a few lines. . . . Mrs. Pullen [has been] on the stand three days and has made lots of false statements swearing to one thing at one time and later on, dispute it. . . . It looks dark for Dan," he wrote.[35] By the

10.2. The Baxter-Pullen trial witnesses, including not only the defendants and the witnesses for the defense but also the witnesses for the prosecution, in June 1893. David T. Smith, Harriet's brother, is the first man on the left in the back row and is probably the photographer. WASHINGTON STATE LIBRARY MANU-SCRIPTS COLLECTION, A. WESLEY SMITH PAPERS, 1853–1935, M.S. 172

midpoint of the trial, when the plaintiff's witnesses had completed their testimonies, the case against the Pullens looked strong indeed.

Baxter seemed to target Hattie, accusing her of appropriating luxury items from the store, such as six birdcages, three music boxes, and the riding hats. He even stated during the trial, "I believe [Dan] was honest until he was married."[36] As she and Dan answered each of Baxter's accusations on the stand and witnesses for the defense testified, however, a different picture of Hattie's lifestyle emerged. Hattie explained that she had bought just one of the six birdcages and had sold the others. The account books showed that the Pullens had actually paid for the music boxes twice. Dan was concerned about being honest, and Hattie was uncertain about whether or not she had paid for them, so he insisted they pay again.[37]

Hattie's testimony revealed that she had ordered the riding hats during a visit to Seattle with the governess. Because the two women wanted their initials affixed to the hats, they had to leave Seattle without them. Hattie arranged to have them added to Baxter's regular merchandise shipment. She paid the haberdasher for the hats and made a present of two of them to the governess. Baxter had not bought them at all, as he had claimed.[38]

The Pullens employed the governess for only six months. After that, the school district paid her as a public school teacher. As school in the area was sometimes only in session three months a year, the governess conducted lessons both at the school and in the Pullens' home, where she boarded. People may have been unaware of the details of the arrangement.[39]

Financial records produced at the trial proved that Dan had duly accounted for the money that the spying Baxter had seen him take out of the till to pay the sheep shearer.[40] Hattie and Dan had paid cash for the materials for their house, and their lumber had not been shipped by the Washington Fur Company, contrary to Baxter's and Carnes's claims. In the end, the details of Hattie and Dan's lengthy testimonies mitigated against their purported extravagance. Dan's abstemious ways also helped to take the edge off the couple's alleged lavish spending. He used no tobacco, liquor, tea, or coffee, and wore only the cheapest and plainest clothing.[41]

Another issue concerned the accusation that the Pullens charged their customers exorbitant prices to line their pockets. Both Dan and Hattie admitted that their prices were high, as much as 50 percent above cost.[42] The Pullens' attorneys, however, brought in a merchant from Port Angeles who ran a store similar to the one in La Push to show that the 50 percent markup was typical of such businesses in remote places. He also proved that it was Baxter, not Dan, who had established the high-markup policy.[43]

Concerning their income, Dan and Hattie testified that it did indeed exceed the salary that Baxter paid Dan. They took in the additional money managing their respective post offices, boarding guests, renting land, and selling farm products, and therefore could afford their lifestyle without stealing.

Many of the people who signed affidavits and later testified during the trial revealed under cross-examination that either Baxter had pressured them into signing or they had some kind of ongoing conflict with Dan Pullen, and thus were likely to be prejudiced against him. John Carnes, who had presented such a damning picture of the Pullens, for example, ended his testimony by admitting that he and Dan had "quarreled about a fence."[44]

Baxter's case began to fall apart. A second dressmaker admitted under cross-examination that Baxter had paid her to travel from Seattle to testify at the trial. A Quileute admitted that Baxter had paid her at the time she signed the affidavit. Another Quileute stated later that he was working for Baxter at twenty-five dollars per month by the end of the trial. Examination under oath revealed that a Quileute who had signed an affidavit that he had overheard certain incriminating things said in conversations between Dan and Hattie did not speak or understand the English language.[45]

The Pullens and their lawyers through examination and cross-examination were able to account for virtually every one of the items Baxter accused them of having converted. It was the analysis by the Pullens' accountants, however, that was particularly compelling. They showed that the Pullens had recorded in their business ledgers or personal account books the items they allegedly had stolen. Dan stated on the stand that he had no prior knowledge of bookkeeping, and that Baxter had taught him everything he knew about how to maintain the books. Baxter had instructed him not to record goods lost or damaged in shipping or unloading, which would have explained some of the so-called "stolen" merchandise.[46]

Because of Dan's business inexperience, the accountants had to recalculate nearly seven years' worth of financial records, another costly expenditure for the Pullens. The laborious endeavor, however, allowed them to refute Baxter's accusations and conclude: "We found evidence that the defendants were very inexpert book keepers and they made blunders as often against themselves as in their own favor. We examined the books for the purpose of determining this point and we find that every evidence indicated that they had kept the books honestly."[47] The Pullens' accountants also rightly pointed out that it was necessary to look at both sides of the business—the store sales and the sealskin trading—something the plaintiff's accountants had chosen not to do, to Baxter's advantage. While the store generally operated at a loss (something Dan maintained Baxter had known would be the case from the beginning), the sealskin trading earned a handsome profit for the company.[48] That, they argued, was evidence of Dan Pullen's faithful service.[49]

It is worth noting that Baxter's collaborator in spying, E. M. Williams, turned out to be a true scoundrel. A year after his arrival in La Push, the police arrested him near Seattle on charges of grand larceny in an unrelated matter. There were outstanding warrants for his arrest on charges relating to a number of fraudulent transactions. A newspaper article referred to him as a "full-fledged confidence man."[50] And Baxter himself had been involved in a great deal of litigation during his lifetime,[51] even admitting during the trial, "I was instrumental in causing the [Pullens'] land contest. I have threatened to put them in the penitentiary." If unknown to them before, Hattie and Dan now knew the initial cause of their land troubles.[52]

Despite the many people that Baxter was able to find who agreed to disparage the Pullens' reputations, some in the community supported them from the beginning. One January 1893 anonymous newspaper article stated that the people of Quillayute country "know and have a warm attachment for 'Dan' Pullen. Especially attached to him are those who have enjoyed the abundant hospitality of his splendid home, where as kind and sweet tempered a wife as any home can claim, makes the guest, the visitor or the wanderer, as the case may be, feel at home. Mr. Pullen's numerous friends regret exceedingly that he is the victim of the machinations of an unscrupulous capitalist, who seems to be endeavoring to wrench the hard earned comforts of an industrious life time, for private gain. All hope to see him victorious."[53]

The trial lasted twenty-eight days, twenty-one of which were devoted to examining fifty-five witnesses. Because Dan had considerable hearing loss and Hattie had assisted him in the store consistently, she was a particularly important witness. She was on the witness stand seven days and asked over four thousand questions, "the longest examination of any woman as a witness on the Pacific coast," according to her lawyers.[54] Newspaper coverage described the proceedings as "an apparently endless lawsuit" and "one of the longest if not the longest civil cases ever tried in the state."[55] One exasperated juror penned a poem, published in the local press, suggesting the trial had lasted about seven years. Near the beginning of the trial his new bride sat in the courtroom, he wrote, but as the trial's end approached, he felt like he had been there quite some time:

> And when the defense consented to rest
> And the summing-up was begun
> My six bright little children came to court
> To see which side had won.[56]
> (Anonymous)

Today, the documents concerning the case in the Clallam County Courthouse include the statement of facts, affidavits, motions, subpoenas, depositions, stipulations, court orders, writs of attachment, sheriff's notices, requests for extensions, lists of exhibits placed into evidence, 182 pages of testimony, the judge's 52 pages of jury instructions, and the judgment—an exhausting 592 pages. A newspaper report concluded, "The costs of the trial will be enormous . . . a luxury in which only millionaires should indulge in but once during a lifetime. The sympathy of the public doubtless was with the Pullens, as the evidence adduced from day to day by the plaintiff, did not appear to warrant or justify the charges made in the complaint. The verdict of the jury, therefore, was quite generally approved."[57] When it was over, after twenty-two hours of deliberation, the jury found in favor of the defendants on June 26, 1893.[58]

" 'Plug' "

The Baxter case, however, wasn't really over for Dan and Hattie or for Clallam County. Baxter immediately filed a motion for a new trial, which the judge denied. More than three years later, the county had to place a levy on the Washington Fur Company's assets in an attempt to recover its costs in connection with the case. Both the sheriff and the man the court had appointed custodian of the Pullens' animals were unable to recover from Baxter what he owed them. And most dispiriting for the Pullens, a year after the trial, Baxter initiated an appeal to the Supreme Court of the State of Washington. Again, the Pullens had to hire lawyers. They responded to Baxter's proposed statement of facts with a slew of blistering amendments. Those amendments must have scared Baxter off. He apparently dropped the effort because nothing more of the case appears in the court records.[59]

At this point, the Pullens were deeply in debt. They had spent enormous sums in legal fees and in making arduous trips to and from Seattle, Port Townsend, and Port Angeles to meet with their lawyers and to appear in court for both the Baxter case and their ongoing land contest. Between 1882 and 1891 Dan had increased his land holdings tenfold. Land was considered the cornerstone of an empire at the time. But in 1890, in the throes of their dispute with the Land Office and the Office of Indian Affairs, the Pullens began borrowing money and mortgaging property. In 1892, in desperation, they borrowed one thousand dollars from Hattie's brother Olly and sold him a large parcel of land. They mortgaged the rest of their land for another forty-five hundred dollars.[60] Mortgages at the time had terms as short as one year, so the pressure on Hattie and Dan began to mount quickly. Hattie testified that just as Williams was beginning his investigations in 1892, "our household expenses . . . increased largely. I had a sick baby and was unable to attend to the kitchen myself and everything went wrong. We had no vegetables at that time and no milk."[61] From that point on, the Pullens' financial situation deteriorated.

Although the Baxter conflict was finally behind them, the Pullens' income had decreased by more than half with the loss of Dan's job as store manager and trading agent. Some of the land they had once been able to rent was no longer theirs. Paying taxes, mortgage debts, and lawyers was beginning to be more than they could handle. To make matters worse, a deep, nationwide economic depression, the worst in the country's history, started in the spring of 1893. Trouble began with a steep drop in the United States gold reserves, which triggered a financial panic. Corporate bankruptcies, bank failures, and mass layoffs followed. Unemployment rates were staggeringly high. Because Seattle was still recovering from

10.3. Harriet in her riding habit and plug hat, with her farm animals in Skagway, ca. 1904 (Clarence Leroy Andrews, photographer). ALASKA STATE LIBRARY, CLARENCE LEROY ANDREWS PHOTO COLLECTION, P45-322

a disastrous 1889 fire, the Panic of 1893 hit that city particularly hard. What lay ahead for the Pullens was unclear.

Four years after the trial ended, Hattie's hat, the infamous emblem of extravagance, was still in the possession of the court. She had to appeal through her lawyer to retrieve it, which she did in February 1897. The court document describes it as a " 'plug' ... being evidence used at the trial of this case."[62] A plug is a bowler or derby hat with a stiff, rounded crown and a brim. A photograph taken years later shows Hattie posing with her farm animals and wearing what is probably the very same hat.

To Court Again

The relief and joy Hattie and Dan experienced on June 26, 1893, over the not-guilty verdict vanished when the reality of a recent decision in their other legal battle set in. A letter dated June 23, 1893, from the Indian agent at Neah Bay demanded that the Pullens vacate their home and La Push land claims within sixty days. The Department of the Interior had finally rendered a decision, which instructed the commissioner of Indian

Affairs to remove the Pullens from the premises. They had lost their latest appeal in the land contest.[63]

If nothing else, Dan and Hattie Pullen were persistent. Their response to the letter was to go to court again, this time to get a restraining order against the Indian agent charged with removing them. Their lawsuit against the agent began in August 1893 and would drag on for years.[64]

Again in waiting mode, the Pullens continued to live in their La Push house. Their children now attended public school with other settlers and some of the Quileutes.[65] The "popular seaside resort" mentioned in the newspaper article and cited at the end of the previous chapter suggests that Hattie was running a kind of resort hotel, an endeavor that would serve her well in the future. The income derived from this small business helped the Pullens to make ends meet.[66]

They also continued farming and ranching. The area had not lost its rural character. By the early 1890s, Quillayute country had established its Annual Harvest Home Fair for which all the neighbors gathered to show off their produce, animals, canned goods, and needlework. Harvey B. Smith, Hattie's youngest brother, showed his unusual pet, an elk named Zeke, who he had raised from a calf and trained to wear a harness and pull a sled. Dan Pullen showed his vegetables, among which were "some uncommon fine onions."[67] Despite the urbane and genteel appearance of their "the seaside resort" dwelling, still an anomaly in Quillayute country, Dan and Hattie's life in La Push was isolated and lived close to nature.

In the early 1890s, the predictions of La Push's potential as a trans-portation hub continued.[68] The press regarded the outcome of Dan's case as the key to that future. The *Leader* ran a series of editorials and articles that made its position clear. One states, "We hope [Pullen] will win the case for two reasons. First, in equity it should belong to him, and, second, if the government should win the case and the disputed land [is] laid aside as an Indian reservation it would retard further material develop-ment of this valley."[69] Placing the blame squarely on the Quileute people, another editorial declares, "Were it not for the [Pullen] suit . . . it would be an easy thing to get capitalists interested in building and operating a sawmill. . . . A small handful of Indians have caused all this trouble for the settlers."[70]

Three days later, a journalist stated, "The reservation never has been and never will be any use to the noble red man."[71] A newspaper editor at about the same time opined, "The idea of giving the Indians the choicest and best located land in the country is foolishness. They never farm the land, are too lazy to work, and a rocky hillside would answer their purpose as well as the richest agricultural land."[72] He went on to point out that settlers had moved onto the Makah reservation at Neah Bay, only to be later removed by the US government. From the point of view of the *Leader*, no good had come from that decision; surely the government had learned its lesson, the editor asserted, and would pave the way for progress at La Push. It was within this spirit of the possibility of impending economic development, shadowed by the lingering court case, that the Pullens lived their lives at La Push in the mid-1890s. With such support within their community, for a while, it may have been difficult for them to believe that they might not win the battle.

"Shocked the Moral Sense"

The land contest with the US government proved to be the last straw for the Pullens. The entire episode represents a microcosm of what historian Donald Worster has proposed in his essay "Beyond the Agrarian Myth" when he characterizes the development of the American West as a process "plagued by racism, ethnocentrism, brutality, misunderstanding, and rage."[73] Given the complexity of the land case and its importance to Hattie's future, a summary of how the case unfolded is useful.

The treaty the US government had made with the Quileute people in the 1850s, more than a decade before Dan arrived in the area, called for them to relinquish their lands in exchange for money. The government paid for the land but allowed the Quileutes to stay put. Many settlers, including Dan, however, believed it was only a matter of time before the federal government moved them.

The US government surveyed the land and officially opened La Push and the surrounding area for settlement in 1882, so Dan and other settlers began to make land claims. In 1889, the US government created the Quileute reservation, with a proviso allowing settlers with legitimate prior claims to stay. Dan, who had proved up on his Preemption claim in

1884, believed his land claim was legitimate, even though the Local Land Office held up his patent while conducting its investigation. He believed the land was rightfully his and that, eventually, a patent would be his as well.[74]

The US government, on the other hand, had evidence that Dan had repeatedly intimidated and assaulted members of the Quileute tribe. The land at La Push had been the homeland of the Quileute people for as long as anyone could remember.[75] In spite of the government's failure to move them when a reservation was first set apart for their use in 1873, the government continued to recognize their legitimacy, as evidenced by the establishment of the Indian Agency School at La Push and the funds provided for rebuilding the village after the 1889 fire.

George Chandler, First Assistant Secretary of the Department of the Interior, explained his decision to have the Pullens evicted in a letter of March 1, 1893:

> *This little peninsula has been their harbor and their refuge for ages. By their own labor and skill as fishermen they have always been and are now self supporting. To deprive them of this landing place and thus destroy their own usefulness and deprive them of the only vocation they are capable of pursuing, would be a cruelty that is abhorrent to our policy.*[76]

To support his contention that the Pullens were trespassers, Chandler cited language in an 1877 US Supreme Court opinion in *Atherton v. Fowler*:

> *The generosity by which Congress gave the settler the right of pre-emption was not intended to give him the benefit of another man's labor, and authorize him to turn that man and his family out of their home. It did not propose to give its bounty to settlements obtained by violence at the expense of others. . . . To erect a dwelling-house did not mean to seize some other man's dwelling. It had reference to vacant land, to unimproved land; and it would have shocked the moral sense of the men who passed these laws, if they had supposed that they had*

extended an invitation to the pioneer population to acquire inchoate
rights to the public lands by trespass, by violence, . . . and other crimes
of less moral turpitude.[77]

The US government's position regarding the rights of Indian peoples
had changed. Many believed it was time to atone for the country's past
transgressions against other Indian peoples.

Despite the contradictions in the various iterations of the government's position, the decision to give the Pullens' land back to the Quileute
people really boiled down to an ethical decision stemming from what
"shocked the moral sense," as the Supreme Court opinion put it. Dan may
have conformed to the letter of the law in making and proving up on his
land claims, but his deplorable and at times criminal behavior toward his
Quileute neighbors outweighed that issue.

The government never prosecuted Dan in spite of his use of threats,
bribery, and assaults to try to get what he wanted. In the years before 1889,
when President Cleveland created the approximately one-square-mile reservation, the agents at Neah Bay maintained that they did not have the
authority to take action against Dan because the Quileute people did not
live on a reservation.[78] In the case of the September 1889 fire and the sus-
picion that Dan was responsible, to accuse him formally was perhaps too
serious a step to take in the absence of any evidence or Euro-American
witnesses. By the time anyone publicly accused Dan of setting the fire, Dan
was dead and his immediate family long gone from Quillayute country.

"SUDDENLY BECAME INSANE"

Waiting for a decision in their latest appeal against the Indian agent
charged with evicting them proved enormously stressful for the Pullens.
Foreclosure on their properties was looming. They had not been able to
pay their taxes and legal bills since 1893. Dan and Hattie both looked for
a way out. Then, in August 1896, a newspaper article reported that Dan
had suddenly become "insane." The full text of the short piece is, "Daniel
Pullen, a prominent farmer of Lapush, Wash., suddenly became insane
last Sunday and left his home and has not since been seen or heard of. It
is believed he has committed suicide."[79]

CHAPTER ELEVEN

Skagway 1897–1902

"STACKS OF YELLOW METAL!" THE FRONT PAGE OF THE *SEATTLE POST-Intelligencer* trumpeted the astounding news on July 17, 1897.[1] The steamer SS *Portland*, back from the Yukon and packed with newly rich prospectors and "a ton of gold," had docked in Seattle, as had another steamer from the Yukon three days earlier in San Francisco. The rush was on. News of the strike had trickled into the press across the nation beginning in 1896, but accelerated quickly with the dramatic arrival of the steamships filled with gold-laden miners.[2] As historian Pierre Berton described it, "There had been nothing like the Klondike before, there has been nothing like it since, and there can never be anything like it again."[3]

Hattie heard the news as it spread around the world, reported in newspapers everywhere, and, along with thousands of others, decided to try her luck. She made her La Push exit boldly in the summer of 1897. Like her parents before her, she went west—and north—to America's only remaining frontier, Alaska. As she told it in later years, her governess, cook, or neighbor, depending on when and to whom she told the story, had suggested she go to where the Klondike Gold Rush had just begun. Hattie joined one of the largest human migrations in history.

Less than two months after the gold rush began, Hattie arrived in Port Angeles. In a letter dated September 3 to her brother Wesley, she informed him that his turnip seed awaited his pickup in her post office, and that she had made her way north on horseback. She asked him to keep an eye on her home, and closed with "I may go to Alaska," a mere hint of her plans to the folks back home.[4]

From Port Angeles, she moved on by mail boat to Port Townsend with plans to go to Seattle for another boat bound for Alaska. "A Woman Without Fear," datelined "Port Townsend, Sept. 4," appeared in a local newspaper and tells the story of her trip: "The terrors of the Dyea and Skaguay passes have caused many strong hearts to quail, but it remains for Quillayute, on the west coast of Washington . . . to furnish a heroine. She arrived today on the mail boat from down the straits in the person of Mrs. Dan Pullen, who with three [of her] children was [two or three words obliterated] several months ago. Mrs. Pullen continued to sow and reap and care for her family, and success crowned her efforts."[5]

Someone had scratched out one mysterious phrase in the clipping of this article pasted into Hattie's scrapbook. What could those unreadable words have said? They probably referred to something that Hattie was ashamed of, or they told a different story than the one she wanted to believe, or tell. Did they say, "alone and broke," or "left alone," or "deserted by Dan" or "widowed?" The words are impossible to decipher. It seems the newspaper issue no longer exists, so cross-checking with an original has not been possible. The article continues:

> *Two weeks ago the Klondike fever pervaded her isolated home. The result was she gathered together her grit, her . . . children and six horses and started for Neah Bay. . . . Mrs. Pullen proposes to utilize her six horses to carry her children and outfit over the [Yukon] divide. Mrs. Pullen says she expects to get over the pass this fall.*
>
> *The largest item in her outfit is clear-cut grit. She is a slender, red-haired woman, who tips the scales at 125 pounds . . . [and] says she would not take a partner for the trip, even if the Prince of Wales was to offer his assistance. The assertion is ventured that people who keep posted on matters pertaining to the Chilkoot pass will never read of Mrs. Dan Pullen sitting on the beach weeping.*[6]

The article suggests that Hattie planned to look for gold. That was not to be—at least, not at first.

To prepare for her trip, Hattie left her youngest son, Chester, age seven, in Quillayute with his aunt Sarah, Dan's sister, and placed fifteen-year-old

Mildred in boarding school at Ellensburg Normal, a state school in central Washington, which in its early years was tuition-free.[7] Hattie sent her two older boys to stay with Dan at a logging camp in Port Gamble. He had left La Push some time before, but, contrary to the newspaper report, had not committed suicide. As it had been in his youth, his job now was as a "bull puncher," driving a team of oxen to pull or skid the felled trees across a road made of heavy wooden planks.

There is a certain irony in Dan finding himself back on a skid road. The term, originating in nineteenth-century Pacific Northwest logging camps, evolved over time into "skid row," a term referring to a place of poverty or, figuratively, to the state of impoverishment. In Seattle, the skid road leading to an early and important logging operation, today Yesler Way, ended up becoming the edge of the district of the down-and-out. Murray Morgan in his *Skid Road: An Informal Portrait of Seattle* calls it "the place of dead dreams."[8] The proud and once-wealthy landowner was back to the life he had led thirty years before—on "skid road."

As Royal recounted, Dee, at twelve, was old enough to be a skid greaser, a job that involved oiling skid roads to help the logs move faster. Royal, only ten, had to clean out the stables and work in the kitchen with the Chinese cook.[9] Along with finding a safe harbor for each of her children, Hattie found someone in Port Townsend to care for her beloved horses. Her initial plan to use them "to carry her children and outfit over the divide," as the newspaper article had put it, was overly ambitious. She wisely chose to leave the horses and the children behind and make a reconnaissance of the situation in Skagway alone. Their future rested on her shoulders. At thirty-seven, Hattie had to make a fresh start. Placing herself in the middle of the Klondike Gold Rush seemed like the way to do it.

Even if she and Dan were to win their still-pending lawsuit against the Indian Agency and Dan had returned, their financial situation was dire. Their debts had continued to mount. There seemed to be no way to remedy the situation. For Hattie, the gold rush in Alaska promised fortune—or at least a job and a way to survive.

Reinvented Herself as Harriet

As Hattie began her new life in Alaska, she reinvented herself as Harriet—Mrs. Harriet Smith Pullen. Eight days after her arrival in Port Townsend, a newspaper announced her as its new special correspondent in the goldfields of Alaska. The article declared: "In securing the services of such a fluent and entertaining writer as Mrs. Pullen as its representative in the North, the *Leader* . . . will from time to time give its readers fresh, authentic and interesting news from the pen of its special correspondent."[10] Harriet was, for the first time, following the example of her father, finding her voice in published written words and striking out for new territory when life at home became unsustainable.

Aboard the SS *Rosalie* as she approached her final destination, Skagway, Alaska, a town that would change her life forever, Harriet penned an article that followed her six-day journey, heading north through the waters off British Columbia, Canada, and southeastern Alaska. Accompanying her were forty-five other passengers, twenty-two horses, two cows, a few boxes of chickens, and assorted baggage and freight. The boat wound up through the Inside Passage, around islands, through various narrows, gulfs, straits, sounds, and channels. It tied up at wharves, and passengers disembarked briefly at several ports. It was a smooth and comfortable trip, marred only by a brief spell when, as Harriet put it, "the steamer rolled about just enough to upset the land lubbers, who groaned in bitterness of spirit."[11]

As they reached the trip's final day, Harriet wrote, "As night shut in, we . . . tied up at the wharf at Juneau in a downpour of rain that was simply discouraging. Notwithstanding this everyone took in the town."[12] The high point of the journey was watching the disembarkation, without benefit of a wharf, of a party with twelve horses bound for the goldfields.

On Sunday morning—a lovely day, with the sun shining on the tremendous beauty of the Davidson glacier—we are about to put on shore, at this end of the Dalton trail, a party with 12 horses who are going to make the attempt over the longest of the many routes into the land of gold. The horses are about to plunge into the icy water.

11.1. The SS *Rosalie* that Hattie took to Alaska, docked in Skagway, September to October, 1898 (Harrie Clay Barley, photographer). NATIONAL PARK SERVICE, KLONDIKE GOLD RUSH NATIONAL HISTORICAL PARK, KLGO 60766

Wait! Talk about walking the plank! You should have seen the way these poor beasts stepped out on the gang plank, overbalanced it and plunged into the icy waters. But the captain had put the nose of his vessel close to the beach, so it was only a plunge and a few strokes and the animals landed, all dripping, on the sand. All were landed safely and are now eating grass and rolling in apparent comfort and satisfaction.[13]

The *Rosalie*'s last stops were Dyea and Skagway, bases of operations for would-be prospectors—known as stampeders—seeking gold in the Klondike. Harriet's newspaper calling, while not entirely over, seems to have been short-lived. Even though she promised at the end of her article to write again after settling in Skagway, she seems never to have written another report for the *Leader*. She had other, more pressing concerns to manage. The journey north as Harriet presented it, however, seemed an auspicious beginning to her new life in Alaska.

Hat in Hand

The stampeders, most of them men, landed in Skagway to get the lay of the land and to finish outfitting themselves for the hard and hazardous trip up the White Pass Trail, known as "the Heartbreak Trail,"[14] into the Klondike goldfields in Canada's Yukon Territory. By the fall of 1897, there were about three thousand people in Skagway.[15] Before hordes of stampeders had started arriving in July, the place was Captain William Moore's homestead and a tiny village called Mooresville. The newcomers simply ignored the existing property claims, moved in, and began building.[16]

Here was the start of the White Pass Trail, leading to Bennett Lake, the Yukon River, and the goldfields beyond. For several miles, it was a beckoning, level road, wide enough for wagons. But then it narrowed so that parts of it were not much more than a crude, rocky footpath hacked through the woods and ascending the mountainside, a difficult route for people and animals alike.

Nestled amid glaciers and snowcapped, often cloud-shrouded mountains on three sides, Skagway spread back from the natural deepwater harbor and beach on a floodplain between steep slopes blanketed with trees. There were muddy streets, wood-plank sidewalks, and some rough-hewn frame buildings that housed stores, warehouses, dance halls, gambling houses, and saloons, some with upstairs rooms for prostitution. Many residents lived in tents.[17] An ever-changing cast of characters filled the place as people landed, gathered their outfits, and moved to and from the goldfields.

A woman who had arrived in Skagway two weeks before Harriet postponed her departure from the steamer for fear of what she would encounter onshore. She described the scene. "Towards evening with fear and dread, I actually ventured ashore. To my surprise I found a surging crowd of people busy as bees rushing hither and thither—but everything

11.2. Skagway street scene in the summer of 1897 (Asahel Curtis, photographer). UNIVERSITY OF WASHINGTON LIBRARIES, SPECIAL COLLECTIONS, A. CURTIS 46009

was orderly and quiet. No one attempted to rob or mob. Everyone was kind. . . . There was no evidence of violence or crime—nothing but kindness."[18] Journalist Tappan Adney, in Skagway writing for *Harper's Weekly* in August 1897, observed, "Excepting the gamblers, there are few who might be said to represent a disorderly element. And this, no doubt, is due to the fact that every man here, except those who have come up from the nearby towns of Juneau and Sitka, has had to have the price to get in. This is no country for tramps and loafers." He described the motley assortment of stampeders who had come to make their fortunes as "photographers, newspaper men, physicians, mining engineers, farmers, lumbermen, and clerks."[19]

The once affluent and imperious Hattie, now Harriet—humbled but most likely, in the words of the newspaper, not "on the beach weeping"—arrived in frenzied Skagway with hat in hand. The place swarmed with people, rushing to find their fortune. Nearly penniless, Harriet just needed a job.

FOUND HER VOICE

Here, on the shore of Skagway Bay in September 1897, Harriet Smith Pullen's story begins, a story she fashioned herself. I've told the story of her early life through the lens of her father's diary and the La Push years through the court documents of her legal wranglings, but for the Skagway part of the story, I am able to use her own words. In Skagway Harriet found her voice, albeit primarily through the writings of those who talked to her. The published accounts of her Skagway years are numerous, but, with few exceptions, they stem from interviews, either first- or second-hand. Barrett Willoughby (aka, Florance Barrett), a journalist and author of several books, came to Skagway in the late 1920s to interview Harriet.[20] She published Harriet's story five times between 1930 and 1941. Willoughby's 1930 *American Magazine* article, "Mother of the North," formed the basis for the radio-play script, *Queen of Heartbreak Trail,* quoted in the first chapter of this book.[21]

As Harriet recounted her story to Willoughby, upon her arrival in Skagway, she and her fellow passengers had to be "put ashore in small boats."[22] A journalist who came to Skagway on the *Rosalie* on September 12, 1897, in all likelihood the same day Harriet did, described his landing, a challenge for which he donned rubber boots "and waded for half a mile through mud and water to a dry spot, where the landing was made.... Steamers find hard work in dropping into good anchorage and in getting scows alongside for unloading. ... All goods are loaded on scows, run as far in as possible on high tide and unloaded at low tide."[23] Although Captain Moore had constructed a rudimentary wharf in the 1880s, he charged a toll and his structure was incapable of handling the traffic. Many captains chose to offload using lighters (flat-bottomed barges used to transport animals, passengers, and goods to and from a moored ship).[24]

Deposited on the beach after her steamship journey, Harriet had just seven dollars in her pocket. "Frightened and alone I stood shivering in the cold North wind. While I was trying to make up my mind where to go, a man in a red mackinaw stopped in front of me and looked me over," Harriet told Willoughby.[25] Her conversation with the man in the red raincoat led to a job cooking in a tent for eighteen men who were building a new wharf.[26] Harriet reported how she could not stand upright in the tent because slabs

11.3. Landing supplies by lighter on the beach at Skagway, Alaska, in the summer or fall of 1897 (Asahel Curtis, photographer). UNIVERSITY OF WASHINGTON LIBRARIES, SPECIAL COLLECTIONS, A. CURTIS 46104

of bacon and ham hung from the ridgepole. The place was dirty and disorganized. It smelled of rancid grease and smoked meats. Food scraps littered the dirt floor, and piled on a makeshift table were dirty tin plates. "The strangeness and sordidness of everything sickened me," she recalled.[27] But her years on the prairie, making do in sod houses and helping her mother prepare food in primitive conditions for a family of ten, had prepared her for this challenge. She washed the pots and pans with ashes, got to work cooking, and by the time the men showed up that night, had dinner on the table. Her pay was three dollars a day. She noted she had never paid her cook back in La Push more than twenty dollars a month, but prices were steeply inflated in Skagway at the time, so her pay didn't go far.[28]

For dessert, Harriet baked dried-apple pies. By "building pies," as a newspaper account put it, she became famous.[29] She fashioned pie pans by flattening and reshaping old gallon-size tin cans with a hammer.[30] Harriet claimed to have made "enough dried-apple pies to pave a road from 'town to the top of Chilkoot pass,'" a distance of many miles.[31] The income from the pies allowed her to send for her children three months later.

But where would they live? Soon after she arrived in Skagway, Harriet had found on the beach an abandoned miner's cabin, so small she had to sleep on the table.[32] When a friend's husband had to leave Skagway, the woman came to stay with her. The friend slept on the table while Harriet spent her nights on a cot suspended from the ceiling.[33] Harriet's older sons, Dee and Royal, twelve and ten, arrived in December. She recalled in her interview with Willoughby that they slept on a mound of straw in one corner of the cabin. The boys collected discarded crates on the beach from which she built bunks, chairs, cupboards, and shelving. She took deep pride in her ability to improvise.[34]

Harriet picked up her journalist's pen at least once more during her early months in Alaska. She wanted to communicate to the folks back home what was going on in Skagway. A November 1897 article in the *Seattle Daily Times* quotes a letter Harriet wrote to its editor: "In Skaguay bay the rise and fall of the tide yesterday was 24 feet. The town was flooded. People have been going up and down the streets in boats. There is no serious damage done."[35] She went on to make an ominous prediction, as quoted in the newspaper: "It is my private opinion that a great deal of damage will result when the December high tide comes, and that next June when the high tide and flood from the rising river occur at the same time, the whole town is liable to be swept away."[36]

This *Seattle Daily Times* piece prompted the *Skaguay News* to print a defensive front-page editorial dated December 10, 1897, under the title "Pernicious Truth Users." It railed against Harriet for reporting to the Seattle newspaper that Skagway had been flooded, which the editor maintained was untrue. Although the *Skaguay News* editor accused Harriet of having "a lively imagination" and "exclusive sources of information," it is likely that she was accurately reporting her personal observations and opinions to a city hungry for information about the Klondike Gold Rush.[37] At least one photograph from October 27, 1897, shows the ground floors of dozens of buildings in Skagway underwater, with numerous logs

11.4. A flooded Skagway street in about 1901. ALASKA STATE LIBRARY, PHOTO COL-
LECTION, SKAGWAY-STREET-SCENES-08

and debris floating among them.[38] Harriet lived and worked near the waterfront at the time and undoubtedly experienced the rising tides and flooded streets firsthand. The editor's own newspaper had reported a few weeks earlier on the high tides that had "greatly inconvenienced" people living near the tide flats.[39] The little controversy was important enough to the *Skaguay News* editor, however, that he addressed the issue yet again a week later, writing, "The *News* denies . . . [Mrs. Pullen's assertion] and says that 'the main business portion of the town is high and dry at all times.'"[40]

Harriet offered additional observations in her letter to the editor, "Everything is very quiet here, and there are many idle men. I could not advise anyone to come here, not even my own family—everything is so uncertain. . . . This is a dreadful place for petty thieving. Tools are often stolen when the men are at work; saws, hammers, axes are continually being stolen."[41] Harriet's comments about "idle men" and "petty thieving" were not the result of a "lively imagination." Surely, among the thousands of stampeders who descended upon Skagway in 1897 there were a number of idle men. Some measure of petty thievery in a nascent town that only in December 1897 had held its first election is not surprising.[42] Additionally, many of the men in Skagway who were finding the trek to the goldfields more challenging than they had anticipated were short on resources; the clogged White Pass Trail had left some stranded. There were also frequent incidents of claim jumping. Harriet was not overstating at all, just communicating what she thought most important. So in spite of this accusation by a newspaper editor intent on protecting—or even creating—the emerging town's reputation, there seems to have been much truth in what Harriet wrote. She was a "truth user." The "pernicious" aspect was in the eyes of the editor. Harriet was speaking her mind, kicking up a bit of controversy in the process.

She seems not to have written letters to the editor again. Might she have been chastened by the *Skaguay News* editor's response to her letter? That seems unlikely. She was probably just too busy to write. Moreover, the intense interest in the Klondike in the lower forty-eight during the first few months of the gold rush was beginning to wane.[43]

There was one part of Harriet's Skagway-arrival story that she repeatedly left out. That was the part about Dan. Harriet had some explaining to do when Dan showed up in Skagway in December 1897, accompanying their two older sons, because she had been telling everyone she was a widow. Why she promoted this idea and clung so tenaciously to it in the years to come is a mystery. Was there shame attached to having been deserted by a reputedly "insane" husband, assuming that this is what happened when Dan disappeared? Was it a self-protective measure for a woman alone in an untamed, gold-rush town where women were few? Or was it wishful thinking on her part? The interlude of Dan's sudden disappearance in 1896 may have given Harriet an idea of what life could be like without him.

Dan, who remained in Skagway with the family for a time, at fifty-five in 1897 was too old to continue doing the kind of physical labor he had done in his youth. According to Royal, his severe hearing loss made it difficult for him to keep most jobs.[44] He was, however, able to construct lean-tos on the sides of Harriet's waterfront cabin where the parents and two boys slept. Before long, he had built a two-story house for the family, which soon included the other two children and Dan's older sister Sarah. Harriet's plan was to use this structure as a boardinghouse, but the venture did not last long.[45]

IF SHE HAD HER HORSES

At some point in early 1898, Harriet realized that if she had her horses, the ones she had raised from colts and left in Washington, she could make a considerable amount of money packing the miners' supplies toward the goldfields. Willoughby wrote the story of the landing of Harriet's horses, much of it quoting Harriet's words:

> *"My own horses—I loved them next to my children. The thought of bringing them to Skagway filled me with anguish. But I knew that with them I could make the money necessary to get my babies a better home, better clothes, and an education. So I sent for the horses."* . . . *The day the steamer arrived with Mrs. Pullen's pets, it had come to anchor out in the bay because all four wharves were double lined with vessels unloading cargoes. Amid that bedlam ashore no one had time to help anyone but himself, so the courageous woman took a skiff and started out alone to the steamer. "I rowed to the ship, tied my boat under the Jacob's ladder that dangled over the side of the hull, and climbed aboard. Through an open hatch I looked down into the hold. There were my horses! I don't know how I got down there with them, but I did. And they hadn't forgotten me. They nuzzled me and whinnied, and I—well, I threw my arms about the neck of my beautiful saddle horse, Babe, all that was left me of a happy, sheltered past, and cried."[46]*

According to Harriet, she had to get the horses off the boat quickly. With no one to help her, she had to do it alone. The freight clerk thought she was crazy. "Don't you realize it's a quarter of a mile to shore, and the wind's kicked up a sea already?" he asked, according to Willoughby. "Only an experienced man can swim those seven horses from here to the beach."[47] She was going to do it anyway. The deckhand brought Babe up from the hold. Harriet stood below in the bobbing skiff and called out for Babe to jump. The horse jumped, or the deckhand pushed her, and she landed in the water. Harriet tied a rope to a ring in her halter and rowed the skiff through the choppy sea with Babe swimming behind. Each of the horses followed; soon they were onshore—dry, blanketed, and eating hay.[48]

HAULING

Harriet began hauling supplies from Skagway to White Pass City on the newly completed Brackett Wagon Road, which ascended the Skagway River valley.[49] From there, after a trek over a sled road to the Summit of the White Pass and a narrow trail to Bennett Lake, a trip of more than forty miles, stampeders then had to build boats and paddle them across lakes and down rivers, portaging in between, some five hundred miles to the Klondike goldfields.[50] When they crossed into Canada at the Summit, the border officers required of every would-be miner enough food for a year, plus equipment such as a tent, stove, and tools, which amounted to about two thousand pounds.[51] The authorities knew that the oncoming cold weather would force many of the stampeders to spend the winter in the Yukon, waiting for the spring thaw so that they could make their way down the Yukon River. The Canadian government wanted to avoid mass starvation among people unaccustomed to the harsh climate and the wilderness survival conditions they would encounter. With such prodigious quantities of provisions required, the demand for packers and freighters was enormous. Freighting on the Brackett Wagon Road, while an improvement over doing so on the muddy, rock-strewn White Pass Trail, was still challenging. On the length of it, day after day, were a stream of wagons and overladen mules and horses, driven by cursing men. Harriet and her six-horse team joined the queue.

A January 1898 newspaper article stated, "The Klondike rush of 1897 is fast becoming an uninteresting topic to the general public, yet there remains to be written one very vivid chapter. The story of the Klondike horses has not been concisely presented, despite the fact that it shows a destruction of animals equaled only in histories of battles and under conditions of cruelty unparalleled in a chronicle containing the doings of civilized men."[52]

Writer Jack London joined the stampeders in Alaska in 1897. He and a travel companion, Fred Thompson, each described the dead horses. Thompson noted in his diary concerning the White Pass Trail: "At the point where the Skagway trail comes in, and all along the hillside up from Bennett [Lake], there are hundreds of dead horses that have been used on the Skagway trail and here have played out—died for want of food, bad usage, or shot after no more use could be got from them. Parties coming off the Skagway trail tell me there are enough dead horses and mules along the trail to lay them side by side, so that one can walk on horse flesh the entire length (fifty miles)."[53] People soon dubbed the White Pass Trail, the Dead Horse Trail.

As the annual freeze began, London holed up in a cabin near a crossroads and spent the long winter listening to miners' tales, gathering material he later used in his stories.[54] In one of his short stories published a few years later, London wrote poetically of the Dead Horse Trail as described to him by the stampeders who passed through his cabin:

Freighting an outfit over the White Pass in '97 broke many a man's heart, for there was a world of reason when they gave the trail its name. The horses died like mosquitoes in the first frost, and from Skaguay to Bennett they rotted in heaps. They died at the Rocks, they were poisoned at the Summit, and they starved at the Lakes; they fell off the trail, what there was of it, and they went through it; in the river they drowned under their loads, or were smashed to pieces against the boulders; they snapped their legs in the crevices and broke their backs falling backwards with their packs; in the sloughs they sank from sight or smothered in the slime, and they were disembowelled in the bogs where the corduroy logs turned end up in the mud; men shot them, worked them to death, and when they were gone, went back to the beach and bought more. Some did not bother to shoot them— stripping the saddles off and the shoes and leaving them where they fell. Their hearts turned to stone—those which did not break—and they became beasts, the men on the Dead Horse Trail.[55]

Tappan Adney, the *Harper's Weekly* journalist, spent sixteen months in the Klondike and observed, "The story of the Skagway trail will never be written by one person. It is a series of individual experiences, each unique, and there are as many stories as there were men on the trail. How much of the awful destruction of horses was caused by the trail, and how much by the ignorance and cruelty of the packers, will never be known."[56]

Harriet, a woman on the Brackett Wagon Road, had her own stories to tell. She told Willoughby about what many say were thousands of dead animals in Dead Horse Canyon, where the animals fell to their deaths or the stampeders dumped them when they died on the trail: "Bury them? No. There was hardly time to bury the human dead, let alone horses. Some days I drove through atmosphere so tainted with decaying flesh that I had to wear a handkerchief over my nose."[57] Harriet helped those on the road less knowledgeable about animals than she was. Encountering a man weeping beside his stubborn mule who refused to walk another step, she assessed the problem, unloaded the beast's burden, and repacked it in such a way that the mule would resume walking. It was her Quileute neighbors in La Push who had taught her this packing skill.[58]

Historian and Alaska booster Herb Hilscher published one of Harriet's stories after meeting with her several times in the 1940s. One time on the wagon road, she came upon a crazed man tearing at his horse's broken ankle. The animal had wedged its leg between two rocks. Harriet pulled out her revolver and put the horse out of its misery. Enraged, the man came after her. She leveled the gun at him and quietly suggested maybe he too needed to be put out of his misery. That ended the confrontation. Harriet always carried her revolver with her.[59]

Another time, according to a writer who knew her, Harriet encountered a large boulder blocking the road, its position threatening to overturn wagons. Many stampeders had simply passed it by, working gingerly around it. She, on the other hand, got down from her wagon, and using a crowbar, pried the boulder loose, sending it over the cliff. She said to the men who looked on, "That should make it a little easier for you men. I'm sorry I didn't think of it before." One driver who witnessed the event said, "Darn it, we all felt like two bits and looked as foolish as we felt, but none of us had gumption enough to help her. The way she looked at us poor fish, made us fairly shrivel, but she was a good sport and never rubbed it in afterwards."[60]

When asked if she had ever been fearful among all those rough men, she told Willoughby, "Some days . . . I'd have given anything in the world if I'd had a husband to look out for me."[61] Where Dan might have been at this time is a mystery, but wherever he was, Harriet seemed to have felt she was alone. One scholar has speculated it was not Harriet at all who did the freighting, but rather Dan.[62] Evidence, however, suggests the contrary. Harriet, an accomplished horse handler, was a woman of notable grit and physical strength. In an April 1898 letter from Skagway to her brother Wesley in La Push, she wrote, "I had been on the trail all day hauling & I was all worn out . . . [from] working like a slave."[63] As to whether her older sons did the hauling, as others have suggested, Royal and Dee were just ten and twelve in early 1898 when Harriet's horses arrived. Royal stated in an oral history, "The family didn't help her haul freight."[64]

Harriet told one writer, "I like horses—used to them, you know."[65] Her horse-handling expertise dated from her younger years. One anonymous story about her by someone who knew her claimed that Harriet had learned to ride "the wildest horses, and could handle her rifle with the ease and precision of a cowboy."[66] Riding, probably bareback, on the Dakota prairie, raising horses in La Push, and making journeys like the one she and her cousin made with the cattle drive in 1886 prepared her well for managing horses on the Brackett Wagon Road in Skagway, allowing her to earn a good living when she needed it most.

CHAPTER TWELVE

The Independent Entrepreneur

FAR REMOVED FROM HER LA PUSH HOME AND FRUSTRATED AT HER inability to control any aspect of the situation in Washington, Harriet awaited the court's final decision about her property and worried about the stewardship of her house. Before she left Washington, Harriet had arranged with her sister-in-law Annie, David's widow, to manage the La Push house and to take over her postmaster position.[1] According to their agreement, Annie was to pay for provisions left in the house and replace firewood as she used it. Any money she received from the sale of produce from the Pullens' garden, she was to turn over to Harriet. Earnings from boarders and horses she pastured would be Annie's to keep. The sheep the Pullens had left were to go to Wesley. He was to send any profits from wool or meat to Mildred at school.[2]

In an April 20, 1898, letter to her brother Wesley, Harriet expressed her ire toward Annie, who had apparently sold what rightly belonged to the Pullens, including a stove and pipe, dishes, chairs, and nine sheep:

> *After I got through reading . . . [Annie's] letter to Dan, I came very near taking the boat for home the next morning. I did not sleep a wink. . . . I wrote . . . for her to get out quick as she could if she could not live up to her agreement. . . . I feal like I should be tempted to have her arrested if I was down there. . . . I think it's pretty tough to have my own folks rob me of what few things I have. . . . I feal like I could kick Annie all over the place. . . . She hadn't any athoraty to sell any of my things. The idea of her writing to Dan. These things are my own personal property. Dan hasn't any thing to do with it.[3]*

In July 1898, more bad news came in a letter from the Pullens' lawyer. The judge had dismissed their complaint against the Indian agent. In order for the appellate court to hear the case again, it would have to include the commissioner of Indian Affairs and the Secretary of the Interior as defendants. The Pullens' lawyer, taken by surprise at the outcome, wrote:

The case was dismissed on the authority of a case decided by the Supreme Court of the United States, wherein the Court held that suit against the Indian Agent alone is insufficient, that the Chief of the Indian Bureau and Sec. of the Interior were necessary parties—there have been many cases brought as I brought yours and there has heretofore been no decision such as this, so I do not feel at all in fault for not anticipating the same—the court held that it was too late to amend by adding other parties so there was nothing to do but submit to dismissal—there has been no decision upon the merits, and the action can be brought again if you desire.[4]

The lawyer, however, also told her that he did not wish to be involved, as the Pullens still owed him a large sum of money. Dan Pullen then wrote to the judge handling the case to "hereby give notice" that he would "have to employ another atty," one more effort on Dan's part to find the justice he thought was his.[5]

One month earlier, the sheriff, acting on orders from the court, had removed from the house Annie and all of Harriet and Dan's belongings, including furniture, books, pictures, and an organ, and stored them offsite. One irony in the sheriff's removal was the fact that a boarder in the house, an L. B. Baxter, remained in residence. In La Push to run what had been the Pullens' trading post, he was the son of their nemesis, Sutcliffe Baxter, who had brought the spiteful fur trading company lawsuit against them.[6]

Dan did not follow up on his notice to the judge, either because he could not find legal representation or because he was exhausted. After fourteen long years, the battle was over. There would be no compensation as a result of the court proceedings for the loss of the house and property, even though John McGlinn, the Indian agent who had urged the government to take the Pullens' land for the Quileutes in the first place, believed they should be "paid a fair valuation for" it.[7]

Harriet appears to have considered taking the fight to a higher authority. She wrote to one of her lawyers some months later inquiring about making a claim through the US Congress for compensation for their lost property. The lawyer responded, but in June 1899, he wrote that he had had no reply from Harriet.[8] It seems the Pullens were directing their attention elsewhere. They had finally given up. Harriet was saying "good-bye" to the past. One might view the outcome as the government winning by default, because although there were more legal remedies the Pullens could have pursued, they chose not to. The mortgage holder foreclosed on most of what Clallam County properties they still owned. With interest past due, they owed nearly $6,000 on a $4,500 loan, plus unpaid property taxes. The county sheriff held the foreclosure auctions in 1899 and 1900, but by that time, the Pullens were long gone, physically and emotionally, from Clallam County.[9]

In early 1901, in a letter to Wesley, A. J. remarked that he had heard that Harriet would be home soon. "It is 2 bad that she should loose all they had in Clallam Co. U may have some influence to help her get a home. The Baxter suit & the Indian department have ruined them financially. & lawyers. Hattie has worked hard to live and raise her family and she should have a good home. U are well fixed financially, and if U can do anything 2 help her I hope that U will,"[10] he wrote in his characteristic shorthand. It seems unlikely that Wesley helped Harriet at this point. The family may not have known it, but Harriet wasn't coming back to La Push.

GREAT GAMBLE

In May 1898, when the White Pass & Yukon Route railway began construction on its run from Skagway to Whitehorse, Yukon Territory, Harriet knew the long line of horse- and mule-driven packers on the Brackett Wagon Road would vanish upon the railway's reaching White Pass Summit, slated for early 1899.[11] With her packing business soon to be defunct, Harriet decided to try her luck in the great gamble of placer gold mining.

By early 1898, most of the claims in the original Klondike Gold Rush territory had already been taken, but in August of that year gold was discovered near British Columbia's Atlin Lake, only about seventy-five miles from Skagway.[12] Gold fever had struck Skagway once again. Sometime that summer, as Harriet told one of her interviewers, she set off for Atlin with another woman, a waitress in a restaurant where she had worked. They loaded up their outfits on one of Harriet's horses and planned to take turns riding a second horse, later sending the horses back with a returning miner. Among the items Harriet probably packed besides her pistol were heavy gum shoes, snow glasses, a broad-brimmed netted hat, and gloves to protect her hands from mosquitoes—all recommended in a December 1897 *Skaguay News* article aimed at women who planned to venture "on this really perilous journey. . . . It takes strong healthy, courageous women to stand the terrible hardships that must necessarily be endured."[13] When a miner offered Harriet ten dollars to transport his outfit too, she and her travel companion both ended up walking while the horse earned the money.

The scene at Atlin was as challenging as Skagway had been one year earlier. To get across the lake to the gold, the miners needed boats. One enterprising man had brought a portable sawmill with him and was busy felling trees, cutting the logs into lumber, and building scows. Harriet negotiated for one of his scows for one hundred dollars. The story she told was that she took the ten dollars she had earned packing for the miner, used it as a down payment on the scow, and sold passage to ten prospectors at ten dollars each. With that, she paid for her boat and gained a crew at the same time.[14]

Arriving at Atlin, Harriet discovered that she knew many of the prospectors from her time in Skagway. Through them, she located and made some mining claims. Her experiences homesteading in the raw and vastly differing Dakota and Washington wildernesses had prepared her to manage in rugged and untamed British Columbia. Harriet's dreams of finding gold, however, ended abruptly when she fell on some rocks and broke her wrist. She sold passage on her scow again, this time to men who had given up looking for gold, and returned to Skagway.[15] She later lost her mining claims because she was ignorant of the "alien" laws of Canada, which disallowed claims of noncitizens.[16]

WORKING "AT HOME"

Back in Skagway, the family continued to live on First Avenue near the harbor in the house Dan had constructed. By 1900, the population of Skagway had fallen from its gold rush peak of ten thousand or more to about three thousand.[17] In the census that year, the Pullen family numbered seven—two parents, four children, and Aunt Say (Sarah). It lists Dan as the head of household, as a logger in Washington, and as a carpenter in Alaska, where he worked for the White Pass & Yukon Route for a time, but had been unemployed for three months.[18] The census lists Harriet as working "at home."[19] According to Royal, however, Harriet spent her first several years in Skagway employed outside the home in various capacities—cooking in the tent and working in a clothing store, hotel, and restaurant.[20] By 1901, she actually would be working "at home," managing her own business establishment.

Although Harriet's bid to find gold at Atlin had been unsuccessful, another gold mine awaited her—a burgeoning tourist trade. With the gold rush winding down, Skagway looked to new ways to support its economy. As early as July 1898, the *Skagway Daily Alaskan* reported on summer tourists who were coming to Skagway.[21] Harriet, thinking back to her days boarding guests in her La Push house, saw an opportunity in a stately mansion recently built by Captain Moore, the original Skagway town site owner. In 1901, he leased it to Harriet to use as a boardinghouse. Two-storied, with many dormered rooms that could serve as guestrooms and bay-windowed ground-floor spaces for a large dining room and drawing room, it was on the edge of town, away from heavy traffic and the busy commercial area. A broad porch surrounded two sides.[22]

Captain Moore, who had once operated tugboats on the Mississippi River,[23] had topped its second story with a riverboat-inspired room called the "Texas." The Texas deck of a steamboat (named for, at the time, the largest state) was the topmost deck, which held the captain's quarters, right next to the pilothouse. Other cabins also bore the names of states; hence, the term "stateroom."[24] Painted pea green, the house was a showplace, just waiting to be filled with guests.[25] Harriet claimed to have rented all of her rooms even before she opened for business on July 10.[26]

12.1. The Pack Train Saloon in August 1897, before Harriet worked there.
NATIONAL PARK SERVICE, KLONDIKE GOLD RUSH NATIONAL HISTORICAL PARK, DR. JOHN H.
WALKER COLLECTION, KLGO SE-64-3961

Harriet's goal was to provide comfort and good food in homelike surroundings.[27] She said to Willoughby three decades later, "I've never learned to be a hotel-keeper. I'm still only a home maker."[28] To equip the place as a boardinghouse, she bought mattresses and bedding and bartered with a man who had a load of fine furniture for a dance hall that never opened. In exchange for the furniture, she granted the man accommodations, but shortly after she opened for business, he pulled up a van and took back all of the furniture. He had decided to open a competing hotel. Harriet recounted the scene:

So there I was with my house full of railroad officials, judges, lawyers and their wives—for court was in session again—and I hadn't a dresser, or a bedstead, or even a stool in the place! Fortunately, I did own the mattresses and the bedding. I dashed down town immediately and ordered delivered to my house a load of lumber and all the empty

boxes I could find. Then I hunted up a carpenter and some helpers.
When night came I had a box dresser, a box chair, and a rough bedstead
in every room. My competitor, who had planned on an exodus from
the Pullen House, waited in vain. My blessed guests liked me well
enough to put up with those makeshifts until I could get something
better.[29]

Placed on their sides, bedside egg crates, Royal recalled, had two
shelves, "one for the chamber pot and one for a pitcher and bowl. The
lamp could go on top."[30] As stampeders left Skagway after the gold rush,
Harriet accumulated their discarded furniture.[31] Another money-saving,
improvised solution was to manufacture drinking glasses from discarded
beer bottles. To accomplish this, according to one of her interviewers, she
tied a sturdy string dipped in coal oil below the neck of a bottle, lit the
string with a match, and then dashed the heated bottle into icy water.
Grinding the raw edge in sand yielded a perfect drinking glass.[32]

Life in a meagerly appointed sod house, watching her father barter
for all kinds of goods and services and her mother find ways to equip the
accommodations after a journey in a covered wagon, prepared Harriet for
this start-up business venture. Moreover, she had spent nearly a decade
welcoming guests as boarders and diners in her La Push home and had
trained and supervised her cook, Sam. And by early 1902, Dan was gone
for good, so she was on her own.

The business flourished. Within a few months, a newspaper was
reporting on events at the hotel. Harriet's scrapbook includes several
pages with clippings from 1901 and 1902. From them, we learn that to
help keep her guests entertained, she acquired a piano and a Ping-Pong
table.[33] She gave a Monday-night, "cozy little dinner party" for five,[34] and
hosted other gatherings, including a summer solstice party, a Halloween
party, and a farewell party for court officials at the end of the district
court session. The women came "elegantly gowned" and the men were
"resplendent in full dress."[35] The guest list for some parties included as
many as forty people. An August 1902 article said of Harriet's boardinghouse, "This is probably the best appointed and best managed boarding
house in the North.... The house is beautifully furnished and lighted with

electricity throughout. The board furnished is the very best the market provides, and it is served in a manner that would do a credit to the fashionable boarding houses of the large cities."[36]

Harriet's son Chester turned thirteen in December 1902, and Harriet hosted a "jolly" birthday party for him. According to newspaper coverage, it included twenty guests and featured a "novel . . . serving of 'Jack Horner's pie.' The pie was a huge, round, shallow basket in the form of a conventional pie and encrusted with a newspaper cover. This was pierced with holes, through each of which issued a string." The guests gathered around the pie, took a string in hand, and repeated in unison the Mother Goose rhyme. At the word "plum," everyone jerked their strings, at the end of which were "pretty presents." In the evening, the party concluded with a sleigh ride, by which the guests were driven to their homes.[37]

Even when not the party's host, Harriet could be the center of attention. Another article reported that at a barn dance, a "'way down east hop,'" decorated as a "good old farm barn after the harvest season, . . . 75 couples . . . tripped the light fantastic till the wee sma' hours." Juicy apples filled a manger. Guests came in costumes associated with rural places. Harriet won a pearl-handled umbrella, her prize for "best sustained lady character."[38] After years of farming and raising cattle, Harriet would have felt right at home in an old farm barn, portraying a character associated with country living.

When not in character, Harriet always dressed elegantly, even if her look was old-fashioned. As a woman who had known her in the 1920s and '30s wryly remarked, "Mrs. Pullen wore the latest of styles of 1898; no matter what year it was." In the early Skagway years, Harriet made her own dresses. Later, according to the woman, she had them made to order, always in the same princess style, with form-fitting bodices and "stays that really gave her a shape . . . [and] the high neck and the long sleeves with the very tight cuffs that went almost up to her elbow, and then strings and strings of beads."[39] Her ankle-length skirts flowed over a substantial bustle. Pulled into her hourglass shape from shoulder to waist in a made-to-measure Spirella corset, she needed help getting dressed each morning.[40]

Harriet took particular pride in her hair. Enlisting the assistance of her young staff, she kept her striking mane in top condition. One woman who had worked as a waitress at the Pullen House recalled that her hair was still "red down to her ankles" well past middle age. She and her coworkers helped wash the hair and "sprinkle corn meal on it, and brush it 100 times. She wore it just like a crown. She was a regal beauty."[41]

Her erect posture, determined stride, and that hourglass shape gave her a commanding and confident air. The thick, stately braid wrapped around her head added inches to her already imposing height. Harriet, five feet, nine inches, was tall for her generation, a time when the average American woman was about five feet, three inches.[42] A "Junoesque woman with an air of command, straight as an arrow" was how one writer described her.[43] She was a woman to reckon with, yet always—at least in her role as hotelier, and even on horseback, where she always rode side-saddle—she was a lady.[44]

Even though Skagway's population was shrinking in the wake of the gold rush, there was a ready-made list of rotating residents for Harriet's boardinghouse, dining room, and parties. A number of mining engineers passed through Skagway after the gold rush on their way to and from the mines. As a port of entry, Skagway was home to US Customs officials. In addition, as the town was the terminus of the White Pass & Yukon Route, railroad officials continued to live there even after construction was complete.[45] The US Army in 1899 established a barracks in Skagway after a forest fire burned them out of their quarters in nearby Dyea. The officers moved into the Pullen House. The army stayed several years to prevent mob rule and to "show the flag" during the ongoing boundary dispute with Canada that continued until 1903. Captain Henry W. Hovey, the commander of the US Army's L Company, 24th Infantry (a unit of African-American soldiers), and other officers not only lived at the Pullen House but were also often guests at Harriet's parties.[46]

In December 1900, the US District Court began holding sessions each year in a building next to Harriet's establishment. Although lawyers and judges made perfect guests at her boardinghouse, having officers of the law nearby turned out to be a bit of a drawback, as Harriet was indicted for conducting her boardinghouse business without a license. She pled guilty,

12.2. "Farewell Banquet to Captain H. W. Hovey" at the Pullen House in Skagway in May 1902 (Harrie Clay Barley, photographer). ARCHIVES, UNIVERSITY OF ALASKA FAIRBANKS, J. BERNARD MOORE FAMILY PAPERS, ALBUM #1, UAF-1976-35-22

and the judge fined her fifteen dollars plus court costs. This, however, was light punishment compared to the one hundred dollars that eighty saloon operators had been fined for similar offenses in January 1899.[47]

Skagway became Alaska's first incorporated city in 1900.[48] Harriet took an active role in promoting the town as a tourist destination. August 5, 1902, was marked as the day three hundred tourists visited the town, a record breaker.[49] The future looked promising, so she leased Captain Moore's house for another year. In August 1903, she briefly considered a move to Juneau to take a position managing the Franklin Hotel but decided to stay put.[50] For a woman never "trained to work," as Willoughby put it, she was working hard and doing well.[51]

ON HER OWN AND ON HER WAY

Harriet and Dan's children were growing up. Skagway established its first school in 1898. Royal recalled attending school there for a short time, but when a teacher threatened to whip him, Harriet said she would whip the teacher. She thought better of that plan and instead removed Royal from the school in 1901 and sent him to Seattle to join Dee, who was boarding with a preacher and his wife in Seattle and attending a public high school.[52] Chester was in school in Quillayute for a time, and by his thirteenth birthday, in 1902, was in Skagway with Harriet.[53] Mildred completed her education at the free school in Ellensburg and, by 1902, had entered nursing school in New York City, where her uncle Harvey H. Smith lived.[54]

Harriet stretched her resources to keep the three older children in school. To supplement the family income, Royal and Chester sold the *Seattle Post-Intelligencer* to tourists and townspeople. Dee carried spikes and served as a water boy for the railroad during the summers.[55] By 1903, he was working as a locomotive fireman.[56] His letters to his mother mentioned his need for money to pay his landlord.[57] Royal recalled that at one time in Seattle, he and Dee ate discarded vegetables as well as chickens they found roosting in trees at night. To cover holes in his apparel, he recounted having to put cardboard in his shoes and paper in the seat of his pants.[58] "I got by," Royal told one interviewer.[59] In 1900, Dee was carefully recording his expenditures in letters to his mother and milking a cow to pay for his shoes, candy, and incidentals. He looked forward to his summers in Skagway, when he could earn more money, and asked Harriet to inquire of steamer officials if he could work his way north on a boat.[60]

Harriet's personal life and marriage also faced challenges. She may have suffered a miscarriage in the spring of 1900. In an October 3, 1900, letter to Wesley, Harriet's mother wrote, "Dan told . . . [Hattie] that I was the cause of her sickness last spring. He forgot to tell that they started to go to a party and carried her heavy baby."[61] It may be that Harriet had been pregnant in the spring of 1900, her "sickness" a euphemism for miscarriage. "Carried her heavy baby" perhaps refers to a pregnancy, as there were no babies in the family in 1900. A letter from Mary Jane to Harriet provides a hint as to the status of the marriage:

12.3. Dee Pullen standing on a locomotive near Skagway in about 1900.
COLLECTION VIRGINIA O. PHILLIPS, OAKLAND, CALIFORNIA

12.4. Harriet and her children, from left: Chester, Dee, Royal, and Mildred Pullen, in Skagway, ca. 1903. AUTHOR'S COLLECTION

*My dear Hattie I received your letter yesterday. Your secret is safe with
me. I did feel awfully guilty as though I was about to lose something
very dear to me but if I should gain an equivalent I would try and
submit to it. You have arrived at that period in life that you should be
your own judge of matters of such vital importance but I will give you
this advice. Try not to be deceived, consider calmly, and study human
nature, and do not be to hasty. The saying is one needs to winter &
summer with one to become acquainted. [I]f you have found your Ideal
I suppose you will be suited. I want to write a little more but dinner
is ready. Goodbye.*
 Lovingly, Mother[62]

This undated letter suggests that Harriet's secret is that she has found
a new love, her "Ideal." If true, there is no record of who the "Ideal" was,
nor is there any confirmation of a miscarriage.

Mary Jane's feeling that she might "lose something very dear to me"
may refer to losing Dan as a member of the Smith family. In spite of Dan's
malicious behavior toward the Quileute people, the Smiths revered him
as the one who had come to their rescue during their bout with typhoid
fever and had pointed them to their good land in Quillayute country.
After working on the railroad for a time, Dan seems to have been away
from the family, perhaps traveling, as early as 1900. In February of that
year, Dee wrote to Mildred, asking where their father was and what he
was doing.[63] Dan's role in helping Harriet get her business off the ground
is unclear. According to Royal, who turned fifteen in 1902, Dan became
"disgusted" with the efforts to start a boardinghouse, quarreled frequently
with Harriet, and left for the Klondike "around 1902."[64] Another suggestion of trouble in the marriage was Harriet's appearance in US District
Court in Skagway on December 12, 1901, to revoke her power of attorney
to Dan.[65]

After making his way from Skagway to the Klondike and down the
Yukon River, Dan worked in St. Michael, Alaska, until he had enough
money to return to Seattle.[66] Dan wrote to A. J. on February 25, 1902,
from a Seattle hotel, "I havent gon to work yet and dont know when I
shall. I am thourley [thoroughly] brock up dont care much what becomes

of me."[67] Five weeks later, A. J. wrote to Wesley, "Why did Hattie turn Dan out? Where is he?"[68] Harriet had decided to fend for herself. She had an excellent role model in her mother, who had single-handedly managed the family of eight children repeatedly while A. J. was away working or in the army. Harriet Smith Pullen, the independent entrepreneur, was on her own and on her way.[69]

Chapter Thirteen

The Pullen House

By the end of the first decade of the twentieth century, Skagway had become a genuine tourist destination. A Juneau newspaper promoted Skagway as a vacation spot "greater in majesty and beauty than the far-famed Switzerland."[1] A 1910 Skagway Commercial Club booklet described the Inside Passage steamer trip as "a luxury and a pleasure. . . . [The steamers] are spacious, comfortable, and the service is excellent." The booklet promised the passenger natural beauty, abundant game, romantic stories, and "thrilling escapades of the early days."[2] Among the thrilling escapades were ones that Harriet recounted to her guests.

After a few years leasing, Harriet bought Captain Moore's property sometime after 1904[3] and began operating the Pullen House as both a boardinghouse and a tourist hotel, a destination to cap an exciting sea journey up the Inside Passage. Harriet even collaborated with travel agents to arrange for travelers to lodge and eat at her establishment.[4]

People regularly commented on how attractive and comfortable the Pullen House was. Author Charlotte Cameron, visiting in 1919, wrote that it had the "air of a real home," although Harriet had insisted that she stay in a special room with a singular view, the "Texas."[5] According to visitors in the 1920s, the common spaces included a "large sun parlor crowded with chairs of every description, brilliant geraniums, a large stone fireplace with a crackling fire, elk, moose, deer, and mountain goat heads, one whole wall absolutely covered thick with framed pictures, diplomas, newspaper articles."[6] The grounds featured a stone-rimmed carriage circle, two trout streams, and a small island connected to the lawn by rustic bridges.[7]

13.1. Harriet with her geraniums in the Pullen House sun parlor, ca. 1920. SKAG-
WAY MUSEUM, 93.01.402

Harriet equipped the Pullen House with modern conveniences and expanded the accommodations in several stages. Said to have been the first hotel in Alaska to have centralized steam heat, the Pullen House also boasted hot and cold running water, with bathtubs adjacent to its twenty rooms.[8] In the 1920s, she moved another hotel to her site to enlarge the main building's accommodations and added a bungalow where families could stay.[9] The property also included a horse barn and groom's cabin.[10]

The letterhead stationery Harriet used in 1918 to promote her business featured the following: "The Pullen House, H. S. PULLEN, PROPRIETOR, The Modern Hostelry of Alaska, ELEGANTLY FURNISHED APARTMENTS, SINGLE OR EN SUITE, ELECTRIC LIGHTS, BATHS, TELEPHONES. TABLES SUPPLIED WITH MILK AND CREAM FROM OUR OWN JERSEY DAIRY. SKAGWAY—The Garden Spot and Summer Resort of Alaska." In the upper-left corner next to all of this text is a large photograph of a long, elegantly set table in the hotel's dining room. Along the left margin is a list of "WHAT YOU CAN SEE AND DO IN AND ABOUT SKAGWAY," twenty-three items in all, from hiking to the Denver Glacier, to seeing an old shipwreck, fishing for salmon, trout, and grayling, taking pictures at midnight, and walking "for miles without crawling thru underbrush and weeds."[11]

Part of the appeal of the Pullen House was Harriet's persona. When asked in an interview, "Can you tell me . . . more about Ma Pullen and the Pullen House?" Lucille Hudson Elsner, born and raised in Skagway, and for a time a waitress in the hotel dining room, answered, "Oh, I could tell stories about Ma Pullen for a week! She was a character. She was a character."[12]

Harriet met her guests at the Skagway wharf driving an old horse-drawn omnibus. It may have started out as a necessary mode of transportation, but as time went by, it became a relic and a tourist attraction. Sometimes she rode to the wharf on horseback. Her guests took advantage of a guided tour of Skagway's sights offered by her friend, Skagway promoter Martin Itjen, in his old streetcar.[13] One anonymous diarist writing in 1927 described how Harriet drove him and his companion in a "great big touring car" to visit a flower garden in town, as well as the home

13.2. "Mrs. Pullen and Pullen House Bus in Early Days," taken between 1904 and 1914, made into a postcard. SKAGWAY MUSEUM, DEDMAN COLLECTION, 1238

of an eccentric neighbor who displayed wild trout that would eat from one's hand.[14]

By the late 1920s, Harriet had become a full-blown "character," not only in her behavior but also in her appearance. One visitor noted she was "a fine looking huge tall woman, high and large of bosom, laced in waist and amply bustled behind. She walked with a goodly stride and toes out, . . . [a] striking figure in her old fashioned blue suit."[15] Another described her as "one of the most peculiar characters I ever expect to see."[16] Despite her odd dress, she maintained a level of decorum. When asked by an interviewer if she had ever worn trousers, given all the work and horse-back riding she had done over the years, she replied, "Men's clothes! . . . Indeed not! I've always been able to handle myself in skirts of suitable length. Do you think I'd permit my boys to see their mother in trousers?"[17]

Although Harriet's persona and hotel accommodations attracted a steady stream of visitors to the Pullen House, she was not a stellar businessperson. Florence Clothier, a traveler on a tight budget, wrote of Harriet in a letter to her family: "That wonderful woman, Mrs. Pullen . . . did an amazing thing, she charged us a total of twelve dollars for our 3 whole days in Skagway. This covered everything and as much as we could eat. She was certainly awfully awfully nice to us."[18] Author Herb

Hilscher visited the Pullen House for one week as a child in 1906. He recalled Harriet's generosity in giving his family the money for steamer tickets so that they could return to Seattle after his father lost everything in a failed attempt to strike gold in the Klondike.[19] Royal stated that her openhandedness, while pleasing to her guests, also worked against the hotel's profits. "If they'd praise her, she'd give them the place," he said in an interview.[20]

Elsner recalled that Harriet was "noted in town for not paying her bills. Well, I mean . . . she always paid them, but I mean, it was a problem. . . . She was always in debt to the bank. . . . She was always behind."[21] Royal commented in an article, "She never got out of debt, since she was a poor businesswoman, and I was forever bailing her out, both before and after I was married. [My wife] Eloise and I always were apprehensive when a letter from Skagway arrived—what new trouble was she in?"[22] Poor businessperson or not, Harriet compensated for her limitations with her skills as a storyteller and performer.

A RACONTEUR

Royal said Harriet had talent as a raconteur from the day she was born.[23] As a waitress who worked for her in the late 1930s put it, "she certainly had the gift of gab and could mesmerize people with her line of bull."[24] Harriet's Klondike Gold Rush tales were theatrical, entertaining, and embellished. Clothier witnessed one of Harriet's storytelling sessions and wrote in her diary in 1928:

> *Mrs. Pullen has dramatic ability and theatric sense. She talks with her whole body, in telling of the dances of the Indian medicine men she imitates the movements of their bodies and she drones out the rythm of the circle of squa's. She has a power that does make a shiver travel up your spine, or a tight feeling come in your throat. She advertised a lecture for the next morning. All the tourists gathered but I believe no towns-people were allowed. She held her audience spell-bound and I think there was more than one damp handkerchief. She was clever in her quick shifts from pathos to burlesque comedy.[25]*

Harriet embroidered some of her stories. For example, according to Clothier, she told her audience that a missionary father had raised her among Indians. One might characterize some of A. J.'s activities at Fort Rice while in the army as missionary-like, but Harriet was not there. There is no evidence of any Indian peoples living near her in Wisconsin or Dakota during her childhood. In Washington, as a teenager, she did cook at the Neah Bay Agency for a short time alongside her father. In La Push, she lived among the Quileute people, but by then she was an adult.

Seemingly in a trancelike state, Harriet concluded her performances with a dramatic change of clothing into an ermine-pelt ceremonial shirt decorated with moose-hide fringe, red wool, and blue, yellow, green, and white glass beads said to have been given to her by a dying Tlingit chief. She often wore additional items of Alaska Native clothing, including an Athapaskan dentalium-shell breastplate.[26] Elsner recalled that the performances took place regularly, and would begin in the late morning. "You'd just see them in there crying. And sometimes they'd take a basket and take a collection up for her. . . . And then she managed to get through just in time lunch was ready. So of course, they'd all pile into the dining room there, and she could serve, oh, somewhere around, I would say, 100, 160 people."[27] Harriet even made available for purchase postcards of herself posed in various ways—driving her horse-drawn omnibus, wearing her Tlingit shirt, standing before the Pullen House, and riding sidesaddle on horseback.

Harriet enlivened tales of the early days of Skagway for her guests not only through her performances but also with her extensive collection of Klondike Gold Rush memorabilia, Alaska Native artifacts, and Russian-American colonial decorative items, displayed behind a locked door labeled "MUSEUM 50 cts."[28] She earmarked the proceeds to help pay for her granddaughter's college education.[29] Objects ranging from valuable antiques and artifacts to items of everyday use, like old newspapers, curling irons, and coffee mills, packed the room.[30] Harriet could show her guests the shoulder holster and first wooden grave marker of legendary swindler Soapy Smith, as well as gold rush–era essentials such as packsaddles, trappers' snowshoes, and mosquito net headgear.

13.3. Harriet in her Tlingit ermine-pelt shirt and Athapaskan dentalium-shell breastplate, with strings of trade beads and a Puget Sound–area Native American basket (undated). COLLECTION WALTER R. AND MARY E. PATTERSON, SEATTLE, WASHINGTON

13.4. A postcard of the Pullen House and Harriet, taken between 1914 and 1916. AUTHOR'S COLLECTION

13.5. A postcard labeled "Mrs. Pullen, Horse, & Dog," taken between 1909 and 1913, looking west on Broadway, just north of Fourth Street in Skagway (Draper & Company, photographer). AUTHOR'S COLLECTION

Notwithstanding her 1880s membership in the Good Templars temperance organization, she had numerous framed advertisements for beer, whiskey, and wine, spirit jugs and bottles, beer steins and tankards. Several "Imperial Tsarist Russian" brass samovars and jardinières reminded visitors of the Russian colony that was once in Alaska. One interviewer described her two dozen long strings of Tlingit trading beads dating from the years of the Russian fur trade[31] as "sparkling rows of sapphire, amethyst, and ruby-coloured glass, . . . each bead remarkably smooth, cut by hand, and of a different pattern . . . a treasure indeed!"[32] Her extensive collection of Alaska Native material also included two museum-quality, fringed, cedar-bark and mountain goat–wool Chilkat dancing blankets, beaded Tlingit ceremonial shirts fashioned from blue-and-red Hudson Bay flannel blankets, and several carved totems.[33]

During the years after the gold rush, Harriet enlarged her collection as Skagway's population headed south, selling off possessions or leaving them behind. She had a dozen slot machines, several pianos, windup phonographs, and three large paintings of nude women that once hung over the bar of a Skagway saloon. Naturally, there were stories to go with each object in the collection. Such entrepreneurial moves drew guests to the Pullen House and helped to develop Skagway's tourist industry.[34]

Harriet also made a name for herself locally by becoming active in the Women's Christian Temperance Union and the women's suffrage movement. She drove her horse-drawn coach around town, picking up women to take them to the polls on Election Day, beginning in 1914. A photograph taken in front of the Pullen House shows Harriet in the driver's seat with reins in hand. A banner across the coach reads, "VOTE Non Partisan Union Ticket."[35] The Alaska Territorial Legislature granted women the right to vote in 1913, six years before the US Congress passed the Nineteenth Amendment, granting the same to women across the country.

DYEA

Seventeen years after starting her business, Harriet found a new way to expand the Pullen House operation. She homesteaded land on the mountainside just east of Skagway but lost everything to a forest fire in 1912.

Relinquishing that homestead claim made her eligible to stake another one. Planning to begin farming, in July 1915 she filed homestead papers for a 320-acre claim on the site of the abandoned town of Dyea, about six miles from Skagway. Farming at a goodly distance from home was something she had experienced in both Dakota and La Push.[36]

Dyea, once a small Tlingit fishing camp, developed suddenly into a gold-rush gateway center in 1897 as the start of a major route to the goldfields, the Chilkoot Trail. About five thousand to eight thousand people set up tents and constructed buildings, creating a boomtown that was all but gone by 1900.[37] In the aftermath of the gold rush, Skagway superseded Dyea, mainly because it had a more-navigable harbor. With the construction of the Brackett Wagon Road and then the White Pass & Yukon Route, Dyea was doomed. It did offer, however, flat, relatively treeless, arable land. With the long, light days of summer, one could make a go of it farming, or so Harriet believed.

Two men had made land claims at Dyea primarily for the purpose of dismantling the town and selling the salvage to merchants in Skagway.[38] With their work done, they wanted out. They both relinquished their land claims back to the US government and offered to sell their improvements and what remained of the town—houses, cabins, barns, outbuildings, and a warehouse—to Harriet.

She took the men up on their offer. Some probably thought she was crazy. Dyea had been abandoned for many reasons. The tidewater receded more than two miles from the southern border of her claim, making a springtime tidal rise and fall of twenty-five feet. The shallow Taiya, or Dyea, River, which ran along the edge of her claim, changed channels occasionally, eating away the land and leaving dry sloughs over the delta. The sandy soil needed tons of fertilizer because it contained little organic material and drained quickly.[39] But Harriet believed she could grow crops and graze cattle where the town once stood. Her plan was to build a farm, or a ranch, as she called it, which would supply her hotel dining room with eggs, chickens, beef, dairy products, and produce.

Getting to Dyea was an ordeal. Traversing the rugged land route was only, as one observer put it, for a strong, athletic man, and only in the summer.[40] Access by water took one and a half hours in a rowboat in good weather, and was treacherous much of the time.[41] Horses and cattle had to be towed on a scow behind the rowboat. Reaching the property during low tide required a two-mile hike across the tidal flats.[42] Sometimes Harriet made the trip alone, having learned a thing or two about rowing in the canoes of La Push. A Skagway acquaintance stated in a letter, "Mrs. Pullen has made this trip at every hour of the day and night . . . and frequently she has rowed a skiff and towed a big scow more than once all by herself . . . and altho I am not fearful of the water and am willing to take the ordinary risks of life I would not do what she has done in this respect."[43]

No stranger to rough seas, Harriet had survived a shipwreck a decade earlier on a trip from Skagway to Quillayute country to visit her mother. As reported on the front page of the Port Angeles *Tribune-Times* on January 18, 1907, Harriet and other passengers left East Clallam headed for Neah Bay aboard a steamship in "the teeth of a howling gale and a snow storm so thick that her master could not see a ship's length ahead." Near shore, the ship struck rocks. The rough seas made it impossible to launch the lifeboats. The captain kept his eight passengers as comfortable as possible through the night, even though the ship was listing badly. In the morning, rafts, lifeboats, and tugboats began unloading passengers, crew, and freight. The newspaper account continued its description of Harriet's harrowing experience: "Mrs. Pullen, although one of the most fearless of the passengers, underwent the most terrible experience of all."[44] Another newspaper account quoted Harriet:

> *I got on the raft with one other passenger and was scarcely on it when an immense big sea lifted the raft high above the side of the boat. In settling back into the water the raft struck on the quarter rail, turning over completely. I was thrown into the water with the raft on top of me. I had presence of mind enough to reach up my hands for something to cling to, and caught one of the slats of the raft. Knowing what was above and that my only hope lay in reaching the edge of it, I worked along the slats to the round log at the side. I got my head out of water and clung on like grim death.[45]*

It was the steamer *Rosalie*, the one Harriet had taken to Skagway ten years earlier, that carried her and the other passengers back to Port Angeles, where friends took her in. With her new venture in Dyea, Harriet would not let a challenge like rough seas or even hindrances like a corset and an ankle-length dress stand in her way.

"An Unlimited Amount of Nerve"

Harriet arranged for her longtime, trusted staff members, Jenjiro and Lena Ikuta, to manage the Pullen House and took up residence on her new homestead claim.[46] For the first four weeks she slept in the barn, and then in a cabin that lacked windows and a door. Her hired man stayed in a shack. They cleared the land and harvested the hay that one of the former owners had planted. In October, Royal joined her. Together they managed a crew of four men, clearing forty acres, putting up fences, and replacing the shingles on the barn.[47] Harriet cooked for the men. She remodeled an old house on the property, planning for Mildred and Mildred's young children to join her.[48] Mildred had apparently left her husband in Washington at this point.

When Royal left the following March, Harriet hired Tom Brown. He and Harriet's Dyea neighbor to the north, Billy Matthews, "were having fights every day over this woman. . . . I had almost more than I could handle," Harriet recalled.[49] Her problems with the Matthews family were just beginning. Brown managed the farm while Harriet went back and forth to her hotel.[50]

One year later, Harriet had her farm up and running. At harvest time in 1916, an article in the *Daily Alaskan* of Skagway reported on Harriet's progressive farming operation, and noted that it took an "unlimited amount of nerve and sticktoitiveness to plank down on one of these locations and work the required improvements." The article went on to say that floods had required Harriet to build a bulkhead and a jetty to keep the river from eating away her land. Three buildings on the property had to be moved to safer locations. Mrs. Pullen, the article continued, would "direct the fall ploughing," and "next summer she will surprise Skagway with some prize strawberries raised on her home place."[51]

Just as the renovated house she had planned to live in was ready, Harriet received a telephone call at Skagway from Tom Brown, who told her that her house had burned to the ground under suspicious circumstances. He had found evidence suggesting that Harriet's neighbor and his own rival in romance, Billy Matthews, had set the fire.[52] In spite of this setback, Harriet carried on. Mildred and her children would soon arrive, so Harriet went to Seattle and replaced everything lost in the fire to render another house on the property habitable.

In 1918, as the time drew near for Harriet to make final proof on her homestead, the government surveyor made his appointed visit. Harriet showed him around. He made sure her claim observed the rights of Alaska Natives, one of whom had an adjoining claim. The surveyor talked to him personally, his son translating, to be certain he was satisfied with the boundaries Harriet was claiming. Either more thoughtful than her husband had been toward the Quileutes or she had learned a lesson, Harriet explicitly asked the surveyor to exclude from her claim a small burial ground that included both settlers and Native Alaskans.[53]

The surveyor's notes on Harriet's homestead indicate that she had three horses and thirty-seven head of cattle, and had raised eleven tons of potatoes and other root crops, fifty tons of oats and hay, and ample "garden truck" and berries the year before. Her dairy had produced large quantities of milk, cream, and buttermilk and a ton of butter, rare treats in Alaska. One hundred chickens rounded out the farm's production.[54] Another visitor to the farm in 1918 reported seeing a "splendid" stable, a blacksmith shop, a storage building, a model dairy, and many acres under cultivation.[55] The farm had rapidly become a productive operation.

Kicked Her Horses, Beat Her Dog

Harriet had made a wise business decision in taking on this property, or so it seemed. The fire at her house, however, was just the first in a string of challenges. Harriet had to let Tom Brown go in 1917 after she found that he had kicked her horses, beat her dog, and used such offensive language that Mildred was afraid of him.[56] Angry and feeling mistreated, Brown then sued Harriet for back wages. Not satisfied with the court's decision, he took revenge on Harriet. The man Harriet hired to take Brown's place heard him say, "She won't ever get this place. Her troubles have just commenced. I'll make it hot for her."[57] Harriet's boatman recounted, "When Mrs. Pullen fired Tom Brown, he got mad and swore that he would not let her prove up. . . ."[58] The smoldering conflict would soon ignite into a firestorm.

William Matthews, the head of the family that was among Harriet's few Dyea neighbors, had been homesteading his 154-acre-claim with his Alaska Native wife and their twelve children for several years.[59] It was his son Billy who was alleged to have burned down Harriet's house. When Harriet arrived in Dyea, for reasons that are not clear, the Matthews family began making life difficult for her. Five of the nine sons in the family were adults, and three others were old enough to create serious mischief. It seems, according to a man who worked for Harriet, the family didn't "want anyone else in Dyea except themselves."[60] They did everything imaginable to try to drive Harriet out.

After Harriet's Dyea house burned, she was reluctant to make accusations, saying, "I have had many obstacles thrown in my way—by whom I do not know."[61] Olaf Dale, whom Harriet hired after firing Tom Brown, stated that one day a structural brace in the barn gave way when he leaned on it. Then a second brace fell. He examined all the braces and reported that "they had all been tampered with and pried loose with a bar (evidently) so that the building would surely have collapsed if a strong wind had come up. Someone had deliberately tried to make that building unsafe."[62] A gable in one of her buildings collapsed. She found other buildings on the property with compromised structural elements, fences torn down, and gates broken. Her tools went missing. Someone tied her boat so low that when the tide came in, it filled with water and she lost the whole vessel. Three other times her boats were set adrift. Someone shot her burro, and when she had a cow slaughtered, its flesh was found to be full of shot.[63] Mildred kept a diary for a time and recorded in it that Billy Matthews had broken their telephone line.[64] Harriet suspected that the Matthews family was responsible for all of the trouble. There was almost no one else living at Dyea.

"I COULD KNOCK IT DOWN IF I WANTED TO"

One day in 1918, while working at the Pullen House, Harriet got a call from Mildred. It was an emergency; Harriet needed to get there right away. George Matthews, another of William's sons, was trying to jump Harriet's claim by moving into a cabin on the property. Harriet found a boatman, and when she arrived in Dyea, Mildred, who had been watching the situation from afar, thought it best if Harriet not confront the culprit. To do so would put her life at risk. Harriet's response, as she told it later, was "Two can play at that game. You go home with the children and I'll see to this."[65]

In later years, an old Alaskan recounted the details of the claim-jumping incident to a writer:

> *A fine figure of a woman she was then. A splendid, red-headed young matron sitting her horse sideways in the long, tight-fitting riding habit of the time, but riding, by gad, like a plains Indian. And she certainly had her dander up that day! She came galloping out of the forest and charged down on the jumpers, skirts a-flying, hair all tumbled to her waist, and a revolver spitting bullets. The jumpers moved off her land pronto. But they kept sneaking back and in order to protect her rights, Mrs. Pullen went over there and lived in the little cabin for a while. Many a time she sat up all night, a Winchester across her knee, watching for the jumpers. In the end she won out.*[66]

A vivid image, especially considering the hair "all tumbled to her waist" was red. Supposedly, it was an eyewitness account, but the "young matron" part of the story is cause for some skepticism, given that she was about fifty-six years old at the time.

Harriet's homestead problems culminated in a challenge to her homestead claim brought by the General Land Office after Tom Brown reported to the land authorities that she had not lived on the property the required length of time. Harriet's recounting of the incidents comes from court testimony, delivered under oath, in *United States v. Harriet S. Pullen*, General Land Office, Department of the Interior.

As Harriet testified, she went to the cabin that day with her six-shooter in her pocket. "They had nailed boards over a few windows. They had set up a door, no hinges. I went in with a match to look around. They had set up a stove and I took the stove outside. Then I went upstairs. I took a long board and knocked every shingle off the house. It was my house and I could knock it down if I wanted to," she said.[67] George Matthews, who witnessed her entry into the cabin, testified, "Mrs. Pullen was standing in the window with a hatchet breaking things up. I came to within six feet of the door and she up with a six-shooter and threatened to shoot me. She threatened to kill me if I came closer. . . . She broke up what we had in there, everything—smashed it up and tore down the house."[68] Harriet continued, "The morning I commenced to tear the house to pieces, the Matthews came down, eleven of them strong, and they started to come into the house to throw me out. . . . When George Matthews came to go in the door I said, 'You stay back.' He said I had no right there—that I didn't live there and that they were going to jump the property."[69]

From the court testimony also comes information on Harriet's subsequent arrest for threatening to shoot George Matthews during his claim-jumping attempt. There were also details of two civil cases brought against her—the one by Tom Brown, for her refusal to pay him back salary, and another by George Matthews, for damaging the cabin's stove.[70]

What could have prompted a successful and ladylike hotelier to act this way? Although Harriet had heretofore never been arrested, she was well acquainted with the world of sheriffs, judges, lawyers, and juries, both as defendant and plaintiff. In an eerie replay of what had happened to Hattie and Dan in La Push, it was happening again to Harriet, but this time, some twenty years later, she was alone. One way to look at it is to say she was better prepared for the long battle this time. She had learned her lessons on how to go up against litigious individuals and the US government. She had fought for her rights in the legal arena. As Royal said of her, "She was the fighter in the family," and now she would put that indomitable, fighting spirit to use again in another long, drawn-out court case.[71]

Despite all of the difficulties Harriet suspected the Matthews family had caused her, she behaved humanely toward them. When Billy's Alaska Native wife, Sophia, became sick in 1919, Harriet offered her telephone to Billy so that he could call a doctor in Skagway. Royal went in a boat to bring the doctor to Dyea while Harriet went to Sophia's bedside and stayed through the night and the next day, nursing her.[72]

"NEWLY DISCOVERED EVIDENCE"

In July 1919, Harriet submitted to the Local Land Office her proofs of property improvements and three years of residency on the homestead. It was then that Tom Brown, acting as a friend of the government, filed his spiteful protest, claiming that she had been in residence only three weeks. In November, the commissioner of the General Land Office in Washington, DC, ordered the cancellation of her claim because, he wrote, she had failed to maintain residence for a period of at least seven months each year for three years as required by law. Harriet asked for a hearing. The matter went to the Juneau Local Land Office, where a clerk began an investigation.[73]

Meanwhile, Harriet had other legal matters to sort out. After her arrest, a jury in Skagway had acquitted her on charges of threatening to shoot George Matthews, concluding that she had a right to defend her claim. Harriet lost the Matthews lawsuit over the destruction of the stove, and although she considered mounting an appeal, she decided against it to avoid the aggravation.[74]

The Homestead land case hearing took place in June 1920. Harriet opened her testimony by describing the vision she had brought to her Dyea property when she began homesteading, giving insight into her thinking: "what a tangled wilderness and what a beauty spot it might be made into. . . . I am tired of this hotel life and want to get away. This will give me a chance. . . . I can make a beautiful home here."[75]

A number of other witnesses testified for both sides under the direction of the same Land Office clerk who had gathered the evidence. He then issued his exhaustive report, recommending the cancellation of Harriet's Homestead claim. Again, as it had in La Push in 1887, word came that the Local Land Office would withhold her final certificate for her patent. The arguments used to recommend withholding, based on the report, were: 1) Harriet had no hard evidence against the Matthews family, who had admitted only to the shooting of the burro; 2) Harriet had made the Homestead claim for trade and business purposes as an accessory to her hotel, not as a bona fide residence; and 3) Evidence showed she had voted in one of Skagway's elections, calling into question her legal residence.

Harriet did not help her case any when she stated in an affidavit, "During 1918, [I] slept about fifty nights on the [Dyea] place off and on. I don't remember the exact days I was over there. I have always considered residence requirements on the homestead to be a farce."[76] The Local Land Office's conclusion: She believed in homesteading by "proxy," and had not met the residency requirements.[77]

Once the disappointing news made its way into Harriet's hands, she went into action. The "fighter in the family" would not back down. In a letter dated February 12, 1921, she asserted her right to apply for a new hearing "on newly discovered evidence."[78] She was well versed in the dogged process needed to go up against the US government, but in preparing her case, she had been led to believe by the Land Office clerk that a lawyer to represent her would be unnecessary.[79] Therefore, she had asked Royal to conduct the examinations and cross-examinations. Perhaps because she had paid lawyers so much in her La Push land battle, she thought it was time to try doing without them. It was a decision she would regret. It is clear from reading the transcript that lawyering was not Royal's forte. Going forward, Harriet would be using the advice of an attorney. With his input, her case became much more persuasive in her favor.

Harriet and her new lawyer gathered affidavits from people who had worked for her and submitted them to the Land Office. Each affidavit made a compelling case that spite had driven Tom Brown and the Matthews family to harass her. Olaf Dale, Harriet's second farm manager, corroborated the claim about the barn having been deliberately structurally compromised, stating, "I have tried to show that the Matthews crowd did everything they could to scare Mrs. Pullen out, and when they saw that they couldn't scare her out, they threatened that they would keep her from getting the homestead when she tried to prove up on it."[80] He and others stated that Harriet's family had lived on the homestead for eighteen months straight, and that she had been back and forth between Skagway and Dyea several times a week.[81] The affidavits supported what the government surveyor had said during the hearing. George Matthews had drawn a gun on him and Harriet while he was there to make the official survey. He stated that the next day Matthews told him, " 'Mrs. Pullen had no right to the land and that he had friends who would see that she did not get [the land].' "[82] Harriet's case grew substantially stronger.

Harriet sent the documents to the General Land Office in Washington, DC. On October 4, 1921, the commissioner issued his ruling— a reversal of the Local Land Office's most recent decision. The basis for the reversal included new rationales. Harriet's family, consisting of her daughter and grandchildren, was always on the homestead. Her frequent trips to Skagway requiring time away from the homestead in order to support her family "became necessary by reason of the fact that her son who managed the business for her was in the United States Army during the war."[83] This, of course, was not true, because Royal never managed the business and had left Dyea a year before the United States entered the war, but a suggestion that she had a son who fought for his country in Europe added to the sympathy quotient. The reversal of the decision, in essence, relied on the concept that "where a man's family resides there also he resides."[84]

Harriet had won the battle, but, not taking any chances, she solicited letters of support from a US senator, who was the chairman of the Committee on Territories, and a retired US Army colonel living in Washington, DC, perhaps someone Dee knew, for by then he was an army officer. The process went ahead without a hitch. In October, the Local Land Office issued her final certificate, which authorized the issuance of her patent. The document, dated February 23, 1922, bore the signature of the patent-signing surrogate of President Warren G. Harding, whom she would meet the following year. Finally, the homestead was hers.[85] A Skagway newspaper reported her victory and said of her property, "she had converted it from a waste tract into what is probably the best agricultural stock and dairy farm in Alaska. . . . Mrs. Pullen . . . is known to more people than any other one woman in the North."[86]

The poetic justice of this chapter in Harriet's life is difficult to overlook. In 1898, Harriet lost one long battle and her land, the upshot of a decision by the General Land Office, only to win another long battle and her own homestead twenty-four years later, again through a decision of the General Land Office. It's worth noting, too, that although the situations vastly differed, in both cases her contests involved close neighbors who were Native peoples.

She continued to work her Dyea land, apparently free of harassment from the Matthews clan. Harriet's empathy may have helped. Although she had heard from her land claim's former owner that they were difficult neighbors, during her court testimony, she said:

"I thought I could get along with them. I told myself that I would be so kind to them that they couldn't find any fault with me. I thought that I could get along with anybody."

"Were you acquainted with the Matthews boys before you went over to the Dyea homestead?" the lawyer asked her.

"No, I had seen them about but didn't know much about them."

"You never had any trouble with them?"

"No," Harriet replied, "they stole some tools from us. We found them and got them back. Billy apologized for it. He wasn't to blame. Some white boys got him to do it."[87]

Perhaps this attitude and the kindness Harriet had extended to Billy Matthews's wife, Sophia, when she was sick helped to mitigate the Matthews family's hostility. According to Harriet, Sophia had said to her from her sickbed, "I am sorry that we have had trouble over here. If I had known there would be any trouble I would never have come over here [to Dyea]. . . . I can't stand up under this trouble any longer. Billy has the money to buy you out."[88] Sophia may have envisioned that as a solution to the conflict, but Harriet had no intention of selling.

Her Dyea land supplied the hotel dining room for years to come, even though, according to Royal, the place was never highly productive.[89] Harriet, however, subscribed to the agrarian myth that had driven her father for so many years. Even when the vagaries of the growing season forced her to import strawberries from Seattle, she would proudly and disingenuously tell her guests they were her prize specimens, fresh from her ranch.[90] At least some of the time, they were.

Chapter Fourteen

New Century

The Quileute Nation

For the Quileute people, the new century brought a welcome resolution to their seventeen-year conflict with the Pullens. Today, the village of La Push, with a population of several hundred people, is still home to the Quileute Nation. The rugged and stunning beauty of its surroundings, including Olympic National Park, makes it a tourist destination for whale watching, storm watching, fishing, surfing, and hiking on the Pacific Northwest National Scenic Trail. The Quileute Oceanside Resort— a string of handsome cabins and camping facilities situated along the beach—is comfortable and welcoming. In the village are a grocery store, a restaurant, a fish hatchery, a seafood company, a marina, and a US Coast Guard Motor Lifeboat Station.

Since 2005, the phenomenal success of Stephenie Meyer's *Twilight* series of books and films about teenage love, vampires, and werewolves has brought broad attention and fans to La Push and to the nearby town of Forks.[1] One of the main characters in the series, Jacob Black, is a Quileute and a shape-shifting, vampire-fighting werewolf. The release of the books and films has spurred fan clubs, tours of the story's sites, and merchandising of all manner of *Twilight*-related products.

The phenomenon has raised questions about commercial exploitation and the role that indigenous peoples should play in the use of their cultural property. An op-ed piece in the *New York Times* in 2010 argued that the Quileutes should be able to participate in decisions concerning their cultural property, citing an incident in which a website publisher sought permission to film in the area from the Forks Chamber of Commerce but neglected to do the same for La Push and the Quileute Nation. The film crew even trespassed into a cemetery and recorded Quileute gravesites. The filmmakers later removed the images from the website at the tribe's request.

Questions remain about the exclusion of the Quileute people from benefiting from the profits engendered by the commercial activity surrounding *Twilight*, particularly given the poverty that many Quileutes live with.[2] The Quileutes themselves have mixed opinions about their new fame. Some are not pleased, but the notoriety has brought opportunities for them to explain accurately their stories, traditions, and culture. With input from a Quileute advisory committee, the Seattle Art Museum mounted a 2010 exhibition, which featured a collection of Quileute objects from the Smithsonian and a timeline of their major historical events. It offered an opportunity for the Quileutes to share their culture with the outside world.[3]

After years of struggle, the Quileute Nation succeeded in regaining some of the land that was once their traditional hunting and gathering grounds when President Obama signed into law the Quileute Tsunami and Flood Protection Act on February 27, 2012. Rising sea levels have raised concern about the vulnerability of the village of La Push, much of which is very close to the sea. Now residents have higher ground on which to build and retreat if necessary.[4]

The Quileute Nation has survived for centuries, and it continues in the twenty-first century, managing its own governance and public municipal services. It has a tribal school, an active senior center, a newsletter, *Bayak: The Talking Raven*, and an ongoing series of cultural and community events such as drum circles, support groups, and, every July, a three-day cultural festival, Quileute Days, open to the public.[5]

A. J. AND MARY JANE SMITH

A. J.'s conflicted approach to life continued for years—devoted to his family and farming, the most tethered of pursuits, on one hand, and committed to more mobile, social endeavors on the other. He even had a dual impulse toward homesteading. To possess and improve his own land was

14.1. A Smith family portrait taken in Quillayute in June 1896, with each family member wearing or holding a flower. Prominently displayed in A. J.'s pocket is a copy of *War Cry*, a Salvation Army publication (David T. Smith, photographer). WASHINGTON STATE LIBRARY MANUSCRIPTS COLLECTION, A. WESLEY SMITH PAPERS, 1853–1935, M.S. 172

one side of the dyad, but an opposing impulse kept asserting itself—to keep moving for one reason or another, for speculation, economic necessity, or simply wanderlust. This duality is the subtext of A. J.'s life story.

A. J. in his later years continued the peripatetic path he had set for himself in his youth. After his move to Seattle in 1880, he struggled to sell books and served as a roving newspaper reporter, roaming around the Puget Sound region. Probably looking for the social contact he so loved, A. J. joined a number of fraternal and service organizations, including the Salvation Army. Combining his Christianity with social service, he rose through the ranks and proudly wears his captain's cap in several photographic portraits.

14.2. The gravestone of Andrew Jackson Smith (1832–1917) and Mary Jane Stewart Smith (1836–1916) at the Quillayute Prairie Cemetery, Quillayute, Washington, in 2015. PHOTOGRAPH BY THE AUTHOR

A multitalented, resourceful, nineteenth-century westering man, he earned a living working at more than a dozen different jobs—as farmer, teacher, town clerk, school clerk, election supervisor, broom maker, cattleman, brick hauler, water deliveryman, sign maker, hotel office worker, surveyor, cook, blacksmith, assistant Indian agent, postmaster, reporter, book salesman, photography canvasser, justice of the peace,[6] and Salvation Army captain. In the Union Army, he served as carpenter, baker, typesetter, printer, mapmaker, and visitor of the sick and wounded. He also wrote poems, preached, exhorted, and proselytized from the Bible, organized Sunday school classes, and raised eight children.

For a few years after A. J. left Quillayute, he and Mary Jane corresponded and visited each other regularly. If the marriage wasn't rocky then, however, it certainly was by the late 1880s. In April of 1886, Mary Jane expressed in a letter to Wesley her wish that A. J. be more judicious with his money, spend less on himself, and find a way to send more to the family.[7] Harvey H. Smith, A. J.'s brother, in an 1888 letter to Mary Jane expressed his deep dismay at her separation from A. J., a "disgrace to me . . . to your children, and . . . to Our Heavenly Father." Harvey then explicitly listed the steps she should follow to mend the rift between them, including making herself more sexually available to her husband.[8]

After several years around the turn of the century living in Pennsylvania, A. J. was back in the Seattle area in 1910. He reported to the census taker that he was divorced, although I was unable to find any confirming documentation. Perhaps he and Mary Jane eventually reconciled. A neighbor recorded in her diary that the two had gone "to the [La Push] beach to camp" in April 1914. Mary Jane, reportedly in a feeble condition in November 1915, at age seventy-nine, died on October 25, 1916, in Quillayute.[9]

A. J. died three months later at an old soldiers' home near Seattle on January 9, 1917, at the age of eighty-four. A. J. and Mary Jane are buried in the Quillayute Prairie Cemetery under a single headstone engraved with their names in adjacent (but not-quite-touching) hearts.

Dan Pullen

After Dan's departure from Skagway, he was "thourley [thoroughly] brock up," as he put it, depressed and at loose ends, living in several Seattle hotels in 1902.[10] Royal recalled that his father attended his football games in Seattle and gave him money when he could, but it wasn't much, as Dan did not work steadily due to his deafness and a back injury from his days working in a logging camp.[11] In Royal's words, his parents "didn't see the same, and he left [Skagway] for the Yukon in, I think, 1902—went down the river in a small boat, worked for a while in St. Michael and took a boat to Seattle, where he lived and worked. Mother divorced him."[12] I could find no record of a divorce.

In April 1910, the census taker listed Dan as living with Wesley Smith and his family, as their "hired man." In twenty-five years, Dan had gone from being the richest man in the West End of Clallam County to being a hired hand, living with his brother-in-law. In his last days, Dan was back in Seattle in failing health, nursed in his last days by daughter

11.3. Daniel W. Pullen and his sons, clockwise from left: Dee, Chester, and Royal, ca. 1906. AUTHOR'S COLLECTION

14.4. Quileute Indians in front of what was once Harriet and Dan Pullen's dining-room windows in La Push, ca. 1900, with the Pacific Ocean and James Island in the distance (A. Wesley Smith, photographer). WASHINGTON STATE LIBRARY MANUSCRIPTS COLLECTION, A. WESLEY SMITH PAPERS, 1853–1935, M.S. 172

Mildred. He died on August 14, 1910.[13] The Masons paid for his burial. According to the stories passed down by descendants of Quillayute country pioneers, Dan Pullen, having lost both his wife and his fortune, died of a broken heart.[14]

Harry Hobucket in his 1934 article reported that in 1909 Dan had returned to La Push after an absence of many years. At the time, the Pullens' house was still standing, looming over the Quileute village and probably being used by the Indian Agency. When a storm damaged the Quileute school building, the Pullens' former residence temporarily served as the school.[15]

In 1930, the US government razed the Pullens' La Push house, by then in a decaying condition, to utilize its strategic location for a US Coast Guard Station. In 1980, the Coast Guard built a new facility on another part of the Quileute reservation. The station today conducts motor lifeboat rescues along the region's treacherous coastline and acts as an outpost of the US Department of Homeland Security. Its old building on the footprint of the Pullens' house became part of the Quileute Tribal School and remains so today.[16]

TRUEST FRIEND

Harry Hobucket's 1934 article, based on information his tribal elders had passed down, added to the story of the 1889 burning of the Quileute village. According to Hobucket, after the fire, Dan and two other men cut down many saplings and stuck them in the ground. They then sent a photograph of the site to the Local Land Office in an effort to support Pullen's assertion that the land had been unoccupied for some time. Hobucket also wrote that Pullen had coerced the owners of the remaining houses on the hill to move them to the beach, "by holding six-shooters at their backs."[17] By the time the US General Land Office heard the case, Pullen had used up all his resources defending himself, and finally, in Hobucket's words, "Pullen decided to give the land back to the Indians."[18]

When Dan died, according to Hobucket, one mourner, a man who had homesteaded near Dan's property in Quillayute, stepped out of Dan's funeral procession and spoke in Chinook to an old chief, Kla-Kis-Ka-Are, who responded, "Rattle his bones, over the stones. He's only a pauper nobody owns. Amen."[19] Hobucket followed the article's text with his own poem, which ends:

And wisest he is in this whole land
Of hoarding till bent and gray,
For all you can hold in your cold dead hand
Is what you have given away.
'Tis then his noblest enemy
May prove his truest friend.[20]
(Harry Hobucket, "The Burning of the LaPush Village on the Quilla-yute Reservation")

Hobucket suggests here that the American way is to hoard, but that in the Quileute traditional culture, wealth is measured by what one gives away rather than by what one possesses, reflecting the same value that underlies the potlatch. In this case, Dan decided, in Hobucket's words, "to give the land back through the Superior Court," and thus, ironically, became the Quileute people's "truest friend."[21]

"I Only Hope They Have as Much Fun"

It is remarkable that given her financial challenges and her remote location in Alaska, Harriet, with only an eighth-grade education herself, made sure her children received university educations, at a time when less than 3 percent of the US population went to college.[22] Chester, the youngest, died in a 1912 drowning accident at Ketchikan while en route back to the University of Washington.[23] Harriet kept his notebooks of outlines for novels and short stories.[24] In his diary, he wrote shortly before his death, "My Mother is a great woman, splendidly tall, fashioned in the beautiful mould of a goddess, magnificently alive, the noblest woman on earth."[25]

Royal graduated from the University of Washington, served in the army during World War I, and eventually took a job in Lead, South Dakota, as a mining engineer for the Homestake Gold Mine, where he worked for several decades.[26] A pioneer of both Clallam County and Skagway who lived to be 103, he became the family keeper of Harriet's story. Interviewed repeatedly by writers, he wrote his own essays about his parents and then published much of that material in a 1987 article.[27]

Dee—in adulthood known as Dan or Daniel—also went to the University of Washington and then the United States Military Academy at West Point, where he was named an all-American in football all four years and captain of the West Point team in his last year. After one game, a reporter for the *New York Herald* wrote, "In the Army eleven stood one man whose red shock of hair shone out like the plume of a knight of medieval days. In the thick of every scrimmage this tawny, tousled top gleamed in the sun like a beacon. This was the bulwark of the Army—Pullen, a Cadet from far-off Alaska."[28] One might wonder how it was that spectators could so easily see his remarkable red hair. He played without a helmet, as was the custom among many players of the day.

When the United States entered World War I, the army assigned Dee, by then a West Point graduate (ranked fourth in his class) and army officer, to the Tank Corps of the American Expeditionary Forces (AEF), a fledgling operation focused on the latest form of military technology.[29] The army leadership believed tanks held the potential to break the stalemate in France.[30] Dee's fellow officer and equal, George S. Patton Jr., described tanks as "saucy looking little fellows and very active. Just like insects from under a wooden log in the forest."[31] They "bucked and reared like a horse," according to one military historian, something Dee, with ample experience riding horses in La Push, no doubt would have appreciated.[32]

At the end of the war, the US War Department awarded Dee the Distinguished Service Cross. His citation reads: "For extraordinary heroism in action in the Bois-de-Cuisy, France, September 26, 1918. Colonel Pullen displayed conspicuous gallantry and leadership . . . in the face of violent machine-gun fire."[33] The French government awarded him the *Croix de guerre, palme en bronze* and the *Légion d'honneur, Chevalier*, and the Belgian government, the *Ordre de la couronne, Officier*.[34] The following month he was wounded in the shoulder by a shell fragment and knocked down by a bursting shell.[35]

After the war, Dee spent four years in the Army Corps of Engineers,[36] but then died of a brain tumor at the age of thirty-eight.[37] Given what we know today about traumatic brain injury, I can't help but wonder if riding in experimental tanks in the midst of machine-gun fire, being knocked down by a bursting shell, and playing eight years of football without a helmet might have contributed to his death. [38]

Mildred returned from nursing school to the Pacific Northwest, where she worked in a hospital.[39] A rift that later developed between mother and daughter prompted Mildred to accuse Harriet, in a letter to Harriet's brother Wesley, of trying to steal her sons. She wrote, "She is a wicked old woman, and as long as I live, I never want to see her."[40] Harriet, on the other hand, claimed in 1920 that Mildred had given away her children to Harriet, and even said she had a written statement from Mildred that the children were hers.[41] By contrast, Mary, Mildred's only daughter, who Harriet raised, is said to have idolized her grandmother Harriet.[42]

When asked by writer Herb Hilscher during one of his Pullen House visits if she wished her children lived closer, Harriet replied, "That doesn't matter, what I prefer. . . . They must have a chance to build their own lives, just as I did. I only hope they have as much fun."[43]

"THE MOTHER OF THE NORTH"

Harriet kept a kind of shrine to Dee and Chester in the "Texas," the room perched atop the Pullen House's second story.[44] A visitor to the room reported observing numerous framed pictures, varsity letters, and other mementos, including a pile of Chester's notebooks on an old desk with her three sons' names carved into the wood. Placed on a chair was Dee's army uniform, the Distinguished Service Cross and other military medals and insignia pinned to the lapel.[45] Harriet also wore forty-three military medals and other insignia from her sons Dee and Royal on her own lapel. They were not only Harriet's signature accessory in her later years but also the butt of ridicule. "They used to make fun of me up in Skagway, wearing medals," she said [to a Seattle reporter]. "I was only wearing three or four then. But when they laughed, I put on all of the rest. I have a right to wear them."[46] One might say, as a feisty and proud mother, she wore her heart on her lapel.

14.5. Harriet, wearing military medals on her lapel in Skagway in 1941 (Harriet Stuart Pullen Phillips, photographer). COLLECTION VIRGINIA O. PHILLIPS, OAKLAND, CALIFORNIA

Harriet was a mother figure to others as well. Elmer Rasmuson, for many decades president of the National Bank of Alaska, grew up in Skagway. According to Hilscher, Rasmuson and his boyhood friends frequently fished in the trout streams that ran through the Pullen House property, each boy bringing Harriet his string of fish. While Harriet couldn't use all those fish, she'd take them all, and, Rasmuson recalled, "hand over a sugar doughnut or a fat slice of hot bread bathed in butter and, dead serious, say, 'A day's pay for a day's work, that's my motto.'"[47]

Her children gone, Harriet created an environment at the Pullen House that brought an ever-changing array of people to her doorstep. Among the visitors were President Warren G. Harding and his entourage, who came to Skagway in 1923. The town of five hundred people "was turned upside down that morning," according to one eyewitness.[48] The president made a speech standing on the porch steps of the Pullen House. Everyone, dogs included, lined up on the hotel grounds and filed into the dining room to shake his hand afterwards.[49]

A woman who worked in the hotel recalled that in the absence of advance notice of the president's arrival, Harriet had put all of her linen tablecloths in the laundry. Always resourceful, she covered the tables with clean bedsheets for the reception that followed Harding's speech. With nothing on hand to serve the unexpected guests, she turned to her cows, milked them, skimmed off the cream, and served everyone a glass of fresh milk.[50] The president's visit, with a mention of Harriet and the Pullen House, prompted next-day coverage in the *Chicago Daily Tribune*, the *Los Angeles Times*, the *New York Times*, and the *Washington Post*.[51]

President Harding's speech that day included the following— thoughts that capture what Skagway may have meant to Harriet:

> *Skagway . . . was developed and made notable in a rush of men seeking to acquire something of material value. That is a motive which is inherent in us. But the longer I live and the more I see of communities and human beings, the more firmly is my belief established that the sweetest thing in the world is the friendship of a few dependable friends. This is the happiness that makes a life of contentment.*

14.6. Harriet, First Lady Florence Harding, and Alaska Territory Governor Scott C. Bone at the Pullen House in Skagway, on July 11, 1923. ALASKA STATE LIBRARY, MARGUERITE BONE WILCOX PHOTO COLLECTION, P70-18

Apparently you have much of that here, . . . and you also live in an atmosphere that tends to cultivate ambition and lofty aspirations.[52]

Barrett Willoughby described a moment sitting with Harriet in the Pullen House during the late 1920s. At a "table across the dining room," Willoughby wrote, "a jolly, gray-headed millionaire from Long Island was hailing her. 'This is like home, Mrs. Pullen!' he called heartily. 'Permit us to drink to you!' And every guest at the table held high a brimming glass of Alaskan cows' milk and drank a health to Harriet Pullen, the Mother of the North."[53] A new kind of mother, Harriet served as proprietor and manager of the Pullen House for nearly fifty years.

Harriet Smith Pullen died in 1947. She ran the hotel until the end of her life. In poor health for a few months, she fell, broke her hip, developed pneumonia, and died within days on August 9, four days before her

14.7. Harriet and two of her dairy cows in front of the Pullen House in about 1905; inscribed on the photograph is "What Made the Pullen House Famous." CLALLAM COUNTY HISTORICAL SOCIETY

14.8. Harriet in Skagway in photographs dated 1920 by Harriet, but taken between 1909 and 1913 (Horace Herbert Draper, photographer). AUTHOR'S COLLECTION

14.9. Harriet (undated). AUTHOR'S COLLECTION

eighty-seventh birthday.[54] She had outlived her husband and three of her four children.

Her grave lies near the Pullen House, nestled against the mountain-side, right next to the railroad tracks. Vibrant scarlet berries of a mountain ash crown the gravestone during the autumn, a reminder of Harriet's vivid red hair. According to one Skagway old-timer, her wish to be buried outside of a cemetery in this unusual spot caused a bit of controversy in town. In the end, Harriet got her way.[55]

After Harriet's death, the granddaughter she had raised continued to operate the Pullen House until the late 1950s, when she could no longer afford to keep the business going because tourist traffic in Skagway had diminished. Yet today, each summer one million tourists descend upon Skagway from huge cruise liners for daylong stays, making it a seasonally busy place indeed. Harriet was instrumental in setting the course for Skagway as the tourist destination it is.

Royal inherited the property, and his son, in turn, sold it in 1966.[56] I saw what remained of the old hotel during a brief 1965 visit to Skagway with my parents. It was in shambles, more than dilapidated, with a tree growing up through the middle of the floor of the sun parlor. The building continued to deteriorate for the next twenty-five years. Meanwhile, a 1970s effort by the short-lived Pullen Foundation failed to raise the funds needed to restore it.[57]

In 1990, the City of Skagway ordered the owner to raze or repair a deteriorated portion of the building. After an attempt to backhoe that section left the rest of the building unstable, the city deemed it a hazard and ordered the demolition of the entire structure, an order the owner complied with.[58] Only the rubble-stone masonry chimney and fireplace, once a part of the sun parlor, remain. In 2013, below the mantel, I was able to make out letters surrounded by small river stones inlaid in cement. They spell "PULLEN."

Today the Pullen House property is adjacent to the Klondike Gold Rush National Historical Park, authorized by Congress in 1976. The National Park Service began acquiring properties in town and hiring staff, and by 1900 was able to open the park officially. It is one of four units of the park and continues to restore historic buildings and

14.10. Harriet in her Tlingit shirt next to the railroad tracks in Skagway, near the Pullen House and the spot where she would choose to be buried (undated). This photograph is one Harriet had made into a postcard. NATIONAL PARK SERVICE, KLONDIKE GOLD RUSH NATIONAL HISTORICAL PARK, KLGO 057565

14.11. The Pullen House sun parlor chimney and fireplace, in 2013. PHOTO-
GRAPH BY THE AUTHOR

Catalogue #861

Catalogue #2060

Catalogue #817

Catalogue #599F

Catalogue #2065

14.12. A page from the auction catalog for the 1973 sale of Harriet's collection, which included these Chilkat ceremonial blankets, a mountain-sheep trophy head, and framed advertisements for wine and beer, probably castoffs from the many saloons of gold rush–era Skagway. AUTHOR'S COLLECTION, COURTESY WALTER PATTERSON JR., PUYALLUP, WASHINGTON to commemorate and interpret the Klondike Gold Rush through its programming.[59]

Harriet's extensive collection of Klondike Gold Rush memorabilia, Alaska Native artifacts, and Russian-American colonial items went to Seattle in 1959 with her granddaughter and formed the basis for a small museum there, where I was able to see it in 1965.[60] In the early 1970s, the granddaughter offered the collection to the State of Alaska. Both houses of the Alaska State Legislature passed a bill for its purchase on the last day of the session, but a reconsideration vote held up the bill until the following year.[61] Unwilling to wait for the legislature to reconvene months later, in 1973 the granddaughter sold the collection of more than 2,200 lots at a five-day, seven-session auction. Unknown collectors near and far now own pieces from what was once Harriet Smith Pullen's collection.[62]

AFTERWORD

SOLID GOLD

In 2003, my mother moved into a nursing home. Concerned that things of value might disappear, I removed some items from her room. One particular pair of gold earrings surprised me. Unlike virtually everything else I found there, I had never seen them before.

The earrings feature a Victorian hinged-buckle motif. About one inch long, they dangle and sway slightly when the wearer moves. Delicate etching and black enamel surround a tiny seed pearl dotting the center. Parts of them are smooth and polished and reflect the light. My research revealed that black enamel combined with gold is characteristic of mourning jewelry, made in England and America in the 1870s, following the death of Queen Victoria's husband.[1] They are unlike anything I ever saw my mother wear—dangly, and perhaps a bit flashy by her conservative standards. I, on the other hand, wear them happily and, for a time, wondered where they came from.

As a child, I often looked through my mother's jewelry box, a favorite pastime. For each heirloom, she would tell me a story. "That was your grandmother's necklace from the Roaring Twenties," and "my great-aunt Lily brought back that pin from a trip to Italy," and "your grandfather gave that necklace to your grandmother for their tenth anniversary," she would say. But these gold earrings were entirely new to me.

I wondered where my mother had kept them all those years. Why had I never seen them? By the time I found them, my mother unfortunately wasn't able to tell me anything about them or how she had acquired them. Although I've always sought out the story behind family heirlooms, I thought the origins of these earrings would remain a mystery.

As I prepared for my 2004 visit to Washington State, I found a letter among my mother's papers. The letter, written by my mother at the age of nine in 1931, said, "Dear Grandmother Pullen, Thank you so much for the lovely box of treasures you sent me. I just love them."[2] Might those earrings have been among the treasures? Further investigation of my mother's papers months later turned up a photograph of Harriet wearing the very same earrings! Below the image is the business identifier of the photographer's studio, including the words, "Seattle, W.T., 1886." If I'd had any question about whether I was actually seeing my earrings in that photograph, they were answered by my mother's handwriting in pencil on a photocopy of the photograph: "I have these earrings, HPP, 1991."

Afterword.1. Harriet Smith Pullen in 1886, wearing the gold earrings (Moore, photographer). CLALLAM COUNTY HISTORICAL SOCIETY

Now I knew that Harriet had the earrings in 1886 when she was twenty-six, five years after her marriage to Dan; however, I still know little about the circumstances of how she acquired them. Dan's brief period of prosperity had probably made it possible for him to buy solid gold jewelry for his wife.

Even though some questions about the earrings remain unanswered, they led me to tell Harriet Smith Pullen's story, a complex one woven with threads of both fact and fiction. It seems fitting, given the many ways, both large and small, that gold makes an appearance in Harriet's life story, that these gold earrings should be the one thing of hers, aside from a few photographs, that have made their way down to me.

Appendix

A Storied Woman

The trajectory of Harriet Smith Pullen's Skagway story has played out for more than a century in chapters in books, in newspaper and magazine articles, in recorded interviews, in letters, and in diaries. An examination of how writers have gathered information and used the story, how the story evolved, and how much of it is believable demonstrates that memory distorts and storytellers embellish, aggrandize, and synthesize their stories into cohesive narratives by eliminating and adding significant details. Writers, in turn, select and focus on various aspects of a rich story, such as Harriet's, that offers multiple entry points and perspectives.

"Hotels, Pack Horses, and Apple Pies"

The story of Harriet Pullen in Alaska reached its zenith nine months after her death when on May 17, 1948, NBC radio aired *Queen of Heartbreak Trail*, which we first encountered in chapter one of this book. The play, derived in part from a magazine article, dramatized Harriet's landing in Skagway with a multitude of vivid sound effects and colorful, sometimes coarse, dialogue. In the play, Harriet is depicted as a refined lady plunked down on a remote beach in the midst of a gold-hungry, sex-starved community of lowlifes. After her debut as a reluctant saloon singer, the establishment's manager asks her to accept drinks from patrons and wear tights for her next performance. She is horrified at the suggestions and manages to escape when fisticuffs erupt between two men vying for her attention. She chooses a more palatable work situation—cooking in a filthy tent. Rising to the challenge of her financial circumstances by baking pies at night, she saves her money and sends for her children.

When an old prospector in the play tells her, "[T]here's three things this town of Skagway ain't got enough of: hotels, pack horses, and apple pie," Harriet sends for Babe, her favorite horse.[1] The play brings the horse-jumping-off-the-gangplank scene (just like the one Harriet had written about in 1897) to a fever pitch. Standing in a scow, Harriet coaxes Babe toward her waiting arms, the horse jumps, landing with a great, audible splash, and Harriet swims her ashore. With Babe's help, Harriet becomes an entrepreneur, freighting supplies for the stampeders, and soon acquires a hotel, the Pullen House, in Harriet's words, "the best goldarned hotel in Alaska!"[2] With that, the playwrights complete this slightly fictionalized storyline with what Skagway needed most and what Harriet Pullen could supply—apple pies, pack horses, and a hotel.

"The Business Woman"

Probably the first author to interview and write about Harriet Pullen was Thomas Martindale. In 1913, he published *Hunting in the Upper Yukon*, an account of an extended hunting trip. He devoted one chapter to three "notable" women whose paths he had crossed during his hunting forays. The chapter's epigraph, four lines from Robert W. Service's 1907 poem, "The Law of the Yukon," is an apt description of Harriet Smith Pullen's life in Alaska. The epigraph reads:

> This is the law of the Yukon
> That only the strong shall thrive,
> That surely the weak shall perish
> And only the fit survive.[3]

Martindale never identified two of the women in his account, referring to them only as "The White Housewife" and "The Indian Woman." The third he named—Harriet Pullen, designated "The Business Woman."[4] Martindale tells Harriet's Alaska story—broke and bereft, she found a way to use her only asset, her horses, to bring some "revenue into the family coffers." He was careful to specify that, as an accomplished equestrian, "*she* was the driver, she was the contractor, she was the wage-winner for the family." She cleared a profit of twenty-five dollars a day (equivalent to more than seven hundred in 2014 dollars[5]) hauling freight and then opened her hotel. Martindale concluded his observations on Harriet by saying, "Mrs. Pullen is easily the most famous personage in this section of Alaska—and this applies to the men as well as to the women."[6] This 1913 book was the beginning of the published Harriet Smith Pullen Skagway story.

STORIES HARRIET TOLD

The stories Harriet told interviewers like Martindale and her other guests became the foundation of her legendary legacy. She used and extended the narrative liberally (some would say unscrupulously) during her lifetime to enhance her persona and the tourist appeal of the Pullen House. Between 1913 and 1930, accounts of Harriet Pullen's Skagway years appeared in newspapers and in two more books. With each publication, writers repeated key elements, adding personal observations and new details. For instance, around 1914 journalist Bessie Beatty wrote an article for the *San Francisco Call* under the title "The 'Big Lady' of Skagway." She added to what Martindale said in his book, noting that soon after her arrival in Skagway, in Harriet's words, she "went to building pies" and took a job cooking for a wharf crew.[7] Beatty called her "perhaps the biggest lady in all the great Territory of Alaska. . . . Her fame has gone far beyond the range of the northern lights."[8]

Agnes Rush Burr in *Alaska: Our Beautiful Northland of Opportunity* of 1919 told of her Pullen House stay and described Harriet as "a graphic portrayer" of the days of the 1897 gold rush.[9] Hearing Harriet's story was, she said, like "turning the pages of a romance."[10] Burr recounted an oft-repeated observation about the Pullen House dining room. Harriet set her tables with Haviland porcelain china and sterling-silver flatware, amenities unexpected in Alaska. She served fresh milk from her farm in special blue-and-white-enameled pans and invited her breakfast guests to skim the cream for their coffee and cereal. Burr also, for the first time, wrote about Harriet's collection of artifacts.[11]

Newspaper articles, for the most part, relied on the books for source material on Harriet's Skagway experiences and helped to spread her story. In 1926, the *Los Angeles Times* reprinted an article from a Seattle newspaper and titled it "Alaska Hotel Owned by 'Mother of the North.'" It noted that "a handful of women became famous because they were able to stand beside the sprinkling of men in the uncounted myriad of gold-rushers who were hard enough to conquer the North—and of all that bright company, the men of the golden North count Mrs. Pullen the brightest."[12] Harriet's oft-used moniker, "Ma" Pullen, stemmed from this article. By the mid-1920s, Harriet was becoming a storied personality, consistently recognized as a strong woman in a man's world.

The National Media

It was 1930 when Harriet Pullen's story entered the national media in full bloom. That year Mary Lee Davis, who lived in Fairbanks and probably interviewed Harriet, retold in *Uncle Sam's Attic: The Intimate Story of Alaska* much of what British world traveler Charlotte Cameron had written a decade earlier in *A Cheechako in Alaska and Yukon*. Davis added, however, anecdotes about Harriet's inventiveness in creating pie pans from tin cans and drinking glasses from beer bottles.[13] The pattern is clear: Each publication repeated information from earlier publications and relied on Harriet's telling of her own story, while adding new information.

It was Barrett Willoughby, however, who brought the story of Harriet's life in Skagway to a broad audience. The first of her five published accounts appeared in 1930. An established author, Willoughby wrote to Harriet in 1926 asking if she might interview her for a magazine article.[14] Sometime in the late 1920s, the interview took place at the Pullen House. The resulting article appeared in 1930 in *The American Magazine*, a publication focusing on human-interest stories. It boasted a circulation of 2.3 million.[15] One month later, the article reappeared in condensed form in *The Reader's Digest*, which reached readers through both subscriptions and newsstands.[16] Willoughby dramatized Harriet's tale with abundant, lengthy quotes of Harriet's words and interspersed them with her own commentary. Willoughby's narrative appeared again in 1933 as one of six chapters about notable Alaskan adventurers and pioneers in a book titled *Alaskans All*. Until now, it was the fullest and most detailed of the more than sixty published accounts of Harriet's years in Skagway.

Macmillan Company published yet another version of Willoughby's interview in *Unsung Heroes*,[17] a 1930 book for young readers, which includes brief biographies of twenty-four Americans, five of them women, who had "triumphed over difficulties . . . without the aid of inherited wealth or position," and had "risen from obscurity."[18] Macmillan then put the material into a 1941 textbook, *The Growth of Democracy*, which includes verbatim passages of Harriet's words from *Unsung Heroes* to tell of her challenging first few hours in Skagway, how she bravely overcame her distress at the "'sordidness'" of her surroundings and resolved to make her way in Alaska.[19] This textbook, devoted to explaining democracy and telling the stories of people who found opportunities within a democratic system, is said to have been used by children across the United States.[20] It was revised and reprinted three times during the following decade.

During a visit to Seattle in 1937, Harriet had the opportunity to tell some of her Skagway story herself in a radio interview broadcast coast to coast on NBC on the *L. C. Smith Typewriter Program*. While in Seattle, she also addressed students at the University of Washington and demonstrated the making of an apple pie from her own recipe.[21]

After Harriet's radio talk and the publication of Willoughby's stories, journalist Bud Branham traveled to Skagway to visit the Pullen House. He attended "Ma" Pullen's eightieth birthday party in 1940 and interviewed her for an article in *The Alaska Sportsman*. The account she told him was what she had told all of the earlier interviewers, except she added new information about her abortive gold-seeking trip to Atlin.[22]

Of all the authors who published accounts of Harriet's time in Skagway, fifteen of them knew her personally or interviewed her, and all of them got more or less the same information from her. Harriet told her very last story to Laura McCarley, who wrote an article published in a Juneau newspaper in 1976. McCarley had known Harriet during her Skagway childhood, and recalled in the article that Harriet often showed off the bed where President Harding had slept, even though the man did not spend the night at the Pullen House. McCarley also had interviewed Harriet in 1947, three months before Harriet died. At the time, Harriet was in poor health, but according to McCarley, her mind was clear. What Harriet recounted was essentially the same story she'd always told, but she included a few erroneous or invented details. For example, McCarley quoted Harriet as saying, "I received over 100 proposals of marriage during the first month I was in Skagway." This and other bits of information appear in print here for the first time, from the mouth of an ailing, eighty-six-year-old woman.[23]

In the half-century that followed Harriet's death, at least six authors in addition to McCarley published pieces based on firsthand experience with Harriet Pullen. Four of them are reminiscences by writers who had met Harriet many years before, including one by famed author and radio broadcaster Lowell Thomas.[24] "She told me her story...," Thomas recalled, "Ma was no shrinking violet!—and it seemed to me that only a frontier like Alaska could have contained the likes of her."[25] Two other publications include recollections by family members who knew her well.[26] A number of other accounts, developed from secondary sources with little or no documentation and rife with misinformation, have appeared in print as well.

Deviate from the Facts

The published results of interviews sometimes deviate from the facts. But whether Harriet was the source of misleading information or her chroniclers simply misunderstood the details she recounted, or used sloppy language in relaying what she had told them, is not always clear. Martindale in *Hunting in the Upper Yukon*, for example, described a "trail" on which Harriet hauled freight with no mention of the Brackett Wagon Road. Instead of just driving her horses and wagon to the foot of the mountain, as Martindale put it, Beatty characterized Harriet's freighting trip as taking her "over the mountains." Both accounts suggest a more arduous route than the wagon road she actually traversed.[27]

That Harriet spoke five Native American or Alaska Native languages, as Burr claimed in *Alaska*, is probably an exaggeration. Given Harriet's experience and the places she lived, however, it is likely she spoke at least three languages in addition to English. According to Royal, she spoke Quileute, and she may have learned some of the Makah language during her months cooking at their agency. Like her sister Jennie, she also probably spoke Chinook, the North Pacific Coast trade language.[28] It would have allowed her to communicate with people from a number of different Indian nations. Harriet or her chroniclers probably exaggerated a bit when it made for a better narrative.

Another example of stretching the truth is found in Harriet's account of the landing of her horses in Skagway in 1898. Beatty stated, "There was no wharf at Skagway then, and the horses were put overboard to swim ashore."[29] Willoughby, on the other hand, described the event thus: "The day the steamer arrived with the Pullen horses, all four wharves were double-lined with vessels unloading cargoes, and the ship had to come to anchor out in the bay."[30] Although we do not know precisely when Harriet's horses arrived, it was sometime before her letter of April 20, 1898, to Wesley.[31] By March 31, there were at least three, and probably four, wharves in Skagway built out over the tidal flats, but again, perhaps they were unavailable at the time her horses arrived.[32] A 1900 newspaper advertisement said of Moore's reconstructed wharf that it was the only one in town that could accommodate "vessels of large tonnage . . . at all times."[33]

In addition to using wharves, there were other protocols for getting horses from the steamers to the beach when there was pressure to keep things moving in the frenzied harbor. Tappan Adney described his landing at Skagway in August 1897 when there was just one not-always-available wharf: "At dawn a call of 'Get up; the horses are being taken ashore!' resounds over the ship. A large scow is ranged alongside the vessel, and the horses are walked aboard on a plank and ferried to the beach, where they are dumped ashore into shallow water. We notice that men from the *Bristol* are taking horses part way, then dumping them overboard and swimming them ashore. . . . We got our personal effects ashore in small boats."[34]

The element of Harriet's story about her single-handedly swimming her horses to shore may or may not be true. That some of the wharves were unavailable is likely true, but the part of the story about there being no wharves, as Beatty stated, is not true. Either Harriet misspoke or Beatty misunderstood. Or maybe Harriet or Beatty wanted to simplify the tale or make Skagway sound more rough-and-tumble than it was. Harriet actually would have thought nothing of unloading a boat—animals included—without a wharf, because in La Push that had been standard procedure for years. As Harriet relayed the anecdote to her granddaughter, the deckhand had told her that she would have to remove her horses from the boat immediately, as the boat wouldn't find room to dock for many days.[35] On the other hand, perhaps Harriet fabricated the entire story, basing it on her recollection of the horse-gangplank scene she had witnessed from the steamer during her initial trip to Skagway. It's impossible to know what really happened with Harriet's horses in early 1898, except to say that she managed to get them to Skagway.

One bit of misinformation that appeared in a number of publications grew out of Harriet's statement to Willoughby during their interview, "I had never been trained to work."[36] That notion, and Harriet's offhand references to her La Push cook and governess, make her sound like a white-gloved lady of leisure who suddenly had to make her way working in a man's world, where strong backs and calloused hands were necessary. Harriet may have never been "trained to work," but she was an experienced pioneer, who, like her father and mother, possessed diverse skills and had worked all her life. Again, this bending of the truth made her anecdotes of resourcefulness even more remarkable.

"Shot Down before My Door"

Exaggeration makes for gripping drama. Jefferson Randolph Smith, otherwise known as "Soapy" Smith, the charming, attention-getting, gangster con man who also curried favor with politicians, was not related to Harriet Smith Pullen, but they knew each other. His Skagway story has become legendary. An examination of what Harriet herself wrote and published about Soapy Smith, and what others have made of her involvement with him, offers a case in point.

Harriet transitioned her account of merely knowing Soapy Smith into an eyewitness claim of having observed Soapy's death in a dramatic shootout on a Skagway wharf on July 8, 1898. Her earliest chroniclers made no claims that she had witnessed the event. Beatty, writing around 1914, called Soapy a "desperado" who "robbed and murdered," but said of Harriet and Soapy only that their shacks were "the width of a street apart."[37] One woman who had worked for Harriet for five summers in the 1920s and listened to her daily storytelling performances stated that she had never heard Harriet claim to have witnessed Soapy's death.[38] Cameron in 1920 judiciously stated, "She was present when 'Soapy' met his end," by which one could conclude that Harriet was present in the town the night the incident took place.[39]

Harriet wrote and published her own account in a nineteen-page booklet, *Soapy Smith, Bandit of Skagway: How He Lived; How He Died*, in 1929. Here she discussed Soapy Smith's influence in Skagway and his death in the famous incident. She recounted how Soapy had persuaded her to participate, presumably on horseback, in a Fourth of July parade four days before his death. She told of seeing him on the street, just before the shooting, carrying his Winchester rifle on his way to the wharf, site of his final confrontation. She wrote that she saw his body afterwards with eleven-year-old Royal, who, she reported, exclaimed, "Why Mamma, that is the man that bought all us kids candy and now he's dead!"[40]

Harriet concluded her booklet with a nuanced assessment of Soapy, a complex man whom she knew personally: "Thus ends our story of Jefferson Randolph Smith, a story of character, of a man taking the wrong trail and mushing to an ignoble end, dying as he had lived, defying law and order."[41] To Harriet, Soapy Smith was a persuasive man with some redeeming qualities but, in the end, "ignoble." She did not state in her published booklet that she had witnessed his death.

By the time Willoughby interviewed her, however, Harriet's portrayal of her role in Soapy's tale began to take on an eyewitness tenor. Harriet told Willoughby that she had heard the "deep rolling tones" of Soapy's "suave voice luring stampeders to his gambling games," and that he had "dashed" by her cooking tent every day.[42] But then, despite what Harriet herself had written at roughly the same time, Willoughby quoted her as saying, "Soapy Smith himself [was] shot down before my door."[43] Did "before my door?" actually mean two blocks away?

The hyperbole increased. A journalist in a Seattle newspaper in 1930 noted that Harriet saw Soapy "drop to the ground, dead."[44] Seven years later, another journalist interviewed Harriet and quoted her as saying, "I saw both men [Soapy and his assailant, Frank Reid] fall."[45] In 1947, she told McCarley, "I heard the shots and saw Smith fall dead." She even told McCarley it had been she who had hitched up a wagon to her team of horses, taking Soapy Smith's body to the morgue after he'd lain dead on the wharf for several hours. This statement is most certainly not true, given material that appears in the numerous reports about the incident. If that had been the case, someone else would have reported it.

What seems to be true is that Harriet was in Skagway the night Soapy Smith died; the event took place two or three short blocks from her waterfront cabin, in a town with a business district roughly four blocks wide and six blocks long;[46] and she likely heard the shots and witnessed the evening's commotion, which many reported consumed the whole town throughout the night. The eyewitness details that Harriet and her chroniclers provided reinforce the story of her involvement with Soapy Smith in 1898 and make the untrue aspects more believable. If Harriet did not actually witness the shooting of Soapy, perhaps it was while standing at her cabin door that she saw the dying Soapy Smith lying at a distance. The bottom line: Having witnessed the death of Soapy Smith strengthened one's credentials as an authentic Skagway Klondike Gold Rush participant.

This example seems to be a case of Harriet and her chroniclers slipping into hyperbole for the sake of a good story. When stories are told and retold, at times second- and thirdhand, with entertainment as the principal value, they are simplified, exaggerated, and rendered a little more exciting, by both the subject of the interview and the author of the story, all with the goal of capturing an audience's interest.

Harriet's various overstatements seem to have led some writers to question all of the stories she told. There is one scholar, for example, who has gone so far as to cast doubt on Harriet's claim that she arrived in Skagway in September 1897 at the height of gold rush fever, even though there is ample evidence to support that she did.[47] If Harriet did not arrive in 1897, but rather in 1898, as this particular author argues, Harriet wasn't there during the heady days of the gold rush, and therefore had to have fabricated all of her accounts of her Skagway struggle during the town's first year. This author bases her assertions on the 1900 US Census, which indicates that Harriet arrived in Skagway in September 1898. Other sources—letters and newspaper articles—prove the census data to have been wrong. It seems Harriet's storytelling and tendency to embellish prompted the author to jump to the conclusion that Harriet had invented *all* of what she said over the years about her first months in Skagway.[48]

Overlooking the real story adds to the narrative in an unfortunate way, because other writers are likely, as we have seen in the evolution of Harriet's story, to repeat the false information.

Concerning the fabricated aspects of Harriet's Skagway story, as historian Ken Coates has aptly pointed out in his introduction to Tappan Adney's 1900 book, *The Klondike Stampede*, when it came to the Klondike Gold Rush, the truth was often elusive. The stampede took place in a remote place at a time when communication was slow. It was a romantic tale of great drama including vast quantities of gold for the taking and unexplored places, a story inhabited by adventurers and dreamers. Such a combination naturally leads to overstatement and misinformation.[49] Adney himself remarked on the role the press played during the Klondike Gold Rush—what he deemed the "adroit manipulation of the story," which led to "the world's acute attack of insanity."[50] This insanity, too, set the stage for many overstated and embellished narratives. As Herb Hilscher put it in a discussion about Skagway in his 1948 book, *Alaska Now*, "If all the Sourdoughs who 'saw' Soapy Smith shot in '98 were rounded up in one place, the Yankee Stadium wouldn't hold them all."[51]

"MRS. P. IS A REGULAR STROLLOP"

Another aspect of stories about Harriet falls into the gossip category. Some stories were told at Harriet's expense, sometimes making her appear foolish. In one, she hired a man to build the stone fireplace and chimney for the Pullen House sun parlor. When the job was complete, Harriet asked him to wait for his compensation. He grudgingly complied. Harriet built the first fire and filled the whole house with smoke. She complained to the man, who promised to fix the situation when she paid him for his work. Harriet paid him, whereupon he "repaired" the chimney by removing a board he had deliberately left in the flue.[52]

Lucille Hudson Elsner remembered the Pullen House cook who could never find his tools and utensils when he needed them. One day he put on a wide belt and attached to it his cleaver, a broom, and a dustpan. Into the kitchen came Harriet with a large group of tourists, and there was the cook in his peculiar getup. According to Elsner, after that, no one, including the boss, ever bothered his equipment again.[53]

Gossip about Harriet also found its way into various writings. Clarence L. Andrews, a customs collector in Skagway for five years around the time of the gold rush, and a photographer who traveled widely, documenting life in Alaska, kept a diary, recording what he observed and heard.[54] In January 1902, Andrews described a rumor circulating around town that he had gone to the Davidson Glacier with Mrs. P[ullen] and there had gotten "in the back of the boat with her and lay between her legs." Andrews continued in the diary, "I never did it or even thot of it," discounting the episode.[55]

Andrews, fascinated with gossip, recorded more of it about Harriet: "I have heard—'Mrs. P. is a regular strollop [promiscuous woman].' . . . 'The Pullen House is just about a fancy house.' 'She cant make a living out of her boarders so has to do things to trip it up.' 'She neglects her children.' &c &c &c—lots more."[56] He also spelled out rumors and hurtful opinions about others in Skagway. But the most damning innuendo was reserved for Harriet. She, however, considered the gossip "petty persecutions and unfair competition."[57]

Harriet, on some level, seems to have provoked gossip. Possibly it was her arrogance, her independence, or her strong character. Maybe people were envious of her. Perhaps her reputation as a storyteller with a propensity to exaggerate created gossip. As recently as 1983, old-timers in Skagway spoke about how offended Skagway residents had been when Harriet told people Dan was dead when he was not.[58] Even today, it is suggested by some descendants of the family that it was she who deserted Dan in the middle of the night when she went to Skagway, and that she was running a brothel there.[59] Clearly, the Pullen House was not a brothel. By contrast, none of the family stories mentions Dan's sudden and mysterious disappearance and purported suicide in 1896. What some people back home in Clallam County seemed to remember was that Dan returned to Washington from Alaska a broken man, while Harriet flourished in Skagway, suggesting that she was somehow at fault.[60] Royal, on the other hand, always maintained that his parents simply did not see eye to eye.[61] Perhaps the only conclusions one might draw with certainty are, there are two or more sides to every story, and no one really knows what goes on behind closed doors.

"I Had Lost My Husband"

Harriet wanted to control not only her destiny but also her story. Sometimes people want to protect the next generation from a nasty truth. This was likely the reason I had never heard an account of the burning of the Quileute village and Dan Pullen's alleged role in it. Some things can be too painful to discuss.

Harriet guided the emphasis in her life story to be on her gold rush years. That's what visitors to Skagway wanted to hear. Her hospitality and the modern amenities of her hotel reassured her guests that Skagway was not so untamed as to be threatening. Her stories, on the other hand, gave them the wild and woolly West they wanted. The sole interview-based narrative in which Harriet even mentions her days in sod houses on the prairie was an unpublished one written by my mother after her summer in Skagway.[62]

A major false thread in Harriet's story that she perpetuated throughout her life is the one about being a widow when she arrived in Skagway. Even though Willoughby quotes Harriet as saying, "I had lost my husband,"[63] the word "widow" consistently appears in virtually every other account (starting with Martindale in 1913) where an author interviewed her after Dan's 1910 death.[64] Authors did not just write that she was a widow. They wrote that she was a widow with four young children, or a widow when she left Washington. In about 1940, Harriet began outright lying, adding specificity to the widow guise, when she told several interviewers her husband had died in 1895, which was fifteen years before Dan's death.[65] That may have been the year her marriage died.

When writers interviewed Harriet, perhaps it was just easier for her to claim that she was a widow when she arrived in Alaska. I have already cited possible reasons for this—shame about a failed marriage at a time when people regarded divorce with scorn,[66] the need to avoid being accused of deserting her husband, or a desire to definitively put her past behind her. Death elicits fewer questions than divorce or desertion. But Harriet stuck to her story. It unquestionably served to make her tale of independence more compelling, and helped her to reinvent herself.

What Are We to Believe?

One writer who became acquainted with Harriet while working in Skagway during the early 1940s managed to summarize her story in 1969 in a compact string of inaccuracies: "The best known figure in Skagway, no pun intended, was famous Ma Pullen. This fine lady had waded ashore from a cattle boat, carrying and pushing her five fatherless kids along with her. Mr. Pullen was dead and Ma was in the gold rush to make her own fortune. She set up a tent and started baking Pullen's Pies & Cakes, [and] soon had her own small building. In [a] short time she was able to build Pullen House." He returned to Skagway years later and "slept in the bed that President Warren Harding had slept in."[67] Harriet was presumably his source for this information.

To recall another example, did journalist Laura McCarley confuse some aspects of Harriet's story in the many years between knowing Harriet during her youth, interviewing her in 1947, and publishing her article in 1976? Had Harriet's memories changed? Or was it just her stories that had changed? As historian Richard White points out in *Remembering Ahanagran: A History of Stories*, his impressive effort to bring together his mother's stories with documented historical fact, people tell different stories at different times in their lives. People change their stories over time, leave out some, and add new ones. People forget things.[68] Memory is porous. Tara Parker-Pope, health and science columnist for the *New York Times*, has observed that "scientific studies show that memories can fade, shift and distort over time. . . . Entirely new false memories can be incorporated into our memory bank."[69] People also consciously fabricate or distort things to make their stories more streamlined, timely, or compelling. And sometimes storytellers change what they have to say just because it is amusing to do so. Harriet's narrative evolved in a variety of ways over time. In reading these accounts, particularly the ones that relied on Harriet as the sole source, the question remains: What are we to believe?

The Mother of the North

Looking back over the one hundred years since people began publishing information about Harriet, I noticed one intriguing aspect of the many accounts of her life—the broad variety of publications that mention her or discuss her years in Skagway. For example, Harriet Pullen is included in histories of the Klondike Gold Rush, such as Pierre Berton's 1958 *The Klondike Fever: The Life and Death of the Last Great Gold Rush*, and in tourist-oriented books on Skagway, such as Howard Clifford's *The Skagway Story*. She makes token appearances in a number of light and humorous books about the Klondike Gold Rush, like Richard O'Connor's *High Jinks on the Klondike*.[70]

It has been surprising, however, to find Harriet in the torrid romance novel, *Golden Torment*, which, by 1996, had gone through thirteen printings. Although it's fiction, the book features several real people, including Jack London. In it, Harriet accompanies Kathy, a younger, fictional character, on a boat to Skagway during the gold rush in 1897. The steamy romance part of the drama centers on Kathy. Harriet's sole appearances in the narrative are as a stable, wise, mature friend, experienced in the ways of the world, but whose great height and vivid red hair scare off men.[71]

Even more of a surprise is Harriet's inclusion in a 1979 Seventh-day Adventist inspirational daybook for young readers, *Heroes in Training*, which includes accounts of laudable actions of people throughout history and in the Bible. Here the heroic aspect of Harriet's story is the way in which she cared for people's needs and shared the gospel while struggling to build her hotel. In real life, Harriet certainly did provide for people, but there is no evidence she spread the gospel.[72]

In recent years, as interest in independent, powerful, and entrepreneurial women has grown, a number of publications have mentioned Harriet. Doris Chapin Bailey's 2008 *A Divided Forest: The Life, Times, and Lineage of Roy Daniel Bailey*, for example, is about a Tlingit orphan who finds a wrecked bicycle, fixes it, and then rides it across the Pullen House lawn, only to be "soundly scolded and chased away by the famous and formidable Mrs. Harriet Pullen."[73] She is also found in books on remarkable pioneer women, such as Gary Peterson and Glynda Peterson Schaad's 2007 *Women to Reckon With: Untamed Women of the Olympic Wilderness*, where Harriet and her cows grace the book's cover.[74] Harriet is even mentioned in *Sarah Palin: A Biography*, published in 2010, which tells of the former Alaska governor and vice-presidential candidate's familiarity with

Skagway (her early childhood home), and the independent, determined women of the Klondike Gold Rush, such as Harriet Pullen.[75]

One might conclude from these publications that the richness of Harriet's Alaska story lends itself to diverse and sometimes contradictory interpretations. It is important, however, to view her remarkable time in Alaska in the context of her entire life. She did not land on the Skagway beach as a woman who had never been "trained to work." Rather, her early years abundantly prepared her for the many challenges she would face in Alaska. Her prodigious skills, all of them developed before she arrived in Skagway, included managing a store and trading post; running a boardinghouse; raising children; homesteading and farming two land claims; raising and packing horses; rowing boats; using guns and hunting game; living among Native peoples; managing lawsuits; telling stories; and making do with limited resources.

Harriet understood that challenges in life, as well as successes, have value. She appreciated hard, consistent work and the power of the individual's will. She brought with her to Alaska all she had learned from her pioneering parents and husband, but in Skagway, she found her voice, her power, and a kind of freedom she had not known before. Even A. J.'s consistent journaling served as a model for her. In watching him write, she learned that a life lived well is a life worth chronicling.

Two unattributed quotations that Harriet copied into a scrapbook reflect her indomitable spirit and the ways she handled her life's challenges: "All experiences have their uses and blessings," and "The material from which success and happiness are built is in our own hands; the building is the work of every day."[76] She could look back on her life and see that every situation she had encountered, even the difficult ones, offered her some benefit, but by talking about selected aspects of her experience, she could control her legacy. Tappan Adney summarized the environment created by the Klondike Gold Rush by quoting a seasoned miner, "Here the man who patronizes a saloon and the man who goes to church are on the same footing."[77] In Skagway, Harriet Matilda Smith Pullen could be her colorful, independent self. She brought with her all she had learned in Wisconsin, Dakota, and Washington and reinvented herself in Alaska as the "Mother of the North."

ACKNOWLEDGMENTS

The stories my mother told me about my family many years ago set the trajectory for this book. She also modeled for me a love of history. In *Queen of Heartbreak Trail*, I have tried to integrate her recollections and the family lore with historical facts. Many people helped to bring this endeavor to fruition.

I am indebted to librarians, historians, and archivists at more than a dozen institutions from coast to coast who generously gave their time and expertise to assist me in locating material. Moving from east to west across the country, my first research stop was Maine. Librarian Mary Grow at the Albert Church Brown Memorial Library in China Village, Maine, pointed me to a mural-sized mid-nineteenth-century map posted on the wall of her library. On it was every existing residence, business, church, and school in the village of China in 1856. It enabled me to locate the nearby Pullen family property where Dan Pullen began life.

During a second trip, this time to Wisconsin, James Hibbard and Angie Reineke of the Southwest Wisconsin Room of the University of Wisconsin Library in Platteville led me to numerous sources with information about A. J. Smith's years on his first homestead. James alerted me to a central concept underlying the Public Land Survey System—a quarter-section came as a totality, the good with the bad. It was in Platteville that my husband Michael Torlen's healthy skepticism for the accuracy of archival records led him to locate an important misfiled deed.

As I continued westward, following the steps of Hattie and her family, in South Dakota, Cleo Erickson of the Austin-Whittemore House in Vermillion provided me with materials on the history of Clay County. Exploring the Prairie Homestead in the Badlands, where one of the few remaining original sod houses is to be found, gave me the visceral feel of the Smiths' Dakota sod house.

My Washington State research began with a telephone call to reference specialist Gary Lundell of the University of Washington Library, who provided me with a copy of one of my happiest early discoveries, a transcript of A. J. Smith's diaries, a gold mine that opened a path to richer discoveries. Later, when I traveled to Washington, Sean Lanksbury, Pacific Northwest and special collections librarian at the Washington State Library, was endlessly accommodating during my many days in his library. He provided me with scans of photographs and a comfortable workstation for examining the contents of twenty boxes of archival material on the Smith family. Kathy Monds Estes, director of the Clallam County Historical Society, and her staff of eager volunteers, including Susan Koehler Bertholl and Virginia Fitzpatrick, sorted through folders of material on the Smith and Pullen families and located and scanned photographs. Sherrill Fouts, past director of the Forks Timber Museum, guided me through her facility and explained many aspects of the early timber industry in the Pacific Northwest and the history of Clallam County. Others in the region, including Kathy Miller at the Clallam County Auditor's Office and Nikki Price at the Clallam County Superior Court, supplied me with important documents. When it came to understanding the gold earrings Hattie wore, Consuelo White, jewelry appraiser and volunteer at the Clallam County Genealogical Society, and Alexandria Rossoff, Seattle jeweler, contributed invaluable observations. Marcia Phillips, a ranger at Olympic National Park, pointed me to Metsker Maps of Seattle, where I found a township and range map that eased my explorations of Clallam County homestead land claims.

During a second visit to Washington toward the end of my research, I spent two delightful afternoons in the archives of Olympic National Park with curator Gay Hunter, finding and copying numerous bits of important new information. Diane Bedell, a ranger at the Klondike Gold Rush National Historical Park in Seattle, opened the park's store as a favor to me. Wendy Coddington and Jennifer Laine of the Washington State Law Library answered my questions about court documents. Seattle vintage photograph dealers Michael Maslan of Michael Maslan Historic Photographs and his colleague Mike Fairley of Fairlook Antiques put me in touch with Walter Patterson Jr., who, in turn, had a wonderful collection of Smith family photographs.

At the end of a ferry trip through the Inside Passage to Skagway, Alaska, those who facilitated my search for information included Jim Simard, head of historical collections at the Alaska State Library, and library assistants Sandra Johnston and Connie Hamann, who repeatedly went in search of folders full of relevant material. Judy Munns, director of the Skagway Museum, made available from the museum's collection two important photographs of Harriet.

Special thanks are due to Karl Gurcke, park historian for the Klondike Gold Rush National Historical Park in Skagway, who kindly offered to read my manuscript for accuracy. His astute comments on the Skagway sections greatly enhanced the text. Any errors or omissions are my own. Karl also allowed me to read and cite his unpublished manuscript on the history of the Pullen House property in Skagway. His National Park System colleagues in Skagway, researcher David Simpson, curator Samantha Richert, and museum technician Deb Boettcher, were helpful as well.

My correspondence with Steve J. Langdon, professor emeritus, University of Alaska Anchorage, Steve E. Henrikson, curator of collections, Alaska State Museum, and Barbara Brotherton, curator of Native American art, Seattle Art Museum, provided me with important information on items in Harriet's collection of Alaska Native material.

Librarians at Purchase College Library, State University of New York, including US government specialist Andrew Pelle and art librarian Kim Detterbeck, aided me at key moments. Carrie Marten, resource sharing librarian, efficiently brought me a steady stream of books borrowed from distant libraries.

Several cousins contributed in a number of ways. Deby Sweren, my family history collaborator, generously shared her deep knowledge of the Smith family, found key pieces of information for me, and commiserated on the frustrations of family history research. Walter Patterson Jr., Kyla Maupin, Samuel Green, and Eleanor Eckert assisted with family photographs and family trees. Maxine Selmer, also a great-granddaughter of Harriet, kindly toured me around Skagway and Dyea and sent me photographs that had been Harriet's. With husband Stan Selmer, former Skagway mayor, she filled me in on recent Skagway history.

Authors Louisa V. North, Vicki Addesso, and the late Beverley Brigandi conveyed continuing interest and support of my project, as did marketing maven Barbara Rich. My daughter, Elizabeth Blake, my siblings, Virginia Phillips and the late Charles Phillips, and my sister-in-law, Nicola Shirley-Phillips, offered steady encouragement. Others who were supportive include director Tracy Fitzpatrick and senior curator Helaine Posner of the Neuberger Museum of Art, art history professors Paul H. D. Kaplan and Michael Lobel of Purchase College, State University of New York, and author Gary Golio. Friends who saw the possibilities in the project include Peter and Victoria Nelson, Michael Dick and Marjatta Rautionmaa, Lucy Hedrick and George Handley, Lanny Epperson, and Susan Gilbert. Attorney Chuck Brackbill answered my questions regarding Harriet's multiple court cases and came up with several marketing ideas related to Alaska.

Rita Rosenkranz, my agent, a pleasure to work with from the start, found a good home for my manuscript. Erin Turner, Meredith Dias, and Melissa Hayes, my editors at TwoDot and Globe Pequot, lent their skills throughout the editing and production processes. Kalen Landow and Jessica Plaskett ably guided the marketing and publicity for the book.

My deepest gratitude goes to my husband, Michael Torlen, who, while writing and painting, found time to help me with editing, photographing, and deciphering handwriting, and to accompany me on my research trips and geographic explorations. As a devoted diary keeper, he had valuable insights into the subtleties of the A. J. Smith diaries. Most of all, from the start of the journey, he has brought me his enduring enthusiasm for the project.

ENDNOTES

Abbreviations Used in the Notes

Annual Report: Annual Report of the Commissioner of Indian Affairs to the Secretary of the Interior

ASL: Alaska State Library Historical Collections, Juneau

BLMGLO: Bureau of Land Management General Land Office

CCHS: Clallam County Historical Society, Port Angeles, Washington

GLO: General Land Office

GPO: Government Printing Office

KLGO: Klondike Gold Rush National Historical Park Archives, Skagway

NARA: National Archives and Records Administration

OLYM: Olympic National Park Archives, Port Angeles, Washington

PSWA: Port Townsend Puget Sound Weekly Argus

WSL: Washington State Library Manuscripts Collections, Tumwater, Washington

Chapter One: Queen of Heartbreak Trail

1   Arthur Arent and Paul Peters, *Queen of Heartbreak Trail*, script #568 (Delaware: E. I. DuPont de Nemours, 1948), 2–4, 14–15, performed by Irene Dunne and others, broadcast on *The Cavalcade of America*. NBC Radio, May 17, 1948.

2   "Filmography," The Irene Dunne Site, accessed March 6, 2013, www.irenedunnesite .com/filmography.

3   Arent and Peters, *Queen of Heartbreak Trail*, cover page.

4   "Radio Broadcast of: Cavalcade of America," Audio Classics Archive, accessed November 25, 2012, www.audio-classics.com/lcavalcade.html.

5   William H. Hamilton to Mrs. J. Ormsby [Harriet] Phillips, June 9, 1948, Wilmington, Delaware.

6   "Irene Dunne on Radio—the '40s," The Irene Dunne Site, accessed March 6, 2013, www.irenedunnesite.com/radio/radio-the-40s.

7   Mrs. Louis [Dorothy] Klahn, "Local History Recalled by Writer," *Port Angeles Peninsula Herald*, November 25, 1976.

8   Dorothy Vera Smith Klahn, *Andrew J. Smith's Miniature Diary* (Port Angeles: Michael Trebert Chapter, Daughters of the American Revolution, [ca. 1978]). The

diary as transcribed by Klahn is in the Washington State Library and the public libraries of Seattle and Spokane.

9 "A man of much enterprise," Alanson did "an extensive business" in lumber and managed a farm. ("Family of Lumbermen—Another Old-Time Singer," *Towanda (Pa.) Bradford Star*, June 11, 1903.) The 1850 Federal Census of Agriculture shows that Alanson's production was considerably larger than that of any neighboring farms. The value of his farm equipment exceeded that of every other farmer in town but one. ("1850 Census Manuscripts," Pennsylvania Historical & Museum Commission, accessed April 20, 2013, www.portal.state.pa.us/portal/server.pt/community/census_manuscripts/2957.)

10 Fergus M. Bordewich, *Bound for Canaan: The Underground Railroad and the War for the Soul of America* (New York: HarperCollins, 2005), 4, 40, 53, 139, 153, 155, 164–65.

11 William J. Switala, *Underground Railroad in Pennsylvania* (Mechanicsburg, PA: Stackpole, 2001, 2nd ed. 2008), 132; Sylvia Wilson, "The Underground Railroad in Bradford County," *Settler, A Quarterly Magazine of History and Biography*, September, 1973, 6; Mrs. George A. Dayton, "The Underground Railroad and Its Stations in Bradford County," *Settler, A Quarterly Magazine of History and Biography*, April 1953, 144.

12 "Washington Monument," National Park Service, accessed May 4, 2014, www.nps.gov/wamo/index.htm.

Chapter Two: Wisconsin 1854–1869

1 Andrew J. Smith, State Volume Patent, Sale-Cash Entry, Wisconsin, Accession Nr: W12300_.125; WI2290__.140, May 15, 1857, Bureau of Land Management, *General Land Office Records* (hereafter cited as BLMGLO), accessed August 11, 2013, www.glorecords.blm.gov/details/patent/default.aspx?accession=WI2300__.125& docClass=STA&sid=lmwi3mmp.ucb; www.glorecords.blm.gov/details/patent/default.aspx?accession=WI2290__.140&docClass=STA&sid=lmwi3mmp.ucb.

2 Annotation by A. J. Smith on the back of a photograph he sent to his daughter in 1900, Smith Family Papers, Olympic National Park Archives (hereafter cited as OLYM), 728:7.

3 *History of Grant County, Wisconsin* (Chicago: Western Historical, 1881), 679; *Grant County Clerk Board Proceedings*, 1, October 8, 1839, 24–25, Archives, Southwest Wisconsin Room, University of Wisconsin, Platteville.

4 Gary Tinterow, "Édouard Manet: *Young Lady in 1866*," 26–31, in Art Institute of Chicago, Metropolitan Museum of Art and Musée d'Orsay, *Impressionism, Fashion, & Modernity*, ed. Gloria Groom (New Haven: Yale University Press, 2013), 29.

5 Andrew Jackson Smith, "In These Hard Times!" 1858, private collection.

6 *History of Grant County*, 870.

7 Broomcorn is not corn, but sorghum. At the very top of the tall plants are tassels bearing flowers. When dried and then shorn of their flowers and seeds, the sorghum tassels are stiff. Gathered into a bundle and attached to a handle, they make an excellent implement for sweeping. Information is courtesy of the broom maker

at Historic Village, Farmers' Museum in Cooperstown, New York, June 7, 2013, and the late Charles Phillips, grower of broomcorn.

8   *Wisconsin Volunteers: War of the Rebellion, 1861–1865, Arranged Alphabetically* (Madison, WI: Democrat Printing, 1914), 929.

9   A. W. Smith, "Friends & fellow citizens, ladies and gentlemen," draft of an unpublished speech, ca. 1930, Smith Family Papers, OLYM, 728:3.

10 Jennie S. Tyler, "Jennie S. Tyler," 37–39, in *Told by the Pioneers: Reminiscences of Pioneer Life in Washington*, 3, Federal Project No. 5841 (Olympia: WPA, 1938), 38.

11 Ed Maupin, interview by Jacilee Wray, October 20, 2000, edited by Ed Maupin, 2010, Smith Family Papers, OLYM, 728:7.

12 Dorothy Smith Klahn, *Mama's Dickey River Homestead* (privately printed, 1991), 142.

13 *History of Grant County*, 853.

14 A. J. had known his cousin Byron M. Smith in Pennsylvania and had corresponded with him for years. Byron, an early Dakota pioneer, had been elected secretary of the Territorial Legislature in 1866.

15 Mark Hufstetler and Michael Bedeau, *South Dakota's Railroads: An Historic Context* (Pierre: South Dakota State Historic Preservation Office, July 1998, rev. December 2007), 8, accessed January 26, 2013, http://history.sd.gov/preservation/OtherServices/SDRailroad.pdf.

16 James S. Foster with Silas Chapman, *Outlines of History of the Territory of Dakota, and Emigrant's Guide to the Free Lands of the Northwest* (Yankton, Dakota Territory: 1870), 26.

17 Foster, *Outlines of History*, 35–36, 39, 50, 101.

18 Ibid., 51.

19 *Manual for the Use of the Legislature of the State of New York* (Albany: Weed, Parsons, 1869), 10.

Chapter Three: Dakota 1869–1877

1   Kathleen Claar, quoted in Ian Frazier, *The Great Plains* (New York: Farrar, Straus and Giroux, 1989), 153–54.

2   Andrew J. Smith, Final Proof Required under Homestead Act May 20, 1862, September 16, 1874, National Archives and Records Administration (hereafter cited as NARA).

3   James S. Foster to Legislative Assembly of the Territory of Dakota, December 10, 1866, quoted in Kingsbury, *History of Dakota*, 1:456–57.

4   M. S. Burr, "Extract of Report to the Legislative Assembly of the Territory of Dakota," 1867, quoted in Kingsbury, *History of Dakota*, 1:471–72.

5   Herbert S. Schell, *History of Clay County, South Dakota* (Vermillion, SD: Clay County Historical Society, 1976), 144–45.

6   *Clay County Place Names* (Vermillion, SD: Clay County Historical Society, 1976), 67.

7   Foster, *Outlines of History*, 57, 58.

8   Ibid., 65.

9 Clay County, Dakota Territory, in *United States Census*, July 7, 1870, 66, USGen Web Archives, accessed April 17, 2014, http://usgwarchives.net/sd/clay/census/1870/clay_66.gif.

10 "Haines' Header, or Harvesting Machine," *Timaru (New Zealand) Herald*, February 22, 1875, accessed April 18, 2014, http://paperspast.natlib.govt .nz/cgi-bin/paperspast?a=d&cl=search&d=THD18750222.2.13&srpos= 19&e=-------10--11----0haines+header--.

11 Royal R. Pullen, "My Mother Harriet S. Pullen" (Unpublished reminiscence, [ca. 1986]), in the author's possession, 1; Harriet Stuart Pullen, "Story about Mrs. Pullen When She Went to Skagway, Alaska, in 1897, as Told by Mrs. Pullen to Harriet S. Pullen, Her Granddaughter, in 1941" (Essay, 1941), 2, in the author's possession. Appointed surveyor general in 1869, Beadle became a renowned educator. A. J.'s time with him was likely during the winters of 1871 to 1873 (recorded in the volumes of his diary that are missing).

12 Andro Linklater, *The Fabric of America: How Our Borders and Boundaries Shaped the Country and Forged Our Identity* (New York: Walker, 2007) 47, 67.

13 Andro Linklater, *Measuring America: How the United States Was Shaped by the Greatest Land Sale in History* (2002; New York: Plume, 2003), 144, 162.

14 I am grateful to James Hibbard of the Southwest Wisconsin Room of the University of Wisconsin Library in Platteville for help in understanding the PLSS.

15 Foster, *Outlines of History*, 97.

16 Linklater, *Measuring America*, 148.

17 A. J. Smith, Final Proof.

18 Andrew J. Smith, Homestead Final Certificate, No. 707, NARA.

19 A. J. Smith to Mary J. Smith, March 20, 1875, *Warranty Deed Record*, D:74, Clay County Register of Deeds, Vermillion, South Dakota.

20 Alexis de Tocqueville, *Democracy in America*, trans. and ed. Harvey C. Mansfield and Delba Winthrop (1840; Chicago: University of Chicago Press, 2000), 2:529.

Chapter Four: "Looking for Better Times"

1 George W. Kingsbury, *History of Dakota Territory: South Dakota, Its History and Its People*, ed. George Martin Smith, 1 (Chicago: Clarke, 1915), 554–55.

2 "The Children's Blizzard," January 2013, South Dakota Historical Society Foundation, accessed April 18, 2014, www.sdhsf.org/news_events/monthly_history_article .html/title/january-2013-the-children-s-blizzard.

3 Oscar William Coursey, *Pioneering in Dakota* (Mitchell, SD: Educator Supply, 1937), 109–10.

4 "Celebrates Her Seventy-Fifth Birthday," unidentified newspaper clipping, [1911], Smith File, Clallam County Genealogical Society, Port Angeles.

5 R. R. Pullen, "My Mother," 1.

6 Ibid.

7 Harold E. Briggs, "Grasshopper Plagues and Early Dakota Agriculture," *Agricultural History* 8, no. 2 (April 1934): 57.

8 Kingsbury, *History of Dakota*, 1:849.

9   Coursey, *Pioneering,* 62, 66–67.

10 Ibid., 67.

11 Kingsbury, *History of Dakota*, 1:589.

12 R. R. Pullen, "The Pullens . . . Strong Pioneers at LaPush," *Strait History*, 2, no. 4 (1987): 2.

13 Kingsbury, *History of Dakota*, 1:332–33.

14 C. D. Wilber, *The Great Valleys and Prairies of Nebraska and the Northwest* (Omaha, NE: Daily Republican Print, 1881), 68.

15 David M. Emmons, *Garden in the Grasslands: Boomer Literature of the Central Great Plains* (Lincoln: University of Nebraska Press, 1971), 138–39.

16 Tyler, "Jennie S. Tyler," 37.

17 Kingsbury, *History of Dakota*, 1:344.

18 Ibid., 1:345.

19 Briggs, "Grasshopper Plagues," 59.

20 "Celebrates Her Seventy-Fifth Birthday."

21 G. K. Warren, January 21, 1858, quoted in Kingsbury, *History of Dakota*, 1:347.

22 "About the Grasshopper," *Sioux Falls Independent*, July 8, 1875.

23 Ibid.

24 "About the Grasshopper"; Briggs, "Grasshopper Plagues," 61.

25 Briggs, "Grasshopper Plagues," 54.

26 Ibid., 57–59.

27 John R. Milton, *South Dakota: A Bicentennial History* (New York: Norton; Nashville: American Association for State and Local History, 1977), 91.

28 Foster, *Outlines of History*, 29–30.

29 "A Word about Grasshoppers," *Sioux Falls Independent*, June 17, 1875.

30 "About the Grasshopper."

31 Ibid.

32 Ibid.

33 Ibid.

34 Linklater, *Measuring America*, 214.

35 "Dakota Territory," *Chicago Tribune*, December 19, 1868.

36 Kingsbury, *History of Dakota*, 1:443.

37 *Yankton Daily Press and Dakotan*, June 5, 1875, quoted in Milton, *South Dakota*, 25–26.

38 Milton, *South Dakota*, 23–24.

39 Ibid., 26.

40 Kingsbury, *History of Dakota*, 1:922.

41 "Wesley Smith, West End Pioneer Dies," unidentified newspaper clipping, January 27, 1938, in the author's possession.

42 Milton, *South Dakota*, 95. The population of Dakota Territory swelled nearly seven-fold from 1870 to 1880—12,000 to 80,000. By 1890, it was 328,000, plus 20,000 Native Americans, counted separately.

43 Coursey, *Pioneering*, 18, 49.

44 Unattributed, "Dakota Land Is Hard to Beat," [1880s], quoted in Coursey, *Pioneering*, 60–61, a song Coursey's mother sang daily.
45 O. E. Rølvaag, *Giants in the Earth: A Saga of the Prairie* (1927; New York: Perennial Classics, 1999), 339. Originally published in Norwegian in 1924 and 1925.
46 Norman Colman, *Report of the Commissioner of Agriculture, 1887* (Washington, DC: Government Printing Office [hereafter cited as GPO], 1888), 143, quoted in Emmons, *Garden*, 173.
47 James Canfield, "Is the West Discontented? A Local Study of Facts," *Forum* 18 (December 1894): 449, quoted in Emmons, *Garden*, 173.
48 Briggs, "Grasshopper Plagues," 62.
49 Andrew J. Smith, Final Receiver's Receipt, handwritten note, NARA.
50 A. J. Smith, autobiographical statement.

Chapter Five: Washington 1877–1881

1 Ruth Pullen Hamilton, "Smith Family History (As Told to Royal Pullen)" (Essay, n.d.), in the author's possession.
2 Frank Leslie, *Frank Leslie's Illustrated Newspaper*, quoted in Jim Murphy, *Across America on an Emigrant Train* (New York: Clarion Books, 1993), 39.
3 Susan Coolidge [Sarah Chauncey Woolsey], "A Few Hints on the California Journey," *Scribner's Monthly*, May 1873, accessed March 2, 2013, www.cprr.org/Museum/Calif_Journey_1873/index.html.
4 Harriet Stuart Pullen, "Story about Mrs. Pullen," 1.
5 Murphy, *Across America*, 58.
6 Robert Louis Stevenson, "Across the Plains," 1883, 99–149, in *The Travels and Essays of Robert Louis Stevenson*, 15 (New York: Charles Scribner's Sons, 1907), 115–16. The article was first published in *Longman's Magazine*.
7 Stevenson, "Across the Plains," 120.
8 Ibid., 137.
9 Ibid., 134.
10 "Local News," *Port Townsend Puget Sound Weekly Argus* (hereafter cited as *PSWA*), December 1, 1876.
11 Cary C. Collins, "Subsistence and Survival: The Makah Indian Reservation, 1855–1933," *Pacific Northwest Quarterly* 87:4 (1996): 180–93.
12 Ann M. Renker, "The Makah Tribe: People of the Sea and the Forest," University of Washington Digital Collections, accessed August 6, 2013, http://content.lib.washington.edu/aipnw/renker.html.
13 "Wreck Report," *Seattle Daily Intelligencer*, January 27, 1877.
14 "Local Matters," *PSWA*, April 6, 1877.
15 Willa Cather, *O Pioneers!* 133–290, in *Early Novels and Stories* (1913; New York: Literary Classics of the United States, 1987), 161.
16 Henry David Thoreau, "Walking," 1862, 49–74, in *Civil Disobedience and Other Essays* (New York: Dover, 1993), 57.
17 Senator Alexander O. Anderson of Tennessee, in *Appendix to the Congressional Globe*, 26th Congress, 2nd session, January 8, 1841, 46, accessed May 6, 2014,

http://memory.loc.gov/cgi-bin/ampage?collId=llcg&fileName=008/llcg008
.db&recNum=280.

18 Kingsbury, *History of Dakota*, 333.

19 R. R. Pullen, "Smith Family History."

20 "Typhoid Fever," Mayo Clinic, accessed August 8, 2013, www.mayoclinic.com/
health/typhoid-fever/DS00538/DSECTION=symptoms; Michael Pollan, *Cooked:
A Natural History of Transformation* (New York: Penguin, 2013), 339.

21 R. R. Pullen, "Pullens," 2. Royal refers to Harriet's "fiery red hair."

22 Tyler, "Jennie S. Tyler," 37.

Chapter Six: Quillayute Country

1 R. R. Pullen, "Pullens," 2, note 1; Quillayute, Clallam County, in Territory of Washington, *Census*, May 20, 1889, 37, lines 12, 17.

2 *Map of Kennebec Co., Maine* (Philadelphia and Augusta, Maine: J. Chase Jr., 1856).

3 China, Maine, in US Bureau of the Census, *Eighth Census of the United States*, June
18, 1860, 35, line 39, NARA, Ancestry Institution, accessed February 21, 2013,
http://search.ancestryinstitution.com.

4 Archer K. Smith, "Cougars and a Bear's Den," 26–27, in *Tragedy Graveyard, The
Starbuck Ghost and Other True Stories: A Collection of Old True Happenings Taking Place Mostly on Washington's Olympic Peninsula* ([Washington State]: Privately
printed, 1997), 27.

5 R. R. Pullen, "Pullens," 1.

6 *Panama Star and Herald*, September 15, 1860, quoted in John Haskell Kemble, *The
Panama Route, 1848–1869* (Berkeley: University of California Press, 1943), 162.

7 Kemble, *Panama Route*, 11, 30, 148, 153, 166.

8 "Maine History Online," Maine Memory, accessed April 22, 2014, www.maine
memory.net/sitebuilder/site/903/page/1314/display?page=3.

9 "Mosaics of the City," unidentified newspaper clipping [ca. January 1893], in scrapbook, Pullen File, Clallam County Historical Society (hereafter cited as CCHS).

10 R. R. Pullen, "Pullens," 1.

11 "Mosaics of the City."

12 J[ay] V. Powell, "Quileute Exploitation and Maintenance of Prairies in Tradi-
tional Times," 2002, in M. Kat Anderson, *The Ozette Prairies of Olympic National
Park: Their Former Indigenous Uses and Management* (Port Angeles, WA: Olympic
National Park, 2009), 85.

13 "Mosaics of the City."

14 R. R. Pullen, "Pullens," 1.

15 "Makah Tribe History and More," Makah Tribe, accessed August 6, 2013, www
.makah.com/history.html.

16 Ross P. Shoecraft, "Bureau of Land Management Field Note," *Land Status and
Cadastral Survey*, Record: 1242142-0000000; State: WA; Meridian: 33; Township:
028-0N; Range: 014-0W; 1879, 436–40, accessed August 10, 2013, www.blm.gov/
or/landrecords/survey/yNoteView1_2.php?R0051WA0436004450.

17 Tyler, "Jennie S. Tyler," 37.

18 David Torrence Smith to Mina Smith, August 5, 1894, Diya [Dyea], Alaska, copy in entry added to A. J. Smith diary transcript.
19 A. J. Smith, "A. J. Smith and Family," October 1879, in the author's possession.
20 Beth Smith to A. W. Smith, May 6, 1908, Fort Atkinson, Wisconsin, A. Wesley Smith Papers, 1853–1935, M.S. 172, Washington State Library Manuscripts Collection, Tumwater (hereafter cited as A. W. Smith Papers).
21 A. J. Smith, "Communicated," *PSWA*, May 29, 1879.
22 A. J. S[mith], "Communicated," *PSWA*, August 21, 1879.
23 A. J. S[mith], "Quileute Items," *PSWA*, September 17, 1880. People referred to cougars as panthers.
24 George Pettitt, "The Quileute of La Push, 1775–1945," *Anthropological Records* 14:1 (Berkeley: University of California Press, 1950), iii, 22.
25 R. R. Pullen, "My Mother," 1.
26 A. W. Smith, diary, January 19, 1880, A. W. Smith Papers.
27 H. M. Smith to A. W. Smith, June 21, 1880, Quillayute, A. W. Smith Papers.
28 A. W. Smith, diary, November 24, December 2, 4, 5–9, 11, 15, 29, 1879, A. W. Smith Papers.
29 Tyler, "Jennie S. Tyler," 39.
30 A. J. Smith, "Quileute Items," *PSWA*, November 5, 1880.
31 Chas. Willoughby, Neah Bay Agency Report to Commissioner of Indian Affairs, August 7, 1879, in *Annual Report of the Commissioner of Indian Affairs to the Secretary of the Interior* (hereafter cited as *Annual Report*) (Washington, DC: GPO, 1879), 146.
32 Untitled notice, *PSWA*, October 29, 1880; Harvey H. Smith to A. W. Smith, February 11, 1881, Yankton, D.T., Smith File, CCHS.

Chapter Seven: The Pullen Family 1881–1889

1 Clallam County, Washington, *Clallam County Auditor's Marriage Book*, 1, 63.
2 Florance (Barrett) Willoughby (hereafter referred to as Barrett Willoughby or B. Willoughby), "Harriet Pullen: Mother of the North," in *Alaskans All* (Freeport, NY: Books for Libraries, 1933), 198. I thank the late Beverley Brigandi for help in describing Hattie's attire and hair.
3 Harriet Smith, photograph, in the author's possession.
4 Annie Dillard, *The Living* (New York: HarperCollins, 1992), 33.
5 "History of IOGT," International Organization of Good Templars, accessed March 7, 2014, www.iogt.us/iogt.php?p=35. Hattie was active in this organization at least until 1887. (H. S. Pullen to A. W. Smith, January 30, 1887, Seattle, A. W. Smith Papers.)
6 "Brief Local Items," *Puget Sound Argus*, March 4, 1881; A. W. Smith, diary, March 18, 30, 1881.
7 A. J. Smith, "Communicated," *PSWA*, February 12, 1880.
8 A. J. S[mith], "Quileute Items," *PSWA*, May 27, 1880, August 27, September 17, 1880.

9 Daniel Pullen, Homestead Proof, Testimony of Claimant, January 8, 1885, application No. 5370, Final Certificate No. 9167, NARA; Daniel Pullen, Serial Patent, Sale-Cash Entry, Washington, Accession Nr. WAOAA 109807, March 14, 1887, BLMGLO, accessed February 24, 2013, www.glorecords.blm.gov.

10 "Seven Ways to Compute the Relative Value of a U.S. Dollar Amount—1774 to Present," Measuring Worth, accessed December 31, 2014, www.measuringworth .com/uscompare.

11 *Washington Fur Co. v. Daniel Pullen and Hattie S. Pullen*, 307 (Superior Court of Clallam County, WA, 1893), (hereafter cited as *Washington Fur v. Pullen*) 173–74, 195, 218. The page numbers from this source refer to those in the microfilm copy of the documents in the Clallam County Courthouse.

12 Royal R. Pullen, interview by Ruth Pullen Hamilton and unidentified man from the CCHS, audiotape, 1980, CCHS.

13 "Quillayute Indians," *Seattle Post-Intelligencer*, [ca.1887].

14 *Washington Fur v. Pullen*, 219.

15 Ibid., 128, 172, 218–19.

16 R. R. Pullen, "Pullens," 1.

17 *Washington Fur v. Pullen*, 461.

18 Ibid., 112, 194.

19 R. R. Pullen, interview, 1980.

20 R. R. Pullen, "Pullens," 2.

21 R. R. Pullen, interview, 1980.

22 *Washington Fur v. Pullen*, 86, 122, 124, 171, 219–20.

23 Notary Public Certificate, Washington, July 22, 1891, Daniel Pullen; Postmaster Certificates, Quillayute, Daniel Pullen, April 19, 1881, Hatty S. Pullen, La Push, January 29, 1883, in the author's possession.

24 A. W. Smith, diary, December 2, 1879; O. W. Smith to A. W. Smith, February 24, 1898, Seattle, A. Wesley Smith Papers.

25 *Washington Fur v. Pullen*, 91, 128.

26 Ibid., 173–74, 193–95, 219.

27 A. J. Smith, "Our Reporters Budget," *PSWA*, January 12, 1883.

28 R. R. Pullen, "My Mother," 1.

29 David T. Smith, *Pullen Ranch: Gold Digger and Sunday (horses), Uncle Mart on Horseback*, 1890, 80.131.15, La Push Photographs File, CCHS.

30 Martha Smith Cutts, recollections, January 5, 1957, private collection.

31 R. R. Pullen, "Pullens," 2; R. R. Pullen, interview, 1980; R. R. Pullen, "My Mother," 2.

32 A. J. S[mith], "Quileute Items," *PSWA*, September 17, 1880.

33 R. R. Pullen, "My Mother," 2; R. R. Pullen, interview, 1980.

34 R. R. Pullen, interview, 1980.

35 Jim Heynen and Paul Boyer, "Royal R. Pullen," 30–31, in *One Hundred Over One Hundred* (Golden, CO: Fulcrum, 1990), 31.

36 R. R. Pullen, interview, 1980.

37 A. J. Smith, "Communicated," *PSWA*, March 25, 1880.

38   A. W. Smith, diary, October 4, 6–9, 14, 1893, A. W. Smith Papers.
39   "The Wreck of the *Leonor*," *Beaver (Wash.) Leader*, [ca. October 1893—early 1894].
40   Tyler, "Jennie S. Tyler," 38.
41   A. J. Smith, "A. J. Smith and Family."

Chapter Eight: The Quileutes

1   Pettitt, "Quileute," iii, 1, 81.
2   Ibid., iii, 1.
3   John Meares, *Voyages Made in the Years 1788 and 1789, From China to the North West Coast of America* (London: Logographic Press, 1790), 157–58, quoted in Kenneth N. Owens, ed., *The Wreck of the* Sv. Nikolai, Alton S. Donnelly, trans. (1985; repr., Lincoln: University of Nebraska Press, 2001), 20.
4   Owens, *Wreck,* 69; J. V. Powell, "Quileute Exploitation," 116.
5   Owens, *Wreck,* 3–5, 31.
6   James Swan, "A Cruise in the *Sarah Newton* (July 18–August 24, 1861)," *Washington Standard*, October 5, 12, 1861, quoted in J. V. Powell, "Quileute Exploitation," 128.
7   "Quinault Treaty, 1856," Governor's Office of Indian Affairs, State of Washington, accessed April 23, 2014, www.goia.wa.gov/treaties/Treaties/quinault.htm.
8   *Executive Orders Relating to Indian Reservation from May 14, 1855 to July 1, 1912* (Washington, DC: GPO, 1912), 196–97, 218.
9   Joseph Hill, "Report, No. 7," to Superintendent Indian Affairs, Olympia, W.T., 48–49, in *Annual Report* (1867), 48–49.
10   R. H. Milroy, "Quinaielt Agency Report to Commissioner of Indian Affairs, No. 64," October 1, 1872, 328–45, in *Annual Report* (1872), 339–40. *Quinault* was spelled "Quinaielt" at the time.
11   Milroy, "Quinaielt Agency Report," 339.
12   Ibid.
13   C. A. Huntington, "Neah Bay Agency Report to Commissioner of Indian Affairs," August 18, 1877, 187–89, in *Annual Report* (1877), 188.
14   Charles Willoughby, "Neah Bay Agency Report to Commissioner of Indian Affairs," August 18, 1881, 161–63, in *Annual Report* (1881), 162.
15   Oliver Wood, "Neah Bay Agency Report to Commissioner of Indian Affairs," August 13, 1885, 187–89, in *Annual Report* (1885), 188.
16   G. A. Heney, "Quinaielt Agency Report to Commissioner of Indian Affairs," September 1, 1874, 334–36, in *Annual Report* (1874), 335.
17   Heney, "Quinaielt Agency Report," August 24, 1876, 141–42, in *Annual Report* (1876), 142.
18   C. Willoughby, "Neah Bay Agency Report," August 7, 1879, 144–48, in *Annual Report* (1879), 146.
19   Ibid., 145.
20   J. V. Powell, "Quileute Exploitation," 144.
21   R. R. Pullen, interview, 1980.
22   A. J. Smith, "Communicated," *PSWA*, February 12, 1880.

23 Edward Holland Nicoll, "The Chinook Language or Jargon," *Popular Science Monthly*, June 1889, 257–61.

24 R. R. Pullen, "Pullens," 3.

25 A. W. Smith to Harriet Gertrude [Gertie] Smith, July 29, 1888, La Push, A. W. Smith Papers.

26 R. R. Pullen, "Pullens," 3.

27 G. B. Hobucket to A. W. Smith, June 24, 1903, Mora, Washington, Smith Family Papers, OLYM, 728:3.

28 A. W. Smith to Gertie Smith, August 4, 1888, La Push, A. W. Smith Papers.

29 J. V. Powell, "Quileute Exploitation," 126–29, 131.

30 Jacilee Wray and M. Kat Anderson, "Restoring Indian-Set Fires to Prairie Ecosystems on the Olympic Peninsula," *Ecological Restoration* 21, no. 4 (2003): 301.

31 J. V. Powell, "Quileute Exploitation," 142–43.

32 Ibid., 141.

33 Ibid., 87, 103–06, 115.

34 Ibid., 85–86.

35 Pettitt, "Quileute," 16.

36 Nora Marks Dauenhauer, "Tlingit AT.ÓOW: Traditions and Concepts," in Seattle Art Museum, *The Spirit Within*, 21–29 (New York: Rizzoli / Seattle Art Museum, 1995), 29.

37 John P. McGlinn to A. W. Smith, ca. 1890, Neah Bay, A. W. Smith Papers.

38 A. J. Smith, "Quileute Items," *PSWA*, August 27, 1880.

39 Pettitt, "Quileute," 86.

40 Ibid., 15.

41 Ibid., 106.

42 Ibid., 111–12.

43 Wood to A. W. Smith, October 8, 1883, Neah Bay, A. W. Smith Papers; W. L. Powell to A. W. Smith, December 17, 1888, Neah Bay, A. W. Smith Papers.

44 A. W. Smith, Quileute census drafts, 1884, 1890, Smith File, CCHS.

45 T. J. Morgan, Department of the Interior, Office of Indian Affairs circular (Washington, DC, March 19, 1890).

46 *Census of the Quileute Indians*, Neah Bay Agency, 1900, 1916.

47 Pettitt, "Quileute," 25, 94.

48 Wood, "Neah Bay Agency Report to Commissioner of Indian Affairs," August 11, 1884, 206–08, in *Executive Documents of the House of Representatives for the Second Session of the Forty-eighth Congress, 1884–'85* (Washington, DC: GPO, 1885), 207.

49 [W. H. Hudson], "Future of La Push, the Indian Town," *La Push Quileute Chieftain*, February 2, 1910.

50 *Neah Bay Industrial School Monthly Report*, July 1, 1881, Smith Family Papers, OLYM, 728:1/1.

51 C. H. Hale to William P. Dole, August 8, 1864, in *Annual Report* (1864), 57.

52 Pettitt, "Quileute," 23–24.

53 Ibid., 24–25.

54 Ibid., 25, 83.

55   R. R. Pullen, "Pullens," 2; Tyler, "Jennie S. Tyler," 38–39.

56   R. R. Pullen, interview, 1980.

57   Tyler, "Jennie S. Tyler," 39.

58   Anonymous transcript of hearing, [ca. 1885], A. W. Smith Papers.

59   "History," Quileute Nation, accessed August 16, 2013, www.quileutenation.org/
      culture/history.

60   Pettitt, "Quileute," 17; J. V. Powell, "Quileute Exploitation," 143; R. R. Pullen,
      interview, 1980.

61   R. R. Pullen, interview, 1980.

62   Ibid.

63   "Camping at Lapush," *Beaver (Wash.) Leader*, July 29, [early 1890s], in A. W. Smith
      Papers.

64   James G. Swan, "The Surf-Smelt of the Northwest Coast, and the Method of
      Taking Them by the Quillehute Indians, West Coast of Washington Territory," in
      Proceedings of the United States National Museum, 1880, 3:43–46 (Washington, DC:
      GPO, 1881), 45.

Chapter Nine: La Push 1889–1897

1   Joe Pullen to A. W. Smith, September 5, 1897, Orting, Washington, A. W. Smith
     Papers; Pettitt, "Quileute," 27.

2   R. R. Pullen, interview, 1980.

3   Wood, "Neah Bay Agency Report," August 13, 1885, 187–89.

4   Harry Hobucket, "Quileute Indian Tradition," *Washington Historical Quarterly* 25,
     no. 1 (1934): 57.

5   W. L. Powell to A. W. Smith, September 16, 1889, Neah Bay, A. W. Smith Papers.

6   Pettitt, "Quileute," 27.

7   A. J. Smith, "Communicated," *PSWA*, March 25, 1880.

8   W. L. Powell to A. W. Smith, January 15, 1889, Neah Bay, Smith Family Papers,
     OLYM, 728:1/7.

9   Tyler, "Jennie S. Tyler," 38.

10   R. R. Pullen, "Pullens," 2.

11   Robert Lyall to A. W. Smith, March 2, 1884, A. W. Smith Papers.

12   Wood to A. W. Smith, September 9, 1884, Neah Bay, A. W. Smith Papers.

13   N. C. McFarland, Commissioner of the General Land Office, Department of the
     Interior (hereafter cited as GLO), *Circular 3 L. D., 371, to US Land Office Regis-
     ter and Receivers*, May 31, 1884. The directive reads, "You are hereby instructed to
     peremptorily refuse all entries and filings attempted to be made by others than the
     Indian occupants upon lands in the possession of Indians who have made improve-
     ments of any value whatever thereon."

14   Harvey H. Smith, Serial Patent, Washington, Accession Nr. WASAA 311380,
     February 7, 1889, Sale-Cash Entry, BLMGLO, accessed February 21, 2014, www
     .glorecords.blm.gov.

15   Geo[rge] Chandler, First Assistant Secretary, Department of the Interior, to the
     Commissioner of the GLO, March 1, 1893, *United States v. Daniel Pullen and*

Hattie S. Pullen, vol. 16–148:12–13, Pullen File, CCHS. The letter, which sum-
marizes the Pullens' land case, was published as a decision in S. V. Proudfit, ed.,
*Decisions of the Department of the Interior and General Land Office in Cases Relating to
the Public Lands, From January 1, 1893, to June 30, 1893* (Washington, DC: GPO,
1893), 209–17.

16 *Daniel Pullen and Hattie Pullen vs. John P. McGlinn as United States Indian Agent*,
Answer (US Circuit Court, Wash. Dist. No. Div., 1898), 17. In September 1884,
agent Wood asked for proper proceedings to cause the cancellation of Pullen's Preemption and Timber claims at La Push. The General Land Office ordered a special
agent investigation into the situation in October.

17 Wood to A. W. Smith, July 25, 1885, Neah Bay, A. W. Smith Papers.

18 Wood, "Neah Bay Agency Report," August 13, 1885, in *Annual Report* (1885),
188–89.

19 Chandler to Commissioner of the GLO, *U.S. v. Pullen*, 14.

20 W. L. Powell to Commissioner of Indian Affairs, November 23, 1885, Neah Bay
Agency Files, doc. 28595, NARA, quoted in Pettitt, "Quileute," 27.

21 W. L. Powell to A. W. Smith, April 3, 1886, Neah Bay, A. W. Smith Papers.

22 Chandler to Commissioner of the GLO, *U.S. v. Pullen*, 11.

23 Ibid., 12.

24 McGlinn, "Report of Neah Bay Agency," August 14, 1890, 222–25, in *Annual
Report* (1890), 224; McGlinn, "Report of Neah Bay Agency," 447–50, August 17,
1891, in *Annual Report* (1891), 449.

25 Chandler to Commissioner of the GLO, *U.S. v. Pullen*, 2.

26 "Quillayute Indians."

27 Ibid.

28 Jacobs & Jenner to Daniel W. and Harriet S. Pullen, retainer receipt, September 5,
1887, Pullen File, CCHS.

29 "A Land Decision in the Case of the United States against Daniel Pullen," *Seattle
Press-Times*, October 15, 1891.

30 *Washington Fur v. Pullen*, 194.

31 Grover Cleveland, "Executive Order, Quileute Reserve, February 19, 1889," in
Executive Orders Relating to Indian Reservations from May 14, 1855 to July 1, 1912
(Washington, DC: GPO, 1912), 923.

32 Cleveland, "Executive Order," 923.

33 McGlinn, "Report of Neah Bay Agency," in *Annual Report* (1890), 223.

34 A copy of a map dated 1915–16 shows the La Push properties still owned by the
family. David T. Smith's claim had by then passed to his brother, Harvey Smith.
Wesley's wife's claim must have been in his possession by then, as she had died
years earlier. (Smith Family Papers, OLYM, 728:7.)

35 W. L. Powell to A. W. Smith, September 16, 1889, A. W. Smith Papers.

36 McGlinn, "Report of Neah Bay Agency," in *Annual Report* (1890), 223.

37 McGlinn to A. W. Smith, December 23, 1889, Neah Bay, A. W. Smith Papers.

38 McGlinn to A. W. Smith, June 23, 30, October 8, 1890, Neah Bay, A. W. Smith
Papers.

39 W. L. Powell to A. W. Smith, December 17, 1888, Neah Bay; A. W. Smith to McGlinn, June 5, 1898, La Push, Smith Family Papers, OLYM, 728:1/7; McGlinn to A. W. Smith, October 13, 1890, Neah Bay, Smith Family Papers, OLYM, 728:1/8.

40 A. W. Smith statement, signed by members of Quileute tribe, November 1890, A. W. Smith Papers.

41 Chandler to Commissioner of the GLO, *U.S. v. Pullen*, 3.

42 "Land Decision."

43 *Washington Fur v. Pullen*, 112, 219.

44 Chandler to Commissioner of the GLO, *U.S. v. Pullen*, 4.

45 J. M. Carson, "The Pullen Case," *Seattle Press-Times*, October 15, 1891.

46 A. J. Smith, "Communicated," *PSWA*, February 12, 1880.

47 Carson, "Pullen Case."

48 "Land Decision."

49 William A. J. Sparks, Commissioner of the GLO, Department of the Interior, *Circular 3 L. D., 371, to US Land Office Register and Receivers*, October 27, 1887.

Chapter Ten: A Man with a Badge

1   "Seven Ways to Compute," accessed August 31, 2015, www.measuringworth.com/uscompare/relativevalue.php.

2   *Washington Fur v. Pullen*, 254, 583–84.

3   Herbert B. Huntley, *The Code of Procedure and Penal Code of the State of Washington* (Seattle: Sunset, 1893), 468.

4   *Washington Fur v. Pullen*, 339, 548, 577–82; D. T. Smith, *Pullen Ranch*, photograph.

5   *Washington Fur v. Pullen*, 339–40, 350–51, 360, 577–82; Daniel Pullen and Hattie S. Pullen to Oliver W. Smith, Warranty Deed, May 10, 1892; Daniel Pullen and Hattie S. Pullen to Oliver W. Smith, Property Bill of Sale, May 6, 1892, A. W. Smith Papers.

6   *Washington Fur v. Pullen*, 306.

7   Ibid., 89, 100, 103, 108.

8   W. L. Powell, "Neah Bay Agency Report," August 15, 1887, 209–11, in *Annual Report* (1887), 210.

9   *Washington Fur v. Pullen*, 231–32.

10 Ibid., 79, 210, 253; "Dan Pullen Wins," unidentified newspaper clipping, [June 27, 1893]; Carson, "Pullen Case."

11 Carson, "Pullen Case."

12 *Washington Fur v. Pullen*, 100.

13 "Mosaics of the City."

14 "In the Quillayute Country," *Port Angeles Beacon*, March 17, 1893.

15 *Washington Fur v. Pullen*, 418–45.

16 Gertie Smith to A. W. Smith, May 15, 1888, Fort Atkinson, Wisconsin, A. W. Smith Papers.

17 G. Smith to A. W. Smith, July 7, 1888, Fort Atkinson, Wisconsin, A. W. Smith Papers.

18 G. Smith to A. W. Smith, June 29, 1888, Fort Atkinson, Wisconsin, A. W. Smith Papers.

19 Wood to A. W. Smith, December 31, 1883, Neah Bay, Smith Family Papers, OLYM, 728:1/1.

20 M. J. Smith to A. W. Smith, June 10, 1888, A. W. Smith Papers.

21 M. J. Smith to A. W. Smith, August 12, [1888], A. W. Smith Papers.

22 A. W. Smith to J. C. Keenan, January 8, 1896, La Push, draft; Keenan to A. W. Smith, March 6, 1896, Neah Bay, Smith Family Papers, OLYM, 728:2/2.

23 Harriet Stuart Pullen, "Story About Mrs. Pullen," 2; Florence Clothier, diary, July 1928, 5, M.S. 136, University of Alaska Fairbanks Archives.

24 *Washington Fur v. Pullen*, 123-25, 404-06.

25 Ibid., 415. John Carnes was murdered in November 1901, shot in the back near his home by an unknown assailant. The case remained unsolved. (A. W. Smith Papers.)

26 *Washington Fur v. Pullen*, 82-92, 102.

27 *Washington Fur v. Pullen*, 87, 91, 128, 183, 197, 226.

28 "Woman Sourdough of Nineties Likes North," *Seattle Post-Intelligencer*, March 28, 1930.

29 Jeff Brady, "Harriet S. Pullen: A Woman Who Never Confessed," 285-91, in Jeff Brady, ed., *Skagway, City of the New Century: The True Story of Skagway, Alaska* (Skagway: Lynn Canal, 2013), 289.

30 B. Willoughby, "Harriet Pullen," 169.

31 R. R. Pullen, "My Mother," 1.

32 R. R. Pullen, interview, 1980.

33 Harriet Smith Pullen [hereafter cited as H. S. Pullen, as distinguished from Harriet Stuart Pullen, her granddaughter] to A. W. Smith, May 26, 1893, Port Angeles, A. W. Smith Papers.

34 *Washington Fur v. Pullen*, 428.

35 Ely Peterson to Winnie Peterson, June 12, 1895 (*sic*), Port Angeles, letter reprinted in Gary Peterson and Glynda Peterson Schaad, "Preacher's Daughter and Alaskan Icon: The Unsinkable Harriet Pullen," in *Women to Reckon With: Untamed Women of the Olympic Wilderness* (Forks, WA: Poseidon Peak, 2007), 34.

36 *Washington Fur v. Pullen*, 97.

37 Ibid., 186–87, 228.

38 Ibid., 50, 87, 91, 128, 182–83, 228.

39 Ibid., 173–74, 193–95, 219–20; Tyler, "Jennie S. Tyler," 39.

40 *Washington Fur v. Pullen*, 89; "Dan Pullen Wins."

41 *Washington Fur v. Pullen*, 42, 198.

42 Ibid., 170–71, 193.

43 Ibid., 165.

44 Ibid., 103.

45 Ibid., 42–48, 117–19, 123–25, 404–06, 447–48.

46 Ibid., 166–98, 210–32.

47 Ibid., 164.

48 Ibid., 130–59, 215–16.

49 "Pullen Wins," [*Port Crescent (Wash.) Leader*, June 27, 1893], clipping in scrapbook, Pullen File, CCHS.

50 "A Dealer in Drafts," *Seattle Post*, undated clipping in scrapbook, Pullen File, CCHS.

51 *Washington Fur v. Pullen*, 37.

52 Ibid., 100.

53 "An Old Settler Here," [January 20, 1893], hand-dated, unidentified newspaper clipping in scrapbook, Pullen File, CCHS. This may have been written by A. J. Smith.

54 "Pullen Wins"; "Still Drags Along," [June 22, 1893], hand-dated, unidentified newspaper clipping in scrapbook, Pullen File, CCHS.

55 "Still Drags Along"; "Dan Pullen Wins."

56 "Caught in the Act," *Beaver (Wash.) Leader*, June 22, 1893.

57 "End of the Baxter-Pullen Case," *Port Angeles Democrat-Leader*, [June 1893], clipping in scrapbook, Pullen File, CCHS.

58 *Washington Fur v. Pullen*, 319, 337; "Pullen Wins"; "End of the Baxter-Pullen Case."

59 *Washington Fur v. Pullen*, 11–12, 32–67, 252–305, 324, 337, 339.

60 Ibid., 175, 195–96, 218–19.

61 Ibid., 195.

62 Ibid., 18.

63 *Daniel Pullen and Hattie Pullen vs. John P. McGlinn as United States Indian Agent* (US Circuit Court, Wash. Dist. No. Div., No. 290, July 12, 1893),11–12, Smith Family Papers, OLYM, 728:7; William H. Sims, Acting Secretary, Department of the Interior, to Commissioner of Indian Affairs, May 25, 1893, Washington, DC, Pullen File, CCHS.

64 Restraining Order, August 17, 1893; Temporary Injunction, October 9, 1894; *U.S. v. Pullen*, Pullen File, CCHS.

65 W. H. Hudson, "Our Pullen," *La Push Quileute Independent*, December 17, 1908.

66 "Camping at La Push."

67 "A Grand Success," *Beaver (Wash.) Leader*, October 2, [mid-1890s]; A. K. Smith, "Zeke," in *Tragedy Graveyard*, 32.

68 "Over One Hundred Skins Taken in One Day," May 21, [early 1890s], unidentified newspaper clipping, A. W. Smith Papers.

69 Editorial, *Beaver (Wash.) Leader*, October 11, 1895.

70 Ibid., October 18, 1895.

71 "The 'Leader' Vindicated," *Beaver (Wash.) Leader*, October 21, 1895.

72 Editorial, *Beaver (Wash.) Leader*, [ca. 1895], clipping, A. W. Smith Papers.

73 Donald Worster, "Beyond the Agrarian Myth," 3–25, in Patricia Nelson Limerick, Clyde A. Milner II, and Charles E. Rankin, eds., *Trails: Toward a New Western History* (Lawrence: University Press of Kansas, 1991), 18.

74 Surveyor General's Office, Olympia, W. T., *Map of Township No 28 of Range No 15 West, Will Meridian Washington Terr'y*, 28-15W-A, May 29, 1882, notes added, 1889; David T. Smith, Serial Patent, Washington, Accession Nr. WASAA 111415,

July 18, 1895; Harriet Bright Smith, Serial Patent, Washington, Accession Nr. WASSA 111403, April 24, 1894, Homestead Entries, BLMGLO, accessed March 4, 2013, www.glorecords.blm.gov.

75 Chandler to Commissioner of the GLO, *U.S. v. Pullen*, 7–9, 12.

76 Ibid., 15.

77 *Atherton v. Fowler*, 96 US 513 (1877).

78 Wood, "Neah Bay Agency Report," August 13, 1885, in *Annual Report* (1885), 188–89.

79 "Daniel Pullen Missing," *Friday Harbor (Wash.) Islander*, August 27, 1896.

Chapter Eleven: Skagway 1897–1902

1   "Gold! Gold! Gold! Gold!" *Seattle Post-Intelligencer*, July 17, 1897.

2   M. J. Kirchhoff, *Clondyke: The First Year of the Rush* (Juneau: Alaska Cedar Press, 2010), 42–48. Kirchhoff cites coverage of the gold strike in the Yukon in the *Boston Journal*, October 31, 1896, and in the *New York Times*, January 31, 1897.

3   Pierre Berton, *The Klondike Fever: The Life and Death of the Last Great Gold Rush* (New York: Basic Books, 1958), 100. The *Excelsior* docked in San Francisco on July 14.

4   H. S. Pullen to A. W. Smith, September 3, 1897, Port Angeles, A. W. Smith Papers.

5   "A Woman without Fear," dateline, "Port Townsend, Sept. 4," [1897], clipping in scrapbook, Pullen File, CCHS.

6   "A Woman without Fear."

7   R. R. Pullen, "Pullens, 3"; Paula Becker, "Washington State Normal School Opens in Ellensburg on September 6, 1891," Essay 5093, November 19, 2005, *The Free Online Encyclopedia of Washington State History*, accessed March 13, 2014; www .historylink.org/_content/printer_friendly/pf_output.cfm?file_id=5093.

8   Murray Morgan, *Skid Road: An Informal Portrait of Seattle* (1951; repr., Seattle: University of Washington Press, 1982), 9.

9   R. R. Pullen, interview, 1980.

10 "Our Alaska Representative," *Beaver (Wash.) Leader*, [Aug./Sept. 1897], clipping in scrapbook, Pullen File, CCHS.

11 H. S. Pullen, "On Board the *Rosalie*," [*Beaver (Wash.) Leader*, September 1897], clipping in scrapbook, Pullen File, CCHS.

12 Ibid.

13 Ibid.

14 Barrett Willoughby, "Mother of the North," *American Magazine*, August 1930, 66; Ella Higginson, *Alaska, the Great Country* (New York: Macmillan, 1908), 431.

15 Skagway Historic District Unit, Klondike Gold Rush National Historical Park, Skagway (hereafter cited as KLGO), *Cultural Landscape Report for the Capt. William Moore Cabin, J. Bernard Moore House, Peniel Mission, and Pullen House Sites* (Denver: National Park Service, 1995), 19.

16 Robert L. S. Spude, *Skagway, District of Alaska, 1884–1912: Building the Gateway to the Klondike*, Occasional Paper No. 36 (Fairbanks: Anthropology and Historic Preservation, Cooperative Park Studies Unit, University of Alaska, 1983), 6–7.

17 William Shape, *Faith of Fools: A Journal of the Klondike Gold Rush* (Pullman: Washington State University Press, 1998), 4–5; Tappan Adney, *The Klondike Stampede* (New York: Harper & Brothers, 1900), 41, 61.

18 A[nnie] H[all] S[trong], "Impressions of Skagway," *Skaguay News*, December 31, 1897.

19 Adney, *Klondike Stampede*, 57, 273.

20 Barrett Willoughby to Harriet Pullen, September 7, 1926, San Francisco, Pullen File, CCHS.

21 B. Willoughby, "Mother of the North," 64–66, 112.

22 B. Willoughby, "Harriet Pullen," 166.

23 T[om] A. Davies, "Was Over Both Trails," *Seattle Daily Times*, October 1, 1897, evening edition.

24 Julie Johnson, *A Wild Discouraging Mess: The History of the White Pass Unit of the Klondike Gold Rush National Historical Park* (Anchorage: National Park Service, 2003), 25. I thank Skagway historian Karl Gurcke for clarification on this point.

25 B. Willoughby, "Harriet Pullen," 166.

26 Harriet Stuart Pullen, "Story about Mrs. Pullen," 2.

27 B. Willoughby, "Harriet Pullen," 168.

28 Ibid., 166; Ruth Pullen Hamilton, "Reminiscences of Royal Pullen," summer 1987, 1, Pullen Papers, KLGO.

29 Bessie Beatty, "The 'Big Lady' of Skagway," [ca. 1914], unidentified newspaper clipping in scrapbook, Pullen File, CCHS. The article says it was written for the *San Francisco Call*.

30 Mary Lee Davis, *Uncle Sam's Attic: The Intimate Story of Alaska* (Boston: Wilde, 1930), 40.

31 Bud Branham, "Gold-Rush Mother," *Alaska Sportsman*, August 1940, 32. Descendants claim Harriet later made fresh green apple pies from apples sent to Skagway from Clallam County. (Eleanor Eckert, Smith family genealogy.)

32 Royal R. Pullen, interview by R. P. Hamilton, March 1988, 1, 4–5, KLGO 45017, Pullen Papers, KLGO.

33 Dona Cloud, "Minerva Troy: Woman Who Made a Difference," *Strait History* 4, no. 2 (1989): 2.

34 B. Willoughby, "Harriet Pullen," 171.

35 "High Tides at Skaguay," *Seattle Daily Times*, November 23, 1897, evening edition. *Skaguay* was an early spelling of Skagway.

36 "High Tides."

37 "Pernicious Truth Users," *Skaguay News*, December 10, 1897, front-page editorial.

38 *High Tide at Skagway, Alaska*, October 27, 1897, photograph by Eric A. Hegg, Yukon Archives 2220.

39 *Skaguay News*, October 29, 1897.

40 "From Skaguay," *Skaguay News*, December 20, 1897.

41 "High Tides."

42 R. L. S. Spude, *Skagway*, 6.

43 "The Martyr of the Klondike," *Skaguay News*, January 22, 1898.

44 R. R. Pullen, "Pullens," 3.
45 R. R. Pullen, interview, 1980, 1, 4–5; R. P. Hamilton, "Reminiscences of Royal Pullen," 1.
46 B. Willoughby, "Harriet Pullen," 177–78.
47 Ibid., 178.
48 Ibid., 180.
49 R. L. S. Spude, *Skagway*, 11. The Brackett Wagon Road opened on March 1, 1898. According to Karl Gurcke, rather than weighing the stampeders' packs, the Canadian border authorities simply surveyed outfits visually and checked receipts to determine whether they contained sufficient supplies.
50 I thank Karl Gurcke for describing the Skagway to Bennett Lake trip.
51 Fred Thompson, *To the Yukon with Jack London: The Klondike Diary of Fred Thompson*, ed. David Mike Hamilton (Los Angeles: Zamorano Club, 1980), note 1, 22.
52 "Martyr of the Klondike."
53 Thompson, *To the Yukon*, 14.
54 Earle Labor, *Jack London: An American Life* (New York: Farrar, Straus and Giroux, 2013), 107–09.
55 Jack London, "Which Make Men Remember," 65–85, in *The God of His Fathers & Other Stories* (New York: McClure, Phillips, 1901), 79–80.
56 Adney, *Klondike Stampede*, 124.
57 B. Willoughby, "Harriet Pullen," 180–81.
58 Harriet Stuart Pullen, "Story about Mrs. Pullen," 2; B. Willoughby, "Harriet Pullen," 182–83; R. P. Hamilton, "Reminiscences," 1.
59 Herb Hilscher, "The Most Unforgettable Character I've Met," *Reader's Digest*, August 1961, 76.
60 "Harriet Pullen—An Alaskan Heroine; HSP's Own Story" (anonymously authored story in the author's possession, written between March 1922 and September 1923 by someone who knew Harriet and had read earlier published accounts about her, typed by R. P. Hamilton), 4.
61 B. Willoughby, "Harriet Pullen," 182–83.
62 Catherine Holder Spude, *"That Fiend in Hell": Soapy Smith in Legend* (Norman: University of Oklahoma Press, 2012), 156.
63 H. S. Pullen to A. W. Smith, April 20, 1898, Skagway, 987.125.32b, Smith File, CCHS.
64 R. P. Hamilton, "Reminiscences," 1.
65 Charlotte Cameron, *A Cheechako in Alaska and Yukon* (London: Stokes, 1920), 53.
66 "Harriet Pullen—An Alaskan Heroine," 2.

Chapter Twelve: The Independent Entrepreneur

1 Henry C. Dierck, "The First Postmaster of Lapush," unidentified postal service newsletter, 1981, 44, in the author's possession, courtesy Walter Patterson Jr. Annie Smith officially took over the postmaster job on April 30, 1898.
2 H. S. Pullen to A. W. Smith, April 20, 1898.
3 Ibid.

4   Chas. K. Jenner to H. S. Pullen, July 7, 1898, Seattle, Pullen File, CCHS.
5   D. W. Pullen to Judge [Cornelius H.] Hanford, July 27, 1898, Skagway, Smith Family Papers, OLYM, 728:7.
6   W. A. Jones, "Daniel Pullen and the Quillehute Reservation, Wash.," September 26, 1898, 105–07, in United States, Office of Indian Affairs, *Annual Report* (1898), 106; "Reservation News," *Beaver (Wash.) Leader*, June 24, 1898; A. J. Smith, "In Defense of Mr. Pullen," November 18, 1898, unidentified newspaper clipping in scrapbook, Pullen File, CCHS.
7   McGlinn, "Report of Neah Bay Agency," in *Annual Report* (1890), 223.
8   Wilson R. Gay to Daniel Pullen, June 23, 1899, Seattle, Pullen File, CCHS.
9   *Edwin S. Marston vs. Daniel Pullen & Hattie S. Pullen, et al.*, foreclosure, June 13, 1892 mortgage, Superior Court of the State of Washington for Clallam County, September 5, 1899, Sheriff of Clallam County to Edwin S. Marston, Sheriff's Deed, March 28, 1901, *Deed Book*, 191–92, 260–63, Clallam County Auditor's Office, Port Angeles.
10   A. J. Smith to A. W. Smith, January 7, 1901, Macedonia, Pa., Smith File, CCHS.
11   Thomas Martindale, *Hunting in the Upper Yukon* (Philadelphia: Jacobs, 1913), 297. The railway opened to the Summit on February 20, 1899 and to Bennett Lake on July 6 of that year. (R. L. S. Spude, *Skagway*, 18.)
12   R. L. S. Spude, *Skagway*, 11.
13   Annie Hall Strong, "From Woman's Standpoint," *Skaguay News*, December 31, 1897.
14   Branham, "Gold-Rush Mother," 30, 32.
15   Ibid.
16   Harriet Stuart Pullen, "Story about Mrs. Pullen," 3; Adney, *Klondike Stampede*, 462.
17   R. L. S. Spude, *Skagway*, 27.
18   R. P. Hamilton, "Reminiscences," 2.
19   Skagway, Southern District, Alaska, 79, line 18, in US Bureau of the Census, *Twelfth Census of the United States*, April 7, 1900, NARA, Ancestry Institution, accessed February 24, 2013, http://search.ancestryinstitution.com.
20   R. P. Hamilton, "Reminiscences," 2; R. R. Pullen, interview, 1988, 4–5.
21   "Summer Tourists Come to Skagway," *Skaguay Daily Alaskan*, July 25, 1898. "Skaguay Day," designated a day of cleanup to prepare for the tourist season, was held on June 8, 1899. (R. L. S. Spude, *Skagway*, 18.)
22   Branham, "Gold-Rush Mother," 32.
23   Johnson, *Wild Discouraging Mess*, 19.
24   "The Texas Deck," KET Electronic Field Trips, www.ket.org/trips/belle/tour/decks/page04.htm. I thank Karl Gurcke for bringing this meaning of the term to my attention.
25   "Capt. Moore Leaves for the Nome Nuggets," *Skaguay News*, April 28, 1900, reprinted in Brady, *Skagway*, 37–38.
26   Martindale, *Hunting*, 297.
27   B. Willoughby, "Harriet Pullen," 189–90.
28   Ibid., 191.

29 Ibid., 190–91.

30 R. P. Hamilton, "Reminiscences," 3.

31 Ibid.

32 Davis, *Uncle Sam's Attic*, 40.

33 "Piano for Pullen House," hand-dated August 9, 1902, unidentified newspaper clipping in scrapbook, Pullen File, CCHS.

34 Unidentified newspaper clipping in scrapbook, Pullen File, CCHS.

35 "Halloween Party," "Very Swell," unidentified newspaper clippings in scrapbook, Pullen File, CCHS.

36 "Good House," hand-dated August 1902, unidentified newspaper clipping in scrapbook, Pullen File, CCHS.

37 "Jolly Birthday Party," [December 1902], unidentified newspaper clipping in scrapbook, Pullen File, CCHS.

38 "This Is It"; "A Huge Success," unidentified newspaper clippings in scrapbook, Pullen File, CCHS.

39 Virginia Burfield, interview by Joanne Beierly, March 13, 1975, 6, KLGO 45021, Pullen Papers, KLGO.

40 Lucille Hudson Elsner, interview by Helen Clark, July 9, 1981, 19–20, KLGO 45016, Pullen Papers, KLGO; Hilscher, "Most Unforgettable Character," 77.

41 Betty Selmer, quoted in Brady, "Harriet S. Pullen," 289. Selmer worked for Harriet in 1928.

42 Examination of Harriet Pullen's dress in the Skagway Museum indicates this was her approximate height. "Average Height for Males and Females in 1912 and 2012," A Hundred Years Ago, accessed April 30, 2014, http://ahundredyearsago.com/2012/02/06/average-height-for-males-and-females-in-1912-and-2012.

43 B. Willoughby, "Harriet Pullen," 191.

44 R. R. Pullen, "Pullens," 2; Brady, "Harriet S. Pullen," 289; "Woman Sourdough."

45 R. L. S. Spude, *Skagway*, 41. By 1910, the population was down to 850; in 1920 it was just 500. (Karl Gurcke, "The Pullen House Complex: A Preliminary Historic Photographic Essay" working paper, KLGO, 2015, 53.)

46 "Skaguay's Troops," *Skaguay Daily Alaskan*, January 1, 1900, reprinted in "Early History of the 24th Infantry, United States Army, Skagway, Alaska—1900," Explore North, accessed March 21, 2014, www.explorenorth.com/library/military/24th_infantry.html; Frank Norris, "Early Military History of Skagway-Dyea," first published in 1992, in Brady, *Skagway*, 375–80; "Farewell Party to Court Officials," *Skaguay Daily Alaskan*, November 24, 1901; "Good House," unidentified newspaper clipping in scrapbook, Pullen File, CCHS; Karl Gurcke, e-mail message to author, April 21, 2015.

47 Unidentified newspaper clipping in scrapbook, Pullen File, CCHS; R. L. S. Spude, *Skagway*, 18.

48 "Skagway History," Skagway, Alaska, accessed May 13, 2014, http://skagway.com/skagway-history.

49 R. L. S. Spude, *Skagway*, 18, 32.

50 William E. Hunt, journal, August 17, 1903, 89, typescript by William H. Hunt, in William E. Hunt Papers, PCA 155, Pullen File, Alaska State Library, Juneau (hereafter cited as ASL).

51 B. Willoughby, "Harriet Pullen," 165.

52 R. R. Pullen, interview, 1988, 6, 7; Jim Heynen, "Pullen, Royal R." (notes from an interview with R. R. Pullen for a book), 3, in the author's possession.

53 D. D. Pullen to H. S. Pullen, October 1898, Latona, Washington.

54 R. R. Pullen, "Daniel Webster Pullen," unpublished article, [ca. 1986], 2, in the author's possession. I thank Deby Sweren for bringing this information to my attention.

55 Mike Sica, "Daughter of Newsboy Returns," 323–25, in Brady, *Skagway*, 323; R. P. Hamilton, "Reminiscences," 2.

56 D. D. Pullen, White Pass & Yukon Route certification of employment, June 14–September 16, 1903, in the author's possession.

57 D. D. Pullen to H. S. Pullen, September 31, 1898, October 1898, Latona, Washington.

58 R. P. Hamilton, "Reminiscences," 3.

59 Heynen, interview summary, 4.

60 D. D. Pullen to H. S. Pullen, September 31, 1898, October 1898; March 19, 1900, Latona, Washington.

61 Mary Jane Smith to A. W. Smith and wife, October 3, 1900, [D.T.], A. W. Smith Papers.

62 M. J. Smith to H. S. Smith, [1898 to 1916], A. W. Smith Papers.

63 D. D. Pullen to Mildred Pullen, February 25, 1900, Latona, Washington.

64 R. P. Hamilton, "Reminiscences," 3; R. R. Pullen, "Pullens," 3.

65 Harriet S. Pullen to Daniel Pullen, Revocation of Power of Attorney, December 12, 1901, no. 32342, *Clallam County Deed Book*, 103, Clallam County Auditor's Office.

66 R. P. Hamilton, "Reminiscences," 3.

67 D. W. Pullen to A. J. Smith, February 25, 1902, Seattle, A. W. Smith Papers.

68 A. J. Smith to A. W. Smith, April 4, 1902, Towanda, Pennsylvania, A. W. Smith Papers.

69 "House Will Not Close," unidentified newspaper clipping in scrapbook, Pullen File, CCHS.

Chapter Thirteen: The Pullen House

1 "Skagway, Alaska," *Juneau Alaska Daily Empire*, undated clipping in scrapbook, Pullen File, CCHS.

2 Skagway Commercial Club Booklet, 1910, repr. in Brady, *Skagway*, 328.

3 Gurcke, "Pullen House," 43.

4 Hunt, journal, August 17, 1903, 89; R. P. Hamilton, "Reminiscences," 3, 5.

5 Cameron, *Cheechako*, 53.

6 Clothier, diary, 4.

7 Cameron, *Cheechako*, 60.

8 Pullen House brochure, ca. 1920s, in the author's possession.

9   Gurcke, "Pullen House," 1–3, 32, 34, 37, 45, 140; Agnes Rush Burr, *Alaska: Our Beautiful Northland of Opportunity* (Boston: Page, 1919), 63.

10 Gurcke, "Pullen House," 2, 161–62. According to Karl Gurcke, the shipwreck was the bark *Canada*.

11 H. S. Pullen to E. C. Hurlbut, May 8, 1918, Skagway, Pullen Papers, KLGO.

12 Elsner, interview, 19.

13 Cameron, *Cheechako*, 53; R. P. Hamilton, "Reminiscences," 5; R. R. Pullen, interview, 1988, 14; Elsner, interview, 3–4.

14 Anonymous, diary, August 5, 1927, 06-03, Skagway File, ASL.

15 Clothier, diary, 4.

16 Anonymous, diary, August 5, 1927; Brady, "Harriet S. Pullen," 289.

17 B. Willoughby, "Harriet Pullen," 195.

18 Florence Clothier to her family, July 25, 1928, Whitehorse, 2, 6, M.S. 136, University of Alaska Fairbanks Archives.

19 Hilscher, "Most Unforgettable Character," 74.

20 R. R. Pullen, interview, 1988, 12.

21 Elsner, interview, 19.

22 R. R. Pullen, interview, 1988, 11; R. R. Pullen, "Pullens," 3.

23 R. R. Pullen, interview, 1988, 14.

24 Inez Knorr, as quoted in Brady, "Harriet S. Pullen," 289.

25 Clothier, diary, 5.

26 Clothier, diary, 6. I thank Steve Henrikson, curator of collections at the Alaska State Museums, for help in identifying this Tlingit shirt and Athapaskan breastplate. The Tlingit shirt is now in the collection of the Seattle Art Museum as *Daa dúgu k'oodas'* (ermine-skin shirt), ca. 1885, accession number 85.359. Chilkoot Jack standing in front of a Dyea store wears the same or similar shirt in an 1898 photo. (Yukon Archives, Anton Vogee fonds, #58.) He is known as the Tlingit who guided the first white man into the Yukon. I thank Barbara Brotherton, curator of Native American Art, Seattle Art Museum, for bringing this photograph to my attention.

27 Elsner, interview, 21.

28 Clothier, diary, 4.

29 B. Willoughby, "Harriet Pullen," 196.

30 Clothier, diary, 4-5.

31 Greenfield Galleries, *Auction: 7 Sessions, by Catalogue*, [*Pullen Alaska Museum Collection*], [Seattle], July 1–5, 1973, lots 756, 760–81.

32 Cameron, *Cheechako*, 61.

33 Greenfield Galleries, *Auction*, lots 847–53.

34 Clothier, diary, 4–5; Lucile McDonald, "Pullen Museum Houses Alaska Relics," *Seattle Times*, May 7, 1961; Greenfield Galleries, *Auction*; "Gold Rush Days: Mementos Bonanza for Klondike Kin," *Denver Post*, July 8, 1973.

35 The photograph, titled "Woman in Front of the Pullen House," probably dated 1914–18, is in the University of Alaska Fairbanks collection, 1980-68-146; Gurcke, "Pullen House," 46.

36 Harriet S. Pullen, Homestead Entry, Final Proof, July 22, 1919, NARA.

37 Karl Gurcke, in an e-mail message of April 21, 2015 to the author, estimates this to have been the peak population of Dyea in 1897–98.

38 H. P. Crowther, Field Notes of Survey of Pullen Homestead, [1918], 16, in General Land Office, Department of the Interior, *United States v. Harriet S. Pullen*, Serial Patent File #850843, Record Group 49, NARA (hereafter cited as *U.S. v. H. Pullen*).

39 Crowther, Field Notes, 17; Olaf Dale, affidavit, March 22, 1921, *U.S. v. H. Pullen*.

40 P. F. McLaughlin, affidavit, February 23, 1921, *U.S. v. H. Pullen*.

41 D. K. Parrott to Register, Juneau Land Office, October 4, 1921, 2, *U.S. v. H. Pullen*.

42 Alfred Manson, affidavit, March 22, 1921, *U.S. v. H. Pullen*.

43 L. S. Keller to To Whom It May Concern, December 17, 1919, Skagway, *U.S. v. H. Pullen*.

44 "Gertrude a Wreck," *Port Angeles Tribune-Times*, January 18, 1907.

45 "Alice-Gertrude a Wreck," *Port Angeles Olympic-Leader*, January 18, 1907.

46 H. S. Pullen, direct examination by Heisel, 66–67, *U.S. v. H. Pullen*; Skagway Town, in US Bureau of the Census, *Thirteenth Census of the United States*, January 18, 1910, 8, Ancestry Institution, accessed February 21, 2013, http://search.ancestryinstitution.com.

47 Norm Smith to Karl Gurcke, January 24, 1994, Anchorage, Pullen Papers, KLGO; H. S. Pullen to D. D. Pullen, December 27, 1915, Skagway.

48 H. S. Pullen, direct examination by Heisel, 68.

49 Ibid.

50 Ibid., 67–68.

51 "Dyea Farm has Large Crop," *Skaguay Daily Alaskan*, October 20, 1916.

52 H. S. Pullen, direct examination by Heisel, 67–68. According to Karl Gurcke, a telephone company built a line between Skagway and Dyea. Harriet testified that Royal installed (but, in reality, probably repaired) a telephone line.

53 Crowther, Field Notes, 15, 17–18. The Dyea Town Cemetery received its last burial in 1921, Sophia Matthews, wife of Billy Matthews. (Karl Gurcke, e-mail message to author, April 21, 2015.)

54 Crowther, Field Notes, 16–17.

55 McLaughlin, affidavit.

56 Manson, affidavit.

57 Dale, affidavit.

58 Manson, affidavit.

59 Skagway, *Thirteenth Census*, 1910, 12; Skagway Town, in US Bureau of the Census, *Fourteenth Census of the United States*, January 24, 1920, 13, USGenWeb Archives, accessed March 27, 2014, http://files.usgwarchives.net/ak/skagway/census/1920/part03.txt.

60 Dale, affidavit.

61 H. S. Pullen, direct examination by Heisel, 71.

62 Dale, affidavit.

63 H. S. Pullen, direct examination by Heisel, 71–72.

64 Norm Smith to Karl Gurcke, January 24, 1994.
65 H. S. Pullen, cross-examination by Royal R. Pullen, June 3, 1920, 74, *U.S. v. H. Pullen.*
66 B. Willoughby, "Harriet Pullen," 194, quoting an unnamed old Alaskan.
67 H. S. Pullen, cross-examination by R. R. Pullen, 74.
68 George W. Matthews, direct examination by Walter B. Heisel, June 3, 1920, 45, *U.S. v. H. S. Pullen.*
69 H. S. Pullen, cross-examination by R. R. Pullen, 74–75.
70 Ibid., 75–76.
71 R. R. Pullen, "My Mother," 1.
72 H. S. Pullen, cross-examination by R. R. Pullen, 77.
73 Frank A. Boyle, Recommendation, Homestead Entry 03945, January 27, 1921, *U.S. v. H. Pullen.*
74 H. S. Pullen, cross-examination by R. R. Pullen, 75–76.
75 H. S. Pullen, direct examination by Heisel, 65.
76 Ibid., 84.
77 Memorandum, Juneau 03945 "FS" EEC, 4, *U.S. v. H. Pullen.*
78 Boyle, Recommendation, 6; H. S. Pullen to F. A. Boyle, February 12, 1921, Skagway, *U.S. v. H. Pullen.*
79 H. S. Pullen to F. A. Boyle.
80 Dale, affidavit.
81 Ibid.; Manson, affidavit; McLaughlin, affidavit.
82 Crowther, testimony, September 28, 1920, 2, *U.S. v. H. Pullen.*
83 Parrott to Register, 4.
84 Ibid., 4–7, 11–12.
85 Senator Harry S. New to Albert B. Fall, Secretary of the Interior, October 5, 1921, Washington, DC; W. P. Richardson to Commissioner, General Land Office, October 19, 1921, Washington, DC, *U.S. v. H. Pullen.*
86 "Mrs. Pullen Wins Homestead Case," *Stroller's Juneau Weekly,* November 12, 1921.
87 H. S. Pullen, direct examination by Heisel, 82.
88 H. S. Pullen, cross-examination by R. R. Pullen, 78.
89 R. R. Pullen, interview, 1988, 12.
90 Elsner, interview, 20, 22–23; Burfield, interview, 6.

Chapter Fourteen: New Century

1 The four books in Stephenie Meyer's series are *Twilight*, 2005; *New Moon*, 2006; *Eclipse*, 2007; and *Breaking Dawn*, 2008.
2 Angela R. Riley, "Sucking the Quileute Dry," *New York Times*, February 7, 2010.
3 Barbara Leigh Smith, "The Twilight Saga and the Quileute Indian Tribe: Opportunity or Cultural Exploitation?" 2010, *Enduring Legacies Native Cases*, Evergreen State College, accessed April 23, 2014, http://nativecases.evergreen.edu/docs/smith-the-twilight-saga-9-3-13.pdf.
4 Emily Foster, "Quileutes Celebrate!" *bá·yak The Talking Raven*, November 4, 2012, Quileute Nation, accessed April 23, 2014, http://talkingraven.org/?p=844.

5   "The Quileute Tribe," "Quileute Days," "*bá·yak* The Talking Raven," Quileute Nation, accessed January 15, 2015, www.quileutenation.org.

6   A. J. Smith, Certificate of Election, Justice of the Peace, Quillayute Precinct, Clallam County, Washington, November 8, 1898, courtesy Tyler Patterson.

7   M. J. Smith to A. W. Smith, April 10, 1886, Quillayute, A. W. Smith Papers.

8   H. H. Smith to M. J. Smith, August 19, 1888, Yankton, A. W. Smith Papers. Harvey wrote, "[L]et him do with you what he will, and your trouble will be over, ah, but you say, that would be sinful. If he uses your body in a way that you think is sinful you should protest mildly but lovingly. . . . It is my judgement better for you to submit patiently and lovingly and live together, than it is to be separated. . . . [H]e may want you to go to Seattle, if so, you just pack up and go with him wherever he wants you to." Mary Jane did not relocate.

9   Jacilee Wray and Doreen Taylor, eds., *Postmistress—Mora, Wash. 1914–1915: Journal Entries and Photographs of Fannie Taylor* (Seattle: Northwest Interpretive Association, 2006), 26, 117.

10 D. W. Pullen to A. J. Smith, February 25, 1902, Seattle, A. W. Smith Papers.

11 R. R. Pullen, "Daniel Webster Pullen," 3.

12 R. R. Pullen, "Pullens," 3.

13 Mora, Clallam County, Washington, in US Bureau of the Census, *Thirteenth Census of the United States*, April 23, 1910, 1, lines 6–12, NARA, Ancestry Institution, accessed February 21, 2013, http://search.ancestryinstitution.com; R. R. Pullen, "Daniel Webster Pullen," 3.

14 Lonnie Archibald, *There Was a Day: Stories of the Pioneers* (Forks, WA: Privately printed, 1999), 151.

15 Ibid., 79; Wray and Taylor, *Postmistress*, 6–7, 56.

16 Archibald, *There was a Day*, 79, 144, 150.

17 Hobucket, "Quileute Indian Tradition," 57.

18 Ibid., 58.

19 Ibid.

20 Ibid., 59.

21 Ibid., 58, 59.

22 Thomas D. Snyder, ed., *120 Years of American Education: A Statistical Portrait* (Washington, DC: National Center for Education Statistics, 1993), 76.

23 Clothier, diary, 6.

24 B. Willoughby, "Harriet Pullen," 196–97.

25 Chester Pullen, obituary, unidentified newspaper clipping, [September 1912], P-356, Obituary File, Clallam County Genealogical Society, Port Angeles; "Harriet Pullen—An Alaskan Heroine," 6.

26 R. R. Pullen, interview, 1988, 8–9.

27 R. R. Pullen, "Pullens."

28 Davis, "Bob Davis Reveals."

29 *Official Register of the Officers and Cadets of the United States Military Academy* (West Point, 1910), 12; "Drain Goes to Tanks Corps," *Spokane Spokesman Review*, May 16, 1918.

30 Dale E. Wilson, *Treat 'em Rough! The Birth of American Armor, 1917–20* (Novato, CA: Presidio, 1989), 13–26, 118.

31 George S. Patton to Beatrice Ayer Patton, March 24, 1918, France, quoted in Wilson, *Treat 'Em Rough!*, 34.

32 Wilson, *Treat 'Em Rough!*, 15.

33 R. G. Alexander, "Daniel Dee Pullen," in Association of Graduates of the United States Military Academy, *Fifty-Fifth Annual Report of the Association of Graduates of the United States Military Academy at West Point, New York, June 11, 1924* (Saginaw, MI: Seemann & Peters, 1924), 96.

34 Original citations and medals, in the author's possession; "Pullen, Army Star, Dies," *New York Times*, September 23, 1923; "Obituary," clipping from a publication, annotated, "Army Journal, September 1923," in the author's possession.

35 D. D. Pullen, "Obituary."

36 Ibid. D. D. Pullen, "Improvements Planned for Norfolk Harbor," *Norfolk Virginia-Pilot*, December 31, 1922; Alexander, "Daniel Dee Pullen," 92; D. D. Pullen, "Obituary."

37 Alexander, "Daniel Dee Pullen," 92; "Asleep Two Weeks, Condition Serious," *Washington Post*, August 17, 1923; Olivia Middleton Blake Pullen to R. R. Pullen, August 9, 1923, Washington, DC, in the author's possession.

38 Charles E. Mulhearn to O. M. B. Pullen, November 21, 1923.

39 Jennie Smith Tyler to Olivia Blake Pullen, March 18, 1923, Seattle, in the author's possession. An undated letter from Mildred to Wesley Smith states that she was working as a nurse. The letterhead reads "Portland [Oregon] Sanitarium, Medical and Surgical." (A. W. Smith Papers.)

40 Mildred Pullen Dale to A. W. Smith, [1920 to 1930], Portland, Oregon, A. W. Smith Papers.

41 H. S. Pullen, direct examination by Heisel, 81.

42 Brady, "Harriet S. Pullen," 288.

43 Hilscher, "Most Unforgettable Character," 77.

44 Cameron, *Cheechako*, 53–54.

45 B. Willoughby, "Harriet Pullen," 197.

46 "Mrs. Pullen, Noted Pioneer, Makes Trip," *Alaska Weekly*, November 17, 1944.

47 Hilscher, "Most Unforgettable Character," 76–77.

48 Burfield, interview, 4–5.

49 "Visit by President Surprises Skagway," *New York Times*, July 12, 1923.

50 Elsner, interview, 21.

51 "Hardings Leave Juneau on Ship to Visit Seward," *Chicago Daily Tribune*, July 12, 1923; Robert H. Armstrong, "Gold Camp Lures Harding," *Los Angeles Times*, July 12, 1923; No title, *New York Times*, July 12, 1923; "Skagway, Once Gate To Goldfields, Paid Visit By President," *Washington Post*, July 12, 1923; Olivia Middleton Blake Pullen to R. R. Pullen, August 9, 1923, [Washington, DC].

52 "President Alters Plans for Return from Pacific Trip," *Washington Post*, July 13, 1923.

53 B. Willoughby, "Harriet Pullen," 198.

54 Brady, "Harriet S. Pullen," 289.

55 "Mrs. Pullen of Skagway Dies," unidentified Seattle newspaper clipping, August 10 or 12, 1947, in the author's possession; Burfield, interview, 6–7.

56 Brady, "Harriet S. Pullen," 291.

57 Dave and Terry to Ethel Montgomery, November 9, 1978, Port Angeles, M.S. 136, University of Alaska Fairbanks Archives.

58 Skagway Historic District, *Cultural Landscape Report*, iii; Charles Wohlforth, "Skagway Forfeits Piece of the Past to Wrecking Crew," *Anchorage Daily News*, December 17, 1990.

59 Skagway Historic District, *Cultural Landscape Report*, ii.

60 Archie Satterfield, "Klondike Festival Skagway Pioneer's Kin Moved Museum Here," *Seattle Times*, March 23, 1972. The museum was first in Lynnwood near Seattle and later moved in 1963 to the Seattle Center.

61 Robert A. Frederick, interview by Wendy J. Adler, "Alaska: Preservation in the Great Land, an Interview with Robert A. Frederick," *Historic Preservation*, January–March 1975, 12–13.

62 Greenfield Galleries, *Auction*; Brady, "Harriet S. Pullen," 291.

Afterword: Solid Gold

1 I thank Alexandria Rossoff, Seattle jeweler, for her help in describing the earrings.

2 Harriet Stuart Pullen to Harriet Smith Pullen, September 27, 1931, [Asheville, North Carolina].

Appendix: A Storied Woman

1 Arent and Peters, *Queen*, 18.

2 Ibid., 26.

3 Robert W. Service, "The Law of the Yukon," excerpt quoted in Martindale, *Hunting*, 279.

4 Martindale, *Hunting*, 279, 281, 285, 293.

5 "Seven Ways to Compute," accessed August 15, 2015, www.measuringworth.com/uscompare/relativevalue.php.

6 Ibid., 293–301.

7 Beatty, "'Big Lady.'"

8 Ibid.

9 A. R. Burr, *Alaska*, 62.

10 Ibid., 64.

11 Ibid., 63.

12 "Alaska Hotel Owned by 'Mother of the North,'" *Los Angeles Times*, June 16, 1926.

13 Davis, *Uncle Sam's Attic*, 39–45.

14 Nancy Warren Ferrell, *Barrett Willoughby: Alaska's Forgotten Lady* (Fairbanks: University of Alaska Press, 1994), 6, 139–43. By 1930, Willoughby had published three popular romance adventure novels set in Alaska, a nonfiction book, and more than a dozen articles on Alaska-related topics; B. Willoughby to H. S. Pullen, September 7, 1926.

15   B. Willoughby, "Mother of the North," *American Magazine*, 64–66, 112; Frank
      Luther Mott, *A History of American Magazines, 1741–1930* (Cambridge, MA: Har-
      vard University Press, 1957), 3:514–15.

16   "Our Founder's Beginnings, Our Company's Birth and Early Years (1889–1938),"
      RDA Timeline, accessed January 21, 2015, www.rda.com/rda-timeline.

17   Barrett Willoughby, "Mrs. Harriet Pullen: A Stirring Tale of a Woman Who Bat-
      tled Alone in the Alaska Gold Field," in Elma Holloway, ed., *Unsung Heroes*, 85–95
      (New York: Macmillan, 1938).

18   Clinton K. Judy, Foreword, in Holloway, *Unsung Heroes*, v, vii, viii.

19   Edna McGuire and Don C. Rogers, "A Woman Who Battled Alone in the Alaska
      Gold Field," in *The Growth of Democracy*, rev. ed. (New York: Macmillan, 1941;
      1952), 265.

20   Brady, " 'Ma' Pullen Tells Her Story," in Brady, *Skagway*, 284.

21   *Skagway Cheechako*, February 13, 1937, as discussed in Cherry Lyon Jones, *More
      than Petticoats: Remarkable Alaska Women* (Guilford, CT: TwoDot, 2006), 9–10.

22   Branham, "Gold Rush Mother," 30, 32; "Ma Pullen Yearns for Alaska's Old Boom
      Days While Greeting the New," *Alaska Daily Press*, February 17, 1937.

23   McCarley, "Harriet Pullen Remembered."

24   L. M. W., "The Roundup," *Mexico Ledger*, May 25, 1948; Hilscher, "Most Unfor-
      gettable Character," 73–78; Margaret E. Murie, "The Inside Passage and Beyond,
      1911," in *The Reader's Companion to Alaska*, ed. Alan Ryan (San Diego: Harcourt,
      Brace, 1997), 35–49, first published in Murie, *Two in the Far North* (New York:
      Knopf, 1962); Lowell Thomas, *Good Evening Everybody: From Cripple Creek to
      Samarkand* (New York: William Morrow, 1976), 92–94.

25   Thomas, *Good Evening*, 93.

26   R. R. Pullen, "Pullens," 1–3; McDonald, "Pullen Museum."

27   Martindale, *Hunting*, 295–96; Beatty, " 'Big Lady.' "

28   A. R. Burr, *Alaska*, 63; R. R. Pullen, "Pullens," 2; Tyler, "Jennie S. Tyler," 38.

29   Beatty, " 'Big Lady.' "

30   B. Willoughby, "Mother of the North," *American Magazine*, 66.

31   H. S. Pullen to A. W. Smith, April 20, 1898, [Skagway].

32   Johnson, *Wild Discouraging Mess*, 114.

33   Advertisement, *Skaguay News*, March 30, 1900.

34   Adney, *Klondike Stampede*, 43.

35   Harriet Stuart Pullen, "Story about Mrs. Pullen," 2.

36   B. Willoughby, "Mother of the North," *American Magazine*, 64; B. Willoughby,
      "Mother of the North," *Reader's Digest*, September 1930, 426; B. Willoughby,
      "Harriet Pullen," 165; B. Willoughby, "Mrs. Harriet Pullen," in Holloway, *Unsung
      Heroes*, 85. Even Harriet's granddaughter repeated the notion in a 1961 interview
      (McDonald, "Pullen House").

37   Beatty, " 'Big Lady.' "

38   Elsner, interview, 1981.

39   Cameron, *Cheechako*, 61.

40   H. S. Pullen, *Soapy Smith, Bandit of Skagway: How He Lived; How He Died* (Skagway: Skagway Tourist Agency, [ca. 1929]), 12–13.

41   H. S. Pullen, *Soapy Smith*, 15.

42   B. Willoughby, "Harriet Pullen," 167–68, 172.

43   B. Willoughby, "Harriet Pullen," 188.

44   "Woman Sourdough."

45   "Ma Pullen Yearns."

46   R. L. S. Spude, *Skagway*, 140.

47   "High Tides at Skaguay," *Seattle Daily Times*, November 23, 1897, evening edition; "Pernicious Truth Users," *Skaguay News*, December 10, 1897; H. S. Pullen to A. W. Smith, April 20, 1898; Chas. K. Jenner to H. S. Pullen, July 7, 1898, Seattle, Pullen File, CCHS.

48   C. H. Spude, *"That Fiend in Hell,"* 154–61; Skagway, in US Bureau of the Census, *Twelfth Census*, 79, line 18. It is worth noting that we know from her mother's letter cited in chapter twelve that Harriet was sick during the spring of 1900, when the census taker visited. Given that, and the fact that both other adults in the Pullen household, Dan and his sister Sarah, were deaf, it is perhaps not surprising that the census taker got the date wrong.

49   Ken Coates, Introduction, in Adney, *Klondike Stampede*, xvi–xvii.

50   Adney, *Klondike Stampede*, 298.

51   Hilscher, *Alaska Now* (Boston: Little, Brown, 1948), 57. A *sourdough* means an old-timer in Alaska.

52   Brady, "Skagway's Entrepreneurial Spirit Born during Gold Rush," 221–24, in Brady, *Skagway*, 224.

53   Elsner, interview, 20.

54   Nicolette Ann Bromberg, "Clarence Leroy Andrews and Alaska," *Alaska Journal* 6, no. 2 (1976): 66–77.

55   Clarence Leroy Andrews, diary, January1902, 164, M.S. 136, University of Alaska Fairbanks Archives.

56   Ibid., September 1902, 174–77.

57   "Harriet Pullen—An Alaskan Heroine," 5.

58   Barbara Dedman Kalen, quoted in Brady, "Harriet S. Pullen," 286.

59   Deby Sweren, e-mail message to author, March 7, 2014.

60   Archibald, *There Was a Day*, 151.

61   R. P. Hamilton, "Reminiscences," 3.

62   Harriet Stuart Pullen, "Story about Mrs. Pullen," 1.

63   B. Willoughby, "Mother of the North," *American Magazine*, 64; B. Willoughby, "Mother of the North," *Reader's Digest*, 426; B. Willoughby, "Harriet Pullen," 165; B. Willoughby, "Mrs. Harriet Pullen." 85.

64   Martindale, *Hunting*, 294; Beatty, "'Big Lady'"; "Mother of Tank Corps Hero Visits," *Port Angeles Evening News*, December 29, 1919, A. R. Dun, *Alaska*, 63; "Woman Sourdough"; Hilscher, "Most Unforgettable Character," 74; Thomas, *Good Evening*, 93.

65 Branham, "Gold-Rush Mother," 26; Harriet Stuart Pullen, "Story about Mrs. Pullen," 1; Laura McCarley, "Harriet Pullen Remembered," *Juneau Southeast Alaska Empire*, November 5, 1976.

66 Robert L. Griswold, "Law, Sex, Cruelty, and Divorce in Victorian America, 1840–1900," *American Quarterly* 38, no. 5 (1986): 721–45.

67 Peter Wood, *Unbelievable Years* (Playa del Rey, CA: Littlepage, 1969), 66, 68.

68 Richard White, *Remembering Ahanagran: A History of Stories* (Seattle: University of Washington Press, 1998), 21, 91.

69 Tara Parker-Pope, "False Memory vs. Bald Faced Lie," *New York Times*, February 10, 2015.

70 Pierre Berton, *The Klondike Fever: The Life and Death of the Last Great Gold Rush* (New York: Knopf, 1958), 159, 359–60, 365; Howard Clifford, "And Women Arrive," in *The Skagway Story*, 2nd ed., 54–63 (1975; Anchorage: Alaska Northwest, 1988); Richard O'Connor, *High Jinks on the Klondike* (Indianapolis: Bobbs-Merrill, 1954), 69, 155.

71 Janelle Taylor, *Golden Torment* (New York: Kensington, 1984), 20–23, 53, 180–81, 228–29, 334, 604–06.

72 Vicki Redden, *Heroes in Training* (Hagerstown, MD: Review and Herald, 1979), March 7 entry.

73 Doris Chapin Bailey, *A Divided Forest: The Life, Times, and Lineage of Roy Daniel Bailey* (Victoria, British Columbia: Trafford, 2008), 29.

74 Gary Peterson and Glynda Schaad, "Preacher's Daughter," *Women to Reckon With: Untamed Women of the Olympic Wilderness* (Forks, WA: Poseidon Peak, 2007), 28–40.

75 Carolyn Kraemer Cooper, *Sarah Palin: A Biography* (Portsmouth, NH: Greenwood, 2010), 4.

76 "Harriet Pullen—An Alaskan Heroine," 7.

77 Adney, *Klondike Stampede*, 269.

Selected Sources

Archives and Special Collections

Alaska State Library Historical Collections, Juneau, Alaska
Bureau of Land Management General Land Office Records, www.glorecords.blm.gov/
search
Clallam County Genealogical Society, Port Angeles, Washington
Clallam County Historical Society, Port Angeles, Washington
Klondike Gold Rush National Historical Park Archives, Skagway, Alaska
National Archives and Records Administration, Washington, DC
Olympic National Park Archives, Port Angeles, Washington
Washington State Library Manuscript Collections, Tumwater, Washington

Books

Adney, Tappan. *The Klondike Stampede*. New York: Harper & Brothers, 1900.

Anderson, M. Kat. *The Ozette Prairies of Olympic National Park: Their Former Indigenous Uses and Management*. Port Angeles, WA: Olympic National Park, 2009.

Archibald, Lonnie. *There Was a Day: Stories of the Pioneers*. Forks, WA: Privately printed, 1999.

Arent, Arthur, and Paul Peters. *Queen of Heartbreak Trail*. Delaware: E. I. DuPont de Nemours, 1948. As broadcast, NBC Radio, *Cavalcade of America*, May 17, 1948.

Berton, Pierre. *The Klondike Fever: The Life and Death of the Last Great Gold Rush*. New York: Basic Books, 1958.

Bordewich, Fergus M. *Bound for Canaan: The Underground Railroad and the War for the Soul of America*. New York: HarperCollins, 2005.

Brady, Jeff, ed. *Skagway: City of the New Century*. Skagway, AK: Lynn Canal, 2013.

Burr, Agnes Rush. *Alaska: Our Beautiful Northland of Opportunity*. Boston: Page, 1919.

Cameron, Charlotte. *A Cheechako in Alaska and Yukon*. London: Frederick A. Stokes, 1920.

Campbell, Patricia. *A History of the North Olympic Peninsula*. Port Angeles, WA: Peninsula, 1979.

Cather, Willa. *O Pioneers!* In *Early Novels and Stories*. New York: Literary Classics of the United States, 1987. First published in 1913 by Houghton Mifflin.

Clifford, Howard. *The Skagway Story*. 1975. Reprinted with foreword. Anchorage: Alaska Northwest, 1988.

Cohen, Stan. *Gold Rush Gateway: Skagway and Dyea, Alaska*. Missoula, MT: Pictorial Histories, 1986.

Coursey, Oscar William. *Pioneering in Dakota*. Mitchell, SD: Educator Supply, 1937.

Crew, Keith, and Douglas Heck. *Prairie Homestead: Meet the Browns and Their Neighbors.* Philip, SD: Prairie Homestead Creations, 1996.

Dahl, Robert A. *After the Gold Rush: Growing Up in Skagway.* Privately printed, 2005.

Davis, Mary Lee. *Uncle Sam's Attic: The Intimate Story of Alaska.* Boston: Wilde, 1930.

de Tocqueville, Alexis. *Democracy in America.* 1840. Translated and edited by Harvey C. Mansfield and Delba Winthrop. Chicago: University of Chicago Press, 2000.

Dillard, Annie. *The Living.* New York: HarperCollins, 1992.

Emmons, David M. *Garden in the Grasslands: Boomer Literature of the Central Great Plains.* Lincoln: University of Nebraska Press, 1971.

Executive Orders Relating to Indian Reservations from May 14, 1855 to July 1, 1912. Washington, DC: Government Printing Office, 1912.

Foster James S., with Silas Chapman. *Outlines of History of the Territory of Dakota, and Emigrant's Guide to the Free Lands of the Northwest.* Yankton, Dakota Territory, 1870.

Frazier, Ian. *The Great Plains.* New York: Farrar, Straus and Giroux, 1989.

Greenfield Galleries. *Auction: 7 Sessions, by Catalogue,* [*Pullen Alaska Museum Collection*]. [Seattle], July 1–5, 1973.

Heynen, Jim, and Paul Boyer. "Royal R. Pullen." In *One Hundred Over One Hundred.* Golden, CO: Fulcrum, 1990.

Hilscher, Herbert H. *Alaska Now.* Boston: Little, Brown, 1948.

History of Grant County, Wisconsin. Chicago: Western Historical, 1881.

Hufstetler, Mark, and Michael Bedeau. *South Dakota's Railroads: An Historic Context.* Pierre: South Dakota State Historical Society, 2007.

Hult, Ruby El. *Untamed Olympics: The Story of a Peninsula.* Portland, OR: Binfords & Mort, 1954.

Huntley, Herbert B. *The Code of Procedure and Penal Code of the State of Washington.* Seattle: Sunset, 1893.

Johnson, Julie. *A Wild Discouraging Mess: The History of the White Pass Unit of the Klondike Gold Rush National Historical Park.* Anchorage: Klondike Gold Rush National Historical Park, 2003.

Jones, Cherry Lyon. *More than Petticoats: Remarkable Alaska Women.* Guilford, CT: TwoDot, 2006.

Kemble, John Haskell. *The Panama Route, 1848–1869.* Berkeley: University of California Press, 1943.

Kingsbury, George W. *History of Dakota Territory: South Dakota, Its History and Its People.* Edited by George Martin Smith, Vols. 1 and 4. Chicago: Clarke, 1915.

Kirchhoff, M. J. *Clondyke: The First Year of the Rush.* Juneau: Alaska Cedar Press, 2010.

Klahn, Dorothy Smith. *Mama's Dickey River Homestead.* Privately printed, 1991.

Labor, Earle. *Jack London: An American Life.* New York: Farrar, Straus and Giroux, 2013.

Limerick, Patricia Nelson. *The Legacy of Conquest: The Unbroken Past of the American West.* New York: Norton, 1987.

———, Clyde A. Milner II, and Charles E. Rankin, eds. *Trails: Toward a New Western History.* Lawrence: University Press of Kansas, 1991.

Linklater, Andro. *The Fabric of America: How Our Borders and Boundaries Shaped the Country and Forged Our Identity.* New York: Walker, 2007.

———. *Measuring America: How the United States Was Shaped by the Greatest Land Sale in History.* New York: Plume, 2003.

London, Jack. "Which Make Men Remember." In *The God of His Fathers & Other Stories*, 65–85. New York: McClure, Phillips, 1901.

Martindale, Thomas. *Hunting in the Upper Yukon.* Philadelphia: George W. Jacobs, 1913.

McGuire, Edna, and Don C. Rogers. *The Growth of Democracy.* Rev. ed. New York: Macmillan, 1952. First published in 1941.

Milton, John R. *South Dakota: A Bicentennial History.* New York: Norton / Nashville: American Association for State and Local History, 1977.

Mott, Frank Luther. *A History of American Magazines, 1741–1930.* Vol. 3. Cambridge: Harvard University Press, 1957.

Murie, Margaret E. "The Inside Passage and Beyond, 1911." In *The Reader's Companion to Alaska*, 35–49. Edited by Alan Ryan. San Diego: Harcourt, Brace, 1997. First published in 1962 by Knopf.

Murphy, Claire Rudolf, and Jane G. Haigh. *Gold Rush Women.* Anchorage: Alaska Northwest, 1997.

Norris, Frank B. *Legacy of the Gold Rush: An Administrative History of Klondike Gold Rush National Historical Park.* Anchorage: National Park Service, 1996.

Owens, Kenneth N., ed. *The Wreck of the Sv. Nikolai.* Translated by Alton S. Donnelly. 1985. Reprinted with preface by Owens. Lincoln: University of Nebraska Press, 2001.

Peterson, Gary, and Glynda Peterson Schaad. *Women to Reckon With: Untamed Women of the Olympic Wilderness.* Forks, WA: Poseidon Peak, 2007.

Pollan, Michael. *Cooked: A Natural History of Transformation.* New York: Penguin, 2013.

Proudfit, S. V., ed. *Decisions of the Department of the Interior and General Land Office in Cases Relating to the Public Lands, From January 1, 1893, to June 30, 1893.* Washington, DC: Government Printing Office, 1893.

Pullen, Harriet S. *Soapy Smith, Bandit of Skagway: How He Lived; How He Died.* Skagway, AK: Skagway Tourist Agency, [ca. 1929].

Rølvaag, O. E. *Giants in the Earth: A Saga of the Prairie.* New York: Perennial Classics, 1999. Originally published in Norwegian in 1924 and 1925. First published in English in 1927 by Harper & Brothers.

Seattle Art Museum. *The Spirit Within: Northwest Coast Native Art from the John H. Hauberg Collection.* New York: Rizzoli / Seattle Art Museum, 1995.

Shape, William. *Faith of Fools: A Diary of the Klondike Gold Rush.* Pullman: Washington State University Press, 1998.

Skagway Historic District Unit, Klondike Gold Rush National Historical Park. *Cultural Landscape Report for the Capt. William Moore Cabin, J. Bernard Moore House, Peniel Mission, and Pullen House Sites.* Denver: National Park Service, 1995.

Smith, Archer K. *Tragedy Graveyard, the Starbuck Ghost and Other True Stories: A Collection of Old True Happenings Taking Place Mostly on Washington's Olympic Peninsula.* [Washington State]: Privately printed, 1997.

Snyder, Thomas D., ed. *120 Years of American Education: A Statistical Portrait*. Washington, DC: US Department of Education, Office of Educational Research and Improvement, 1993.

Spude, Catherine Holder. *"That Fiend in Hell": Soapy Smith in Legend*. Norman: University of Oklahoma Press, 2012.

Spude, Robert L. S. *Skagway, District of Alaska, 1884–1912: Building the Gateway to the Klondike*. Occasional Paper No. 36. Fairbanks: Anthropology and Historic Preservation, Cooperative Park Studies Unit, University of Alaska, 1983.

Stevenson, Robert Louis. "Across the Plains." In *The Travels and Essays of Robert Louis Stevenson*, 99–149. Vol. 15. New York: Charles Scribner's Sons, 1907. First published in 1883 in *Longman's Magazine*.

Swan, James G. "The Surf-Smelt of the Northwest Coast, and the Method of Taking Them by the Quillehute Indians, West Coast of Washington Territory." In *Proceedings of the United States National Museum, 1880*, 43–46. Vol. 3. Washington, DC: Government Printing Office, 1881.

Switala, William J. *Underground Railroad in Pennsylvania*. 2nd ed. Mechanicsburg, PA: Stackpole, 2008.

Taylor, Janelle. *Golden Torment*. New York: Kensington, 1984.

Thomas, Lowell. *Good Evening Everybody: From Cripple Creek to Samarkand*. New York: Morrow, 1976.

Thompson, Fred. *To the Yukon with Jack London: The Klondike Diary of Fred Thompson*. Edited by David Mike Hamilton. Los Angeles: Zamorano Club, 1980.

Thoreau, Henry David. "Walking," 1862. In *Civil Disobedience and Other Essays*. New York: Dover, 1993.

White, Richard. *Remembering Ahanagran: A History of Stories*. Seattle: University of Washington Press, 1998.

Wilber, C. D. *The Great Valleys and Prairies of Nebraska and the Northwest*. Omaha, NE: Daily Republican Print, 1881.

Willoughby, Barrett. "Mrs. Harriet Pullen: A Stirring Tale of a Woman Who Battled Alone in the Alaska Gold Field." In *Unsung Heroes*. Edited by Elma Holloway. New York: Macmillan, 1938.

———, Florance [Barrett]. "Harriet Pullen: Mother of the North." In *Alaskans All*, 165–98. Freeport, NY: Books for Libraries, 1933.

Wilson, Dale E. *Treat 'Em Rough! The Birth of American Armor, 1917–20*. Novato, CA: Presidio, 1989.

United States, Office of Indian Affairs. *Annual Reports*. 1867–98.

Articles

Branham, Bud. "Gold Rush Mother." *Alaska Sportsman*. August 1940, 26–27, 30, 32–34.

Briggs, Harold E. "Grasshopper Plagues and Early Dakota Agriculture." *Agricultural History* 8, no. 2 (1934): 52–62.

Cloud, Dona. "Minerva Troy: Woman Who Made a Difference." *Strait History* 4, no. 2 (1989): 1–4.

Collins, Cary C. "Subsistence and Survival: The Makah Indian Reservation, 1855–1933." *Pacific Northwest Quarterly* 87, no. 4 (1996): 180–93.

Coolidge, Susan [Sarah Chauncey Woolsey]. "A Few Hints on the California Journey." *Scribner's Monthly*. May 1873. Central Pacific Railroad Photographic History Museum. www.cprr.org/Museum/Calif_Journey_1873/index.html.

Dayton, Mrs. George A. "The Underground Railroad and Its Stations in Bradford County." *Settler, A Quarterly Magazine of History and Biography*, April 1953, 142–49.

Findlay, John M. "Closing the Frontier in Washington: Edmond S. Meany and Frederick Jackson Turner." *Pacific Northwest Quarterly* 82, no. 2 (1991): 59–69.

Griswold, Robert L. "Law, Sex, Cruelty, and Divorce in Victorian America, 1840–1900." *American Quarterly* 38, no. 5 (1986): 721–45.

Hilscher, Herb[ert H.]. "The Most Unforgettable Character I've Met." *Reader's Digest*. August 1961, 73–78.

Hobucket, Harry. "Quileute Indian Tradition." *Washington Historical Quarterly* 25, no. 1 (1934): 49–59.

McDonald, Lucile. "Pullen Museum Houses Alaska Relics." *Seattle Times*, May 7, 1961.

Nicoll, Edward Holland. "The Chinook Language or Jargon." *Popular Science Monthly*, 35 (1889): 257–61.

Pettitt, George. "The Quileute of La Push, 1775–1945." *Anthropological Records* 14, no. 1. Berkeley: University of California Press, 1950.

Powell, J[ay] V. "Quileute Exploitation and Maintenance of Prairies in Traditional Times." In M. Kat Anderson, *The Ozette Prairies of Olympic National Park*, 85–158.

P[ullen], H[arriet] S[mith]. "On Board the *Rosalie*." *Port Townsend Leader*. [September 1897].

Pullen, Royal R. "The Pullens . . . Strong Pioneers at La Push." *Strait History* 2, no. 4 (1987): 1–3.

Renker, Ann M. "The Makah Tribe: People of the Sea and the Forest." University of Washington Digital Collections. http://content.lib.washington.edu/aipnw/renker.html.

Smith, Barbara Leigh. "The *Twilight* Saga and the Quileute Indian Tribe: Opportunity or Cultural Exploitation?" 2010, *Enduring Legacies Native Cases*, Evergreen State College. http://nativecases.evergreen.edu/docs/smith-the-twilight-saga-9-3-13.pdf.

"Typhoid Fever." Mayo Clinic. www.mayoclinic.com/health/typhoid-fever/DS00538/DSECTION=symptoms.

Willoughby, Barrett. "Mother of the North." *Reader's Digest*. September 1930, 426–28.

———. "Mother of the North: A Stirring Tale of Alaskan Gold and a Woman Who Battled Alone." *American Magazine*, August 1930, 64–66, 112.

Wilson, Sylvia. "The Underground Railroad in Bradford County." *Settler, A Quarterly Magazine of History and Biography*. September 1973, 1–7.

Wray, Jacilee, and M. Kat Anderson. "Restoring Indian-Set Fires to Prairie Ecosystems on the Olympic Peninsula." *Ecological Restoration* 21, no. 4 (2003): 298–301.

Oral Histories and Interviews

Burfield, Virginia. Interview by Joanne Beierly. March 13, 1975. Pullen Papers, KLGO 45021, Klondike Gold Rush National Historical Park Archives, Skagway.

Elsner, Lucille Hudson. Interview by Helen Clark. July 9, 1981. Pullen Papers, KLGO 45016, Klondike Gold Rush National Historical Park Archives, Skagway.

Maupin, Ed. Interview by Jacilee Wray. October 20, 2000. Edited by Ed Maupin, 2010. Smith Family Papers, Olympic National Park Archives, 728:7.

Pullen, Royal R. Interview by Eleanor Eckert. 1987. In the possession of Deby Sweren, Keller, Texas.

———. Interview by Ruth Pullen Hamilton and unidentified man from the Clallam County Historical Society. 1980. Audiotape. Pullen file, Clallam County Historical Society.

———. Interview by Ruth Pullen Hamilton. March 1988. Pullen Papers, KLGO 45017, Klondike Gold Rush National Historical Park Archives, Skagway.

Tyler, Jennie S. "Jennie S. Tyler." In *Told by the Pioneers: Reminiscences of Pioneer Life in Washington*, 37–39. Vol. 3. Federal Project No. 5841. Olympia: WPA, 1938.

Unpublished Manuscripts, Diaries, and Court Documents

Andrews, Clarence Leroy. Diary. January, September 1902. M.S. 136, University of Alaska Fairbanks Archives.

Anonymous. Diary. August 5, 1927. Skagway File, 06-03, Alaska State Library Historical Collections, Juneau.

Anonymous. Transcript of hearing. [ca. 1885]. A. Wesley Smith Papers, 1853–1935, M.S. 172, Washington State Library Manuscripts Collection, Tumwater.

Atherton v. Fowler, 96 US 513 (1877).

Binford. "Pullen Foundation History of Harriet Smith Pullen." [bet. June and November], 1979, M.S. 136, University of Alaska Fairbanks Archives.

Chandler, Geo[rge], First Assistant Secretary, Department of the Interior, to the Commissioner of the General Land Office. March 1, 1893. In *United States v. Daniel Pullen and Hattie S. Pullen*, 16–148. Pullen File, Clallam County Historical Society, Port Angeles, Washington.

Clothier, Florence. Diary. July 1928. M.S. 136, University of Alaska Fairbanks Archives.

Cutts, Martha Smith. Recollections. January 5, 1957. Private collection.

Daniel Pullen and Hattie Pullen vs. John P. McGlinn as United States Indian Agent (US Circuit Court, Wash. Dist. No. Div., 1898), Answer.

General Land Office, Department of the Interior. *United States v. Harriet S. Pullen*, Record Group 49. National Archives and Records Administration.

Gurcke, Karl. "The Pullen House Complex: A Preliminary Historic Photographic Essay." 2015. Klondike Gold Rush National Historical Park Archives, Skagway.

Hamilton, Ruth Pullen. "Reminiscences of Royal Pullen." Summer 1987. Pullen Papers, Klondike Gold Rush National Historical Park Archives, Skagway.

———. "Smith Family History (As Told to Royal Pullen)." n.d. In the author's possession.

———. "Daniel Pullen." 1986. In the author's possession.

"Harriet Pullen: An Alaskan Heroine (HSP's Own Story)." [March 1922–September 1923]. In the author's possession.

Heynen, Jim. "Pullen, Royal R." Notes from interview for published entry in a book. April 1987. In the author's possession.

Hunt, William E. Diary. August 17, 1903. Typescript by William H. Hunt. William E. Hunt Papers, PCA 155, Pullen File, Alaska State Library Historical Collections, Juneau.

Pullen, Harriet Stuart. "Story About Mrs. Pullen When She Went to Skagway, Alaska, in 1897, as Told by Mrs. Pullen to Harriet S. Pullen, Her Granddaughter, in 1941." 1941. In the author's possession.

Pullen, Royal R. "Daniel Webster Pullen." [ca. 1986]. In the author's possession.

———. "My Mother Harriet S. Pullen." [ca. 1986]. In the author's possession.

Smith, Andrew Jackson. Diaries, 1853–1883. 4 volumes. A. Wesley Smith Papers, 1853–1935, M.S. 172, Washington State Library Manuscripts Collection, Tumwater.

———. "A. J. Smith and Family." [1879]. In the author's possession.

United States of America vs. Harriet S. Pullen. Juneau, Serial No. 03945. Pullen Papers, KLGO, Klondike Gold Rush National Historical Park Archives, Skagway.

Washington Fur Co. v. Daniel Pullen and Hattie S. Pullen. 307. Clallam County, WA: Superior Court, 1893.

Index

About the Author

Former director of education at the Neuberger Museum of Art, Purchase College, State University of New York, and author of *An Uncommon Cape: Researching the Histories and Mysteries of a Property*, Eleanor Phillips Brackbill graduated from Antioch College, earned an MA in art history at Boston University, completed a curatorial fellowship in the Whitney Museum of American Art's Independent Study Program, and studied in the art history doctoral program at City University of New York. Following twenty-five years as an educator, she embarked on a second career writing about history. She lives with her husband near Portland, Maine, and is currently working on her next book, another story steeped in the history of the American West.